Winds of Destiny

Jayne Bullock

authorHOUSE®

AuthorHouse™
1663 Liberty Drive, Suite 200
Bloomington, IN 47403
www.authorhouse.com
Phone: 1-800-839-8640

First published by AuthorHouse 9/12/2007

ISBN: 978-1-4343-3077-2 (sc)

Library of Congress Control Number: 2007905690

Printed in the United States of America
Bloomington, Indiana

This book is printed on acid-free paper.

Dedicated
to those I love

"*Lord, be my rock of safety, the stronghold that saves me.*
For the honor of your name, lead me and guide me."
Psalm 30:3-4

Scotland

Ireland

Forest
of Bowland

*Skipton

*Blackpool   *Keighley

                              *Leeds

*Lytham   *Wakefield

*Liverpool   *Manchester

England

Wales

*Stonehenge

*London

Table of Contents

Preface

$\mathcal{I}$ am a firm believer that most authors are a product of the books they read. I can't help but think that an author's writing and thinking are somewhat influenced by those books. In my story I see the influences of the books I love – Gothic romance intermingled with a bit of intrigue and a bit of history. I love Tolstoy and C.S. Lewis, while Arthurian stories rank among my all-time favorites.

The *Winds of Destiny* is a story that began when I went back to school and was completing my education at Marshalltown Community College and Iowa State University. It was after taking a comparative religion class that my idea was born. I was trying to understand how the numerous sects fit into a world of people with varying lifestyles, ethnicities and beliefs. I wanted to create a story that would outline some of those beliefs and how people dealt with the many stumbling blocks presented by the religious and political powers during the reformation period. It has taken me a long time to complete my project because at first I couldn't make my character work in the story I had begun. In 2006 I revisited my story, changed my main character and began reworking my ideas. The words here are how I thought the story could best be told. I have tried to present a story that I hope will please most people and offer a bit of information.

I wish to thank the many people whom I have worked with throughout the years that have encouraged me to write and listened to my ideas. Thanks to my family, good friend Joan who encouraged me to continue when I had doubts and Donna and Bert Petersen. I wish to thank Mary Duerson, an editor who read the work and offered ways to tweak the project. Without the use of the internet and Encyclopedia Britannica, I would not have been able to verify dates, maps and events to make parts of the story a true piece of historic information. The characters, places and some events are fictitious.

CHAPTER ONE
Memories

I should never have returned. It had been a strenuous journey to say the least, but one that had to be taken. Sometimes, you have to put life in perspective and that means looking back at where you began. Now, in the year 1675, each twist and turn in the road brought me ever closer to a life I had long ago put behind me. My anxiety increased as the spinning wheels of the horse-drawn coach continued to roll on toward my destination, the home of my youth. As I approached the familiar countryside, the old feelings of insecurity, fear and love that childhood brings filled my very soul and revived those long forgotten emotions.

Not expecting a great deal of change in the village close to my home, I was surprised to see how time had left its tale. Weathered wood, sagging roofs, unkempt yards and even dilapidated buildings gave evidence much of the population had moved on. It was eerily ghostly. No one was about as we drove through and I felt sad to see these deathly remnants of a once thriving community filled with love and laughter.

I wondered if we would be lucky enough to find the inn open that was always a welcoming spot at the far end of the village. I had asked the coach driver to stop and was pleased to find the old familiar structure had withstood the elements of time and nature. After our long journey, both of us were looking forward to a short rest and the opportunity for lunch, drink and conversation. The old tavern sign waved in the breeze and was a welcome sight to us weary travelers. I breathed a sigh of relief as I heard the driver holler "Whoa!" to the horses.

"I thin' we be in luck," he said to me as he opened the carriage door.

He checked the horses, gave them a pat and then we went inside. The interior was much as I remembered it from my youth when Father and I would stop in for a bite to eat. I could almost hear the stories being told and the mugs clinking as patrons toasted their latest good fortune or bemoaned their woes. The innkeeper proved to be a friendly sort who was more than willing to tell stories about the locals and the community I had left behind in my youth.

"Welcome, welcome," he said in greeting us. "Good t'see some travelers. I be Brownie and I hope ya' be hungry."

We told him we were and hoped he had something good and hot to eat.

"Where ya' from?" he asked, as he set about getting a warm cup of tea for me and a pint of ale for the driver.

"America," I replied. "Came in at Liverpool, found my driver and a few days ago we started up here from Manchester. Are there any rooms available?" Somehow I thought my visit might be extended and we would need a place to stay for the evening.

He laughed and said there "didna' seem to be such a big crowd these days." I then asked him about the village and what had happened to the shops and homes throughout the years.

"We are a dyin' village," the innkeeper said sadly. "The beckonin' call f'r riches and adventures 'as claimed many a young heart, with our youth off t'seek fortunes in other parts o' the world. Many people moved on, seekin' work in the larger cities and towns. And o' course the many wars called young men t'fight f'r their beliefs."

He set a couple bowls filled with steaming stew in front of us and a plate of bread. It didn't take us long to devour the delicious meal.

"The religious struggles here were too much for young and old alike," the innkeeper went on to say. "Oh, ya'll find a few o' the old'r folk still 'round who stayed on t'eke out a livin' best they could wi' wha' nature provided. But it gets harder all the time. Good thin' my inn and tavern be on a well-traveled road."

After enjoying both the meal and the company, the driver and I were ready to continue our journey. We tentatively reserved a couple of rooms and thanked the innkeeper for the information and the food. Once back in the carriage, we headed on toward our destination.

I had previously given the driver directions, and a short distance outside the village he turned onto the old road leading to our journey's end. I bounced with the movement of the coach on the rough dirt pathway, now filled with deep ruts and grassy tufts. My mind began to take me back in time to those long ago days. Not yet, I told myself. Don't look back – not yet.

I caught muted glimpses of my family's estate through spacious openings in a mass of scraggly trees and bushes. My father had always kept a beautifully, well-maintained woods. Now it was an overgrown timber – branches, limbs and whole trees cluttered the ground. Many of the trees, once fully clothed in shades of green, had deteriorated with age. The wooded area was dense, dark and foreboding.

Then, as if the house knew I was returning, it appeared in a shroud of gray clouds. Through a clearing in the trees I caught the full, breathtaking view of the tall, ancient brick and stucco house. As the carriage turned down the long lane, now little more than a path of over-grown grasses and weeds, I could see that time and Mother Nature had taken its toll on the property. Many of the buildings on the estate were in rubble and the horse barn was missing its roof – the slate tile lay all around the weathered building in broken shards. The driver opened the door for me and I stepped out in front of the house. Before me stood the sad remains of my parents, Thomas and Agnes Grafton. And I, Catherine Grafton, their only surviving child, had returned to the home of my youth.

It was a sad homecoming, but I had expected that. The whole house emitted an air of sadness and gloom. I gazed on a home once widely acclaimed for its elaborate décor and stately façade, now faded in color to a dull gray. Shutters hung askew, chipped and broken tile cluttered the ground, and chimneys lay in scattered piles near the house. The well-groomed gardens, once mother's pride and joy, were overgrown with weeds and other debris. The years had not only taken a toll on the estate but the family who had once lived there. I was almost 18 when my eager adventure took me from them. Since, I had received only a few letters in my later years about how my family had fared and what had happened to our estate. My eyes welled with tears at those lost years. Now I gave myself leave to remember those long ago days when Grafton Manor was filled with our daily lives, our moments of happiness and times of sadness…

* * *

As far back as I can remember I have always been a strong-minded and willful child. Right from my very first squall my father said I had an independent nature. At an early age "no" or "not possible" were eliminated from my vocabulary. That I grew up to be an adventurer was inevitable.

Grafton Manor was my home, a modest estate at the edge of a tiny farming village in the fertile Colne Valley of the Pennines in northern England. My life began under all the normal circumstances and I shared the manor with my parents, two brothers and a sister. We were lucky enough to exist in moderate comfort in seventeenth century England. I always thought our home was a castle and as a very young child I would pretend I was princess of the manor. Much to my pleasure, everyone in the house humored my imagination. Then my little sister arrived to end my reign.

My father, known to some as the landlord, called our home an over-sized tenant farm. We owed our prosperity to sheep rearing and raising grains for market. Father ruled his home, at least in my adolescent mind, like the strict and efficient barrister he had been in his younger years. As a young man he had served in the House of Parliament, but grew weary of city life. His love for the land drew him back to his roots and he became a gentleman farmer. His days became filled with supervising and participating in the mechanics and production of our estate. Even though his barrister years were far behind him, the community always counted on Father to promote a cause he believed in or participate in local politics whenever possible, or necessary.

Grafton Manor dated back to homesteads established after the downfall of the feudal system. Due to the ingenuity

5

of early ancestors, our property had grown from a few acres and a cottage to a large parcel of pasture, forest and crop land, along with the stately structure we called home. My ancestors had always maintained a high standard of living, and it was rumored that some had even been honored guests or companions of reigning royalty. Throughout the years, each generation of Graftons had added land and increased the size of the family dwelling. The current house had been built by a great grandfather and it had been renovated to meet family needs throughout the years.

It took a large staff to work the fields, care for the sheep, tend the yards and gardens, maintain the house and buildings and keep us all neat, clean and well fed. The largest portion of our domestic help and the farm laborers came from the nearby village on a daily basis. Father was a just man, being fair to both tenants and employees. I do give him due credit in this area. He was emphatic that everyone who worked on the farm was free and independent and not our servants. I can remember how he would expound on the fact that they were entitled to be treated fairly and receive adequate pay for their work. In return, he asked for their support and loyalty. A few families lived in small cottages on the estate – there was Edgar, my father's man; Annie, mother's chambermaid; and Molly, queen of the kitchen.

Although Edgar graciously tended and administered to Father's personal needs, he had far greater responsibilities as chief steward of our estate. He and Father worked well together to maintain the farm and increase production. They each had their tasks. It was Edgar who oversaw the farming staff and collected rents from the tenants. He kept accounts and negotiated purchases and sales of farm products at nearby markets.

I can't say I was terrified of my father. But he was a stern disciplinarian and we all experienced fear of him on various occasions. Although he was a considerate man and people generally liked him, he expected the rules of both God and King to be strictly followed by everyone on the estate – from the household to the farm staff.

Inside the manor house, everyone had their place and duties. Even as children, there were strict rules to be followed – with no exceptions. Among myself and my siblings there were the usual childhood jealousies and vying for parental affections. David, the oldest, was father's favorite – at least that was my personal point of view. He gratified all the expectations of our father, which the rest of us were never able to fulfill. I don't think David liked me very much and the feeling was mutual. I'm sure he saw me as just a silly girl with no sense of responsibility. I thought he was stuffy and not much fun. He rarely laughed. When he did, it was usually a joke or amusing tidbit about the farm that he and Father shared.

At age twenty-three, David was one of the most eligible bachelors in the village. He had already been away to university, completing courses in law and philosophy. He talked about becoming a barrister some day which would have greatly pleased my father. But like my father, he truly loved the land and had always taken an interest in what was happening on the estate. Instead of heading off to London like so many young men did, he had returned home to learn about the business of farming.

David could always please and impress Father with his knowledge of the accounts and the production status of our estate. He was a favorite with the farm hands as he sought answers and looked at ways to increase production of the various products. As a result, his logical and exacting answers were most pleasing to Father. I can still picture the two of them in Father's study at the end of a day and hear the steady drone of their voices.

"Father, fleece from the sheep in the south meadow should bring a good price at Skipton next week," David would say. "But, do you think we also should consider taking our next batch of fleece to a bigger market – perhaps over into Leeds? I know it will mean transporting the animals a bit further, but I hear they have an excellent market for sheep."

"David, you have a very good eye and ear for business. I have thought about Leeds or even Manchester. Both would be quite a trip for us. Perhaps we should look at the possibility of other markets," Father would answer.

"Sir, the percentages of animals ready for market is also very good; but, what do you think about forestalling the sale right away? Edgar has heard of a few diseased animals in the district. Perhaps by waiting a bit, we could get a better price."

David always seemed to be repeating every tidbit that Edgar divulged. He worked hard at being the first to hear Edgar's reports. David liked to be the one to report the most up-to-date information to Father.

"I had heard that report, too," Father said in acknowledging the diseased animals. "We might want to take that into consideration when we get ready to go to market next."

And, on and on they would go – David abetting Father's ego with trivial tidbits about the farm that Father probably already knew. But I'm sure he was delighted to hear one of his children taking interest in the business of the estate. David would make a good landlord.

Nathan was my favorite sibling. I think he and I were carved from the same mold. The two of us were always looking for a little fun or a new adventure. He was our dreamer, and more artistic than me. He was always drawing or sketching something and kept a journal of his wispy, dreamy ideas. And he especially enjoyed our library. I think his goal was to read every volume, even if they were dull and boring.

Of course Father was stern with him – I think sometimes too much. Father would explode and tell Nathan that he needed to be more like David, taking an interest in the farm instead of whiling his hours away in idle fantasy. Nathan had lofty ambitions for himself and hoped to pursue those interests when he returned to university for the fall semester. But those dreams never came to fruition. I was deeply saddened and troubled to hear in my later years that he died from a serious injury after a fall from a galloping horse shortly after I left. Oh, how I wish I could have been there; instead, I was off on my own adventures. Maybe it wouldn't have happened. When I heard about his death, it made me sad and I wished there would have been years ahead for us. His own journey was ended and my journey had become one I know he would have been pleased to hear about or even participated in.

Nathan and I always had such wonderful times together – especially when we were off on our many joint adventures. We would ride sedately down the lane as though royalty. When we turned out of sight, we were different people – laughing and making the most of the outing.

"Can you make it to Winston's farm?" He would continually urge me to go farther and farther away from home. This was typical of our adventures.

"We daren't go that far," I would answer. "That's more than a couple hours away."

But I couldn't let the challenge pass. I would toss my head, give my horse Maudie a gentle kick and holler back over my shoulder. "I'll get there before you." Away I would go as fast as the wind.

"Want to bet?" he would answer and soon we were racing abreast across meadows and onto the road to the Winston farm. Nathan liked to visit there often because Madeline and Marcella, the Winston twins, were close to his age. He seemed to find their silliness most attractive.

I always let him win our races. After all, that's what sisters do. If I really had wanted to beat him at his own game, I knew I could. But I also knew just how hard I could push Maudie before she would be wheezing and slobbering. I would usually slow down and let Nathan pass.

"You win," I would say and he would hold up his arms in a victory salute.

Finally, there was my little sister Marianne. She was just turning eleven the fall I left home. I was fond of her and thought of her often after my departure. She was a favorite among the household members – a delightful minx with blond curls and twinkling blue mischievous eyes, while I was the brown-haired, adventurous vixen (or at least that is what Mother would tell us). Even as a small child, Marianne had been the charmer and it was obvious that she would eventually be considered a courtly beauty. She inveigled her way into the hearts of everyone. As she continued into womanhood, I'm sure that charm and enchantment enticed and lured the affections of many young men from the village and the neighboring manors.

Usually we were compatible, often sharing secrets. "Don't tell Father, but...." we'd whisper about a misdeed. She could be mean sometimes, but mostly she was a kind-hearted lass with a happy smile for everyone. I often took the blame when we two were in trouble. Our mission in life was to "become young women," through our daily lessons, sewing and music. I don't think I was a very good role model for her; I was much too independent.

Mother was my ally. She was a very compassionate woman whom I found at an early age could easily be maneuvered for support. Even when I was in trouble, she would secretly give me a smile and nod while Father scolded. As I reached maturity, I wondered about Mother and Father and their relationship. I never felt there was a great deal of love between them; more likely, they were simply tolerable of each other. Mother was the peacemaker and she could more easily cope with Father's sternness than some of us stronger-willed family members.

Under Mother's realm was Annie and Molly. Annie lived on the estate with her husband Tom. He was in charge of the gardens and yards. Besides tending to the needs of Mother, and occasionally we children, she supervised the domestic day staff and kept household accounts.

It was Molly who was my favorite. Her domain was the kitchen and she always smelled of rosemary, an herbal smell I thought was especially pleasing. She came in very early each morning from her cottage on the estate to prepare the day's food while her husband worked the fields. Her specialty was delicious tarts or sweet biscuits, and she must have used secret ingredients because they melted in your mouth. I especially liked to step into her domain where I was welcomed with open arms.

"Ah, and 'ow is me favorite? Ya' be lookin' f'r a treat, now I'll wager Miss Cathy. Eat up quickly a'fore the missus catches ya' sneakin'," she would say as she gave me a quick hug. Only she and Nathan called me Cathy. To everyone else I was Miss Catherine. How formidable that sounded!

"What kinda' mischief ya' be doin' t'day, me pet?" she'd ask, giving me a wink and a grin. I would only smile coyly and enjoy my treat.

Molly was well loved by us all. You could always count on a sample of whatever pastry she was preparing for the day. Nathan enjoyed coming into Molly's kitchen and snitching a bite or two. Even though David and Father were busy, they would often stop by for a mid-morning sweet. Marianne liked to go with me to visit Molly. But I would never brag about getting a treat if she wasn't included. She would go whining to Mother.

I'm not sure why Molly seemed to have a special spot in her heart for me. Perhaps she and I were under a spell by the same stars. Or maybe I was her favorite because she and her husband Marne never had any children of their own to spoil. I was never a shy child and that might have been why we hit it off. I liked to tease Molly and we shared a lot of jokes. She was a happy, jovial person and always chuckling about something. In her kitchen, laughter abounded as she and her staff worked on the monumental task of feeding us all.

Even now, I can still remember the wonderfully delicious aromas that wafted from her kitchen, especially during the holidays or when special guests came to visit. Mother loved to entertain and we always had a multitude of aunts, uncles, cousins and other acquaintances stopping by for short visits. Summer was the best; that was when many of Father's friends and families would travel up from London to spend some time with us.

As with most large estates, we had the usual barn and stable help. This was Hasley's domain. His given name was Ralph Hasley, but no one ever called him anything but Hasley. It was he, along with his five sons, who kept track of the numerous herds of sheep and the horses which roamed our pastures. And it was Hasley and his boys who also kept our meager barns and stables always immaculately clean. I often wondered what kept them at our estate when they could have gone on to a much larger stable and been more amply reimbursed. But there had been Hasleys on our farm as far back as Great Grandfather, so we had their loyalty.

The care of animals was a trade the Hasleys had learned and passed on from one generation to the next. The whole family had a special aptitude for the well-being of animals, but Hasley especially had a knack. He could turn the most vicious animal or tormented beast into a docile creature. And when need be, he could be ever so gentle. I remember on one occasion when Nathan and I were quite young, we had found a small kitten in the woods. She had gotten caught in one of our animal traps.

Nathan spied her first. It was while we were looking for berries to put in one of Molly's delicious pies. The urgency in Nathan's voice caused me to rush over to the thicket into which he was peering.

"Cathy, Cathy, come quickly! Look what I have found! It's a tiny cat, and it's dreadfully hurt!"

"Be careful! Don't touch it!" I warned. Not taking heed of my own advice, I cautiously pulled back more of the underbrush to reveal a tiger-striped kit caught in a gaming trap. She was feebly crying with pain.

"Will it live? Can we get her out, without hurting her?" Nathan asked anxiously.

"I don't know, we'll try," I said, reaching in to gently pet the kit. "A sorry state you've gotten yourself into there little one. Shhhhh, don't be frightened." To Nathan I said, "Even if we get her out, I'm not sure she will live."

The wooden traps that Hasley had designed were no stranger to either of us. As adventurous youngsters and having a Father that felt knowing about nature was an important part of our training, we had helped on numerous occasions with the traps. We had set and released our share to rid the farm of pesky animals or catch a few for eating.

We worked carefully to release the injured animal. It didn't put up much of a fight. Both her front paws were mangled and broken. We carefully wrapped her in my apron, trying not to inflict further pain. I gently carried her back to Hasley who set the bones and nursed her. He fed her herbal concoctions and put poultices on the swollen paws. I never gave the kit much hope, but Hasley worked a miracle on the poor ravaged creature. And though both Nathan and I helped minister to her needs, in the end she took a fonder liking to Hasley than to either of us. She became one of his stable cats, priding him on her mouse-catching abilities.

Our father had high aspirations for his children and must have been sorely disappointed that his goals for some of us were never consummated. He was a strict component of education for all of us and said both men and women should know how to read, write and make decisions based on their knowledge of the world. He especially wanted us girls to be independent woman in a society that didn't encourage that.

"After all, I might not always be around to help with your decisions and choices," he would say. "Besides, how will you teach your own children if you don't have the proper background?"

A succession of tutors flitted in and out of our lives. Most often they chose to live in the village, coming out to our farm each day. Lessons were held in the old nursery, transformed into a school room as we grew older. All of us were encouraged to read, and our library was often filled with one or two family members or other estate people who took advantage of enjoying the many books father had collected. Reading history, geography, Greek classics, ciphering and elocution were required subjects. Each tutor could add other lessons to help us become well-educated and masters of our own small world. Father was not concerned about our own interests and dreams, and the tutors were expected to have the same goals as him when it came to our future. If Father found that they were not of his same belief, they usually were given good recommendations and sent on to some other family.

We each had a turn at attending private schools at one time or another. Father believed a portion of our education relied on the experience of socializing and learning with other children. The boys had spent a couple of terms at a small Catholic academy near Wakefield with a Monsignor Richards as headmaster. Nathan was still attending University when I left the home of my childhood. I had spent a couple of semesters at a girls' school in a nearby community and Marianne would soon be following. Now with my eighteenth birthday only months away, Father had been urging me to settle down and become a "proper young woman."

"It is not seemly for a young girl to be galloping around the countryside as you do," he would say in his weekly lectures about becoming a beneficial member of our society. "As a daughter of the landlord, you need to spend more time helping the people on our estate. You need to join your mother and Marianne on their daily rounds of attending to our families. And you must work on becoming more accomplished in music and the social graces. After all, you will be presented to society next spring."

I would bristle at this thought. It wasn't that I lacked responsibility. It was just that riding across the fields and forests, with the wind in my hair, was more exciting than carrying baskets of food out to the cottages. Many a day I would be able to sneak away on Maudie. Other days I would encounter my father just as I was ready to mount up for a ride.

"The warm days are waning and I want to enjoy them just a bit longer," I would plead.

"All right then," he would say, slapping his gloves against the horse's flank. "Get back home soon and take on the responsibilities I expect of you."

And as usual, I would toss my head, promise to try harder, wave good-bye and ride off in a fast gallop down the lane and across the fields. Many times Nathan would join me, and we both pledged to spend more time on our studies when we returned. Nathan said I egged him on, but I think we each sought out ways to be our own person. I think Nathan and I had a reputation for being impossible children. We had a succession of nursemaids and tutors who left their posts because of the various pranks and misdemeanors the two of us provided. But it was mostly me.

It wasn't that I tried to create havoc throughout our household. Things just seemed to happen; I was a victim of circumstances. As a very young child, I always ran through the house and up the stairway, never walking as "young ladies were supposed to." Sitting quietly just wasn't in my nature which was evident as my clothes were often streaked with dirt or had small tears in them. It wasn't my fault that mud was on the floors from my latest wanderings or spills frequently happened to me. I didn't intentionally drop the ink bottle on the school desk.

Nathan used to tell me I should have been a boy. I was always game for capturing a frog or a very tiny, baby garter snake. Somehow these creatures would find their way into a tutor's drinking cup or be hidden under chair pillows in the school room. Nathan and I were both pretty good at covering up for each other when we wanted to be late for lessons. Sometimes we would just plain skip for the day, hiding until the tutor would give up on us. Some of the tutors found humor in our attempt to "scare" them or "pull the wool over their eyes," while others didn't waste any time in reporting our actions to Father. On many occasions, it was me, not Nathan, who received the discipline for our spontaneous pranks.

I always felt my destiny was not something I could control. And with my adventurous nature, I wasn't sure I wanted to. Could I help it if my actions created situations that were "unseemly for a young lady" (Father's words) or took me to places outside the realm of family and farm? That I sought out adventures was the one flaw in my character which gave way to the displeasure my family would fault me for in later years.

As the months grew closer to my eighteenth year, when I "would be recognized as an accomplished young woman" (again Father's words), I seemed intent on seeking out new avenues of adventure more than ever before. I felt time was closing in on me and I wanted to experience all I could outside the domain of my home before I was forever chastened to what I saw as a boring life of womanly tasks.

I enjoyed riding into the village and seeing the surprise on people's faces as I stopped to talk to them. "Where is your father?" they would say, and I would answer "Oh, I rode in alone." I would even shock some of my friends who thought

I was especially bold in riding out to their distant estates by myself. Venturing farther and farther from our estate was always a temptation. But even on my longest days, I always felt I had to be home in time for the evening meal so as not to suffer complete displeasure from Father. Little did I know how my upcoming adventures would provoke his greatest displeasure. Looking back, it was my spontaneous and independent nature that would settle my destiny. Things also might have been different had it not been for the religious upheaval that had England in its web.

Our family's faith and its connection to English history was an enormous part of who we were and the education we were to receive. Father was always expounding on his political and religious views. We had been practicing Roman Catholics for generations, sometimes worshipping openly and sometimes discreetly, depending on the current king. Father's view was our total way of life. He was adamant we stay true to our faith and its doctrines. As Catholics, our family was part of the anti-Puritan movement prevalent at the time. Father would get into heated discussions about current religious dissension with his London friends, and even on occasion, with Edgar and David. Not on any plateau of thinking, could or would my father or family understand the commitment I would eventually make in regard to religious beliefs.

"It is important that you learn all you can about our faith," Father would say, time and time again. "That is the one thing in life that gives us sustenance. I want you to know about your faith and practice it fervently. It is up to us practicing Catholics to make a difference."

On one occasion, shortly before my adventure took me away from lessons and home, Father surprised us with a visit to the school room. Nathan, Marianne and I were giving the tutor a bad time about having to memorize our catechism. It was a beautiful day and none of us were interested in any kind of lesson, let alone reciting rote answers to the questions "Who made you?" and "Why did God make you?" We were acting silly and making fun of the age old texts when Father came into the room. Seeing our behavior and hearing our "blasphemy," he was outraged. The moment we saw him, we knew we were in for a long and lengthy sermon. We sank down into our chairs with heads lowered, hoping he was too busy to lecture us on the virtues of religion and how it applied to our family. But, no such luck.

"This has been a time of religious trials for all of us and I guess you need to be reminded about these upheavals to understand and appreciate our own faith," he said. "As a Catholic, I am concerned about our being able to worship in our way and follow our beliefs. It is a time when radical groups are striving to gain control of the religious world and creating havoc for our old and established faiths."

Father then launched into a lecture that included England's church history for the latter sixteenth and the beginning of the seventeenth centuries. He said a key factor in that growth was Puritanism, a reformation movement that began in the Church of England during the early 1500s. Little did he know it would continue to create discord for the next two- to three-hundred years. The Puritans thought the national church had not gone far enough in reforming doctrine and structure of the English church. They wanted to eliminate all Catholic influences. However, the Puritans were willing to stay within the church, unlike the Pilgrims or Presbyterians that favored more radical, individual forms of worship. The Puritans only wanted to eliminate the elaborate rituals and ceremonies of the English church. Puritan attack on the established church became popular, especially among the young lawyers, merchants and other professionals of London.

Father continued, saying in those years of conflict each religious group – the Calvinistic Protestants, Puritan reformers and the Catholics – promoted their beliefs to the ruling king. All English people were expected to worship God in the manner that the reigning king chose. A great many Englishmen did not agree with this, and discord resulted. Those refusing to follow the king's wishes were severely punished.

"There have been good times and bad for both us Catholics and the Protestants," Father concluded. "And I can't say that it has been all bad for us since the reformation has brought profit to our farm production. Now that you have heard this lesson, it is your duty to study your catechism and keep the Catholic faith alive."

Father left our school room, leaving us with a challenge to memorize our lessons and learn them well. We were sure that next time there would be no mercy. The memory of that lecture and many other lessons about faith and history would be filed away to be thought about on another day in the distant future.

The morning of my most unforgettable adventure dawned with a beautiful fall day filled with blue sky and bright sunshine. I knew the school room would not see me that day. I had to be out, taking pleasure in galloping across the meadows and feeling the warmth of the golden sun. I asked Nathan if he was game for a day of riding pleasure. He declined saying that he really had to begin to get his things together for school. He was to leave before the end of the week. One last fling, I told myself. Then I can settle in like father wants me to. Unbeknownst to me, fate was awaiting with an adventure that even I could not have imagined.

CHAPTER TWO
The Adventure Begins

I strode leisurely to the stables on that day of days, unaware that I was about to embark on my life's destiny. I was always impressed at how everything was so neat, tidy and in place in Hasley's stables. My eye caught a bad spot in the roof where a few pieces of slate should be replaced. Father would have been proud that I had even given the building a thought.

Hasley hailed me with his usual cheery greeting. "Mornin' Miss Catherine," he said.

"Good morning, yourself," I replied.

"Are ye here f'r Maudie? It do be a fine sunshiny day ta' be out pleasure ridin'. An' where would ya' be off t'a on such a fine day?" he asked.

"I'm not sure, Hasley, but it is indeed a beautiful morning," I said. "It's going to be the kind of day that I can't stay around here and do school work or housework or whatever ladies are supposed to do. As to where I'm going, I think I'll take a long ride, maybe into one of the nearby villages or up yonder there along some of the hills. Maybe I'll ride as far as Skipton. Can't say where my wanderings will take me. Maudie and Mother Nature can lead me where they will. There won't be many more of these beautiful days to be off riding before the weather turns really cold; that is, if my father has his way."

I followed Hasley inside and he began getting gear ready for my ride while I went to Maudie's stall to greet her. The chestnut-colored mare was a fifteenth birthday gift. We two had sought a multitude of escapades.

"How are you doing there, girl?" I asked, as I patted her nose and gave her a big hug. "Are you ready for an adventure today?"

Now, I know people will say horses can't talk, but the way she was prancing around in her stall and nodding her head up and down, I was sure her answer was "Yes!" I really thought of Maudie as my best friend, especially when it came to fun and adventure. She always seemed to know when I needed to turn a dull day into a trip filled with surprises. Like me, she was ready for a day of pleasure in the warm sunshine.

Together Hasley and I got Maudie ready for the ride, putting the saddle and bridle in place and making sure everything was safe and secure – especially the cinch. That was something I always made sure of. I had not paid attention one time and had found myself on the ground, underneath the horse. Thank goodness Maudie was a patient animal.

Maudie was ready to go. "If Father asks about me, you can tell him that as usual I'll be back by dinner," I said as I climbed on the animal's back.

"Ye and ya' father not seein' eye-to-eye 'gain?" Hasley asked.

"For sure – that's how it always is," I said.

"Perhaps the two o' ye will be good friends one day," he said. "Family's important ya' know."

I just rolled my eyes and then gave him a quick wink as Maudie danced around, as anxious as me to be off on our adventure.

"Good luck to ye then," Hasley said. "Be careful Miss and don' get into too much trouble."

Maudie and I turned to leave. I waved good-bye and we galloped down the lane, intent on a day of pleasure. Little did I know then, but by mid afternoon those plans to be home for dinner would be greatly mistaken. I had thought a day's journey across the meadows, through the forest and maybe up to the town of Skipton which bordered the Pennines might provide the excitement I was seeking. Going that far would be a brave thing for me to do. And if Father knew, I was sure he would have sent me to my room for weeks to "think about the consequences."

Much later, I would remember Hasley's farewell words and wonder if he had a premonition or only that I wished to believe his last words were advice for my future. Often I have wondered, when looking back in retrospect, how Hasley and his sons fared in life after my departure.

My journey that day seemed to be adversely against me. From the very first gallop past a small stream, to "Standing Stone" which identified our property boundaries, and to the forest I thought bordered Skipton, my adventure was plagued with problems and inconveniences. The shortcut trail through our timber which I always used to get to the main road was quite muddy and slushy. Thus, I decided to ride along the wooded area a little farther and find a different route that would take me to my destination. Surely there was more than one path.

I wasn't paying much attention to the landscape, and time did not seem of importance. It was pleasurable to just gallop along on Maudie in the warm sunshine and the blue cloudless sky. What a glorious day, I thought. Finally, I spotted a well-used path that would take me through the woods.

"This should get us where we want to go," I said to Maudie, but really more to myself for assurance. We cautiously turned onto the worn trail that appeared to be going in the direction we needed to go. Like the other trail, it too, was a bit muddy. I just hoped it would take us to our destination.

Maudie and I finally reached the small creek that meandered through our woods and on toward the river that would lead into Skipton. I looked for the familiar wooden-plank bridge which connected the trail with the opposite shore. The bridge was no longer visible, nor did I see the familiar stepping stones that we used to skip across during nature outings with either Father or the current tutor. They seemed to have disappeared. The deep, foamy water discouraged me from attempting to cross at this point. Rather than go clear back around to the road, I decided to continue riding downstream along the bank I had been following. I vaguely remembered the banks almost touched at one point further down which might offer a safer crossing.

We followed the boiling water, which twisted, turned and narrowed, for quite a distance. Because there was no time element, I luxuriated in the lush scenery and the calming and peaceful voices of nature. Along the banks were young willows bending low with the weight of a multitude of blackbirds, all chattering noisily amongst themselves. A slight breeze was stirring, and the tall grasses whispered as they brushed against each other. In the distance, I could hear birds whistling for their mates and the continual bubbling and roaring of the stream, all adding harmonious, hypnotic chords to nature's song.

For the most part, the wooded terrain was unusually green for this time of year due to the heavy deluge of rains we had experienced earlier in the week, and in fact, most of the latter part of the summer. Along the creek bank, the carpet of grassy foliage was slightly turning a dusty gold and tan. A few cattails had burst; their fluffy, seedy guts spewing out for the breeze to catch and disseminate. On the other side, trees lined the forest edge with birch and oak leaves. They were beginning to boast traces of brown and orange. The clear blue sky was changing like the seasons, starting to fill with scattered puffs of grayish-white clouds that echoed into infinity.

I hadn't been riding up this way for a long time so I was enjoying the view that nature offered. This lowland area, at the farthest edge of Father's land entitlement, was often flooded so it wasn't usually such a delightful ride. More often, when I would take off on my adventures, I rode in the other direction. I had ridden out with Father and the boys on a couple of hunting excursions, but we didn't hunt much on this side of the rill. That was usually done in the south timber which was much higher ground and less filled with downed branches and trees. This whole area had been left as virgin or native timber, abandoned to exist, decay and rejuvenate itself. As I rounded a bend in the stream, I could see in a meadow area the isolated "Standing Stone." I felt relieved to see the landmark.

"Thank goodness," I said to Maudie. "I was beginning to worry we were lost. But it seems the path we took led us to where I'd hoped it would."

The "Stone," as it was most often called by the family, had been given its name eons ago. The asymmetrical gray rock, easily twenty-six or twenty-seven hands in diameter and about twice as tall, was smooth as glass from years of slow erosion by wind, rain and sun. At one time it had been the worshiping place for a secretive cult before my family had acquired the land. At least that is the tale local gossips and historians tell. My old Grandmother used to say fairies, witches and such met here on dark nights at special times of the year just like they did on the Plains of Salisbury. I wasn't so sure I believed all the old stories since this was just one single large rock and those at Salisbury were grouped together. It was also documented that those stones had special significance in ancient religions. Our stone didn't look very threatening and as far as I could tell, its sole function was just a boundary marker on the northern edge of our estate. I often thought Grandmother made up the witch stories just to scare us so we would not go near the stone. And, I guess her scare had worked, for none of us had ever gotten up the courage to come near here alone. Father had taken us to see it a few times and Nathan and I had ridden through the south timber to get here once. Father didn't believe Grandmother's stories either. He said the "Stone" was most likely a marker for an old Roman road.

I don't know what made me stop. I felt a momentary whisper of nostalgia flare up to greet me, so I dismounted. It suddenly seemed important to I leave my mark – to record my existence for future posterity. My inner soul must have known I would not be returning to this spot again. I don't know why I had that feeling or what prompted my next impulsive gesture. Picking up a small chunk of rock from the ground, I knelt down. On the back side of the "Stone," I brushed the grass aside and began crudely scraping and scratching the date and my initials at the bottom: CG - 1641.

After I finished the task, I stood up, shaking my head, wondering why this moment of nostalgia had seemed so important. I had not been in a hurry before. Now, it seemed time was escaping and we needed to get on with our journey.

"Come on Maudie," I said, mounting the steed which had stood waiting patiently during the interlude. "If we're going to Skipton we need to be on our way. If we're not there by noon, we won't be home for dinner."

I clicked the mare into a brisk, invigorating gallop towards our destination. By late morning we had been able to get across the stream without any incidence, although the crossing spot didn't look the least familiar. With all the raining and flooding this fall, I rationalized it was bound not to look the same as in dry weather. I had not been up to Skipton on my own and wasn't sure how far it was. I had always let Father lead the way and didn't think about directions or other landmarks. I was usually chattering about something and never looked around to see where we were going. We always rode through a forest and I could see a dense forest ahead. I just assumed it was at the edge of our destination, so Maudie and I rode in that direction. Just for a moment, I had the feeling we had been riding far longer than when Father and I had taken our trips to the small town. But with my inattention to the few times we had gone, I just shook my head, shrugged my shoulders and attributed the moment as being anxious to get where we were going.

"Not far now," I said to Maudie. "We are within a stone's throw of that forest ahead. We'll soon be in Skipton with lunch for me and oats for you."

Maudie's ear's perked up and she herself stepped up the pace a bit. Guess she was as anxious as I to get to our destination and take a break. If I had known we made a wrong turn at the "Stone," I certainly would have gone back toward home. I wasn't paying attention as we followed the twists and turns of the swiftly moving, bubbling path of water. I didn't know the stream merged and separated in several places. Much later I learned we did not cross the same waterway we had followed earlier. The watery crossing gave us a false sense of direction and our ride took us too far northward. But at this point I didn't know we were lost and so I urged Maudie on to pursue our adventure.

We reached the edge of the forest and soon found a well-worn trail. It appeared to be a shortcut, heading in the direction I thought we needed to go. We immediately found ourselves in a deep, thick wood, and I had only a moment of apprehension as we entered into the dark shadows. This trail, like many others we had traveled, had been subjected to summer flooding. Right away I felt the chill of the damp, cool forest. The temperature seemed to have dropped drastically. Small puddles could be seen through the undergrowth, while the acrid, musky smell of soggy ground, leaves and felled trees filled my nostrils. I shivered a little as we continued to ride into the murky, green shadows. The sunshine had vanished. The sky had turned gray and I could see dark clouds through the spiny, framework of boughs and lacy patterns of tan, gold and green leaves that was the forest ceiling.

No need to worry I told myself. We'll be in Skipton well before any storm breaks. But in sighting the gray sky, I had unconsciously urged Maudie to hurry a little faster. As most of this adventure had gone slightly awry from its beginning, so my last thought about arriving at our destination shortly would prove to be wrong. It was then I heard the low growling of distant thunder. The storm wouldn't wait – it seemed to be approaching much faster that I had anticipated. The dark shadows around me deepened. Through the limited view of the sky, the clouds boiled and foamed in angry turbulence.

The grumbling and rolling thunder became steadily stronger, while the gusting wind swirled leaves and debris across our path, blinding both of us with fine particles of grit and dirt.

Maudie was becoming extremely skittish and it took all my concentration and strength to control her. I should have stopped then and found some shelter. But I was young and foolish, with a mission in mind.

"Come on Maudie, we only have a short way to go," I said. Or so I thought.

"It's alright girl," I said in soft voice, hoping to relieve her natural animal instincts of approaching danger. "It's just a little storm. We've been in worse."

The thunder was now all around us – snarling, rumbling and crackling with a reverberating boom that jarred and shook the woods, causing the earth to quiver and shake. Suddenly, lightning flashed in a jagged knife-like streak to the ground ahead and exploded in a ball of light, illuminating the entire area. I have always prided myself on my excellent horsemanship. Under the circumstances, I could understand Maudie's distracted state and frightened sense of insecurity. I myself was a great deal more than just a little nervous. You can imagine my frenzy in trying to maintain control over an animal not in any mood to follow directions. She reared, and then bolted in a dead heat away from the trail. I suddenly became aware of the low-lying, heavy branches that we were fast approaching.

I closed my eyes and hung on with all my might, ducking as low as I could into the nape of Maudie's neck to avoid the impact of this potential coup de grace that awaited me. I didn't have time to think about my life or for that matter to whisper a silent prayer. Miracle of miracles! I breathed a sigh of relief as I managed to clear the branches, feeling only the slightest brush of death rub against my right shoulder.

By this time the animal was close to hysteria. I managed to slow her down a little and tried coaxing her with gentle words, a feat that is essentially difficult when you are scared yourself and trying to stay on a wild animal. The droplets of rain turned vicious and it began pelting us with a rapid icy sting. Maudie was still threshing wildly through the entanglement of trees, snorting and wheezing. After several attempts, I finally was able to turn her a little and head in a different direction. I had a glimpse of the trail close by, just off to my left. I managed to coax her onto the muddy trail and felt a bit of confidence we would get through this mess, despite the intensity of the storm. I was sure I could calm the beast and gain control of the situation.

It was at that moment, when Maudie, in her agitated state, somehow tripped and lost her footing. I remember a thunderous crack and another bolt of lightening. To this day I'm not sure what happened next – it might have been the storm itself, a hidden rut protruding out on the trail, or that Maudie was completely exhausted. She skidded, slid and tried to straighten herself, only to totter and lurch in the other direction. I pulled hard on the reins, but to no avail. I didn't even have time to be afraid or feel panic. At one moment I was on Maudie, the next both horse and rider went tumbling. We were tossed into the already electrified atmosphere. I felt the brief whistling of air around my ears as we plummeted apart. I remember hearing a searing, croaking cry and feeling penetrating pelts of rain against my face before I hit the ground and passed into oblivion. That was the last time I saw Maudie.

CHAPTER THREE

Lost in the Woods

I awoke in the arms of fate. In actuality, I awoke to the face of an auburn-haired angel, her umber colored eyes peering concernedly into mine. Could this be heaven? Had St. Peter collected another boarder for his heavenly realm? Surely not! I was too young. Besides, no heavenly music filled my ears. Instead, there was a buzzing, tingling fuzziness and everything appeared hazy-white. I thought if I had passed there would be no pain. But there was a pulsating, pounding at the base of my head and a hot, searing pain through my lower leg which gave evidence I had not been claimed by any heavenly host. I blinked my eyes into awareness, trying to establish the reality of my situation. The aromatic smell of cooking spices and herbs wafted through the air, and at my side was the angel with a warm, welcoming smile.

"So ye be joinin' the livin', eh miss?"

This came from the other side of the bed upon which I rested. I turned my head slowly and met the warm and concerned eyes of the speaker. The snowy, white haired woman had one of those wrinkly kinds of smiles that make you feel warm, cozy and safe. Just knowing I had come under the care of these two women was comforting. The older woman's homespun dress and tan waistcoat was covered with a white, slightly tattered apron. On her head was a white duster bonnet, as clean and white as a fluffy cloud.

I tried to focus my eyes and adjust to the hazy and distorted sunlight streaming through the narrow window. As I looked around the room and saw the rough walls, I quickly assessed I was sheltered in the cottage of a woodcutter or caretaker on some estate. I sensed a simplistic family life with love and warmth radiating from every corner. My brief survey took in the young girl. I guessed she was about my age. She was clad simply like the older woman, but in a blue dress. A brightly patterned knit shawl, haphazardly thrown around her shoulders, gave her cheeks a pink, healthy glow. Her creamy-white face was splattered with freckles. She smiled once more and her brown eyes twinkled with happiness which made her face light up. She seemed delighted the vigil was over and her patient had rewarded her with life. I then returned my gaze to the older woman, answering her greeting with an entourage of questions.

"What happened? Why am I here? My head feels funny – no, it just plain hurts," I said, realizing my voice was almost a grated whisper.

I tried to shift my body a little, and was thanked with sharp pains piercing my head as well as the rest of my body.

"Where am I? Have I been a bother?" I asked softly, trying to assess the situation. "I seemed to be in a bit of a fog." I tried to think back to what might have happened. But my head hurt too badly.

"Well lass," the older woman replied in a heavy Scottish brogue. "We be real worried 'bout ye there f'r a while. Ye's ha' a bad fall and a nasty blow to y'r head. Thought ye may be a gonner. Ye jest moaned and groaned and were so restless.

Tha' were back 'bout five days ago. Ye 'as been sort o' ramblin' in and out of oblivion since then. We ha' tried our best to fix ya' up and I thin' ye be on the mend. Rest be wha' ye need, lots o' rest! No more questions now. Ya' jest lay there and rest a bit longer."

"I must be on my way to...to... to... I'm not sure where ... I don't remember. Everything is blank. I've got to be on my way," I mumbled as I tried to lift myself off the pillow. Again, the searing pain forced me down and the room swam in dizzying, circular sheets before my eyes. I broke out into a cold sweat that made me feel nauseated. "Oh, I... I... I..." I groaned and stammered, all in the same inhale of breath due to the overpowering pain.

"Whoa there, miss," the older lady said as she rushed to the bed and helped tucked me back into the coverlets. "Ya' take it easy! Ye's not ready f'r goin' any wheres yet. A'sides yer head bein' featherblown ye leg is goin' t'need time to heal. And y'r ankle is badly sprained and swollen. Don' thin' ya' got broken bones, but ye do ha' some nasty cuts and bruises. We bandaged ya' best we could and I thin' ye goin' t'be jest fine when ye's strength comes back. It were a good toss ye got and ye is goin' to be sore and not feelin' so good f'r quite o' while."

"Where's my M... M... M... Maudie? Is she alright? I've got to... to... to... g... g... g... go. Oh, I can't remember where... What's happened to me?"

"Don' get y'rself all worked up "said the stern but friendly woman. "It won' help none a'tall. Y'r gonna be a'right. Gi' y'rself time. As t'where ye be? We live somewha' near the For'st of Bowlan'. Don' worry 'bout a thin'. We be talkin' later. Ya' jest snuggle in them covers an' rest y'rself a might longer."

The older woman turned and left the room muttering, "jest rest lass, jest rest," leaving all my questions unanswered.

I did feel the need to close my eyes and not think. The pounding in my head had increased from the futile effort of trying to get up. My body felt numb, except when I moved ever so slightly. Then, the pain welled up like an angry dog. The angel put a cold compress on my forehead. She gently tucked it around my temples and gave me a warm smile that made me feel like I wasn't a burden to her. I managed a feeble smile in return. I again started to ask questions, but she only pressed her finger to her lips, signaling me to be quiet.

"Jest rest," she too said as she turned and left the room.

I was worn out from the few moments of activity and it didn't take me long to fall back into a deep slumber. When I awoke, the room was full of dark shadows. The warm glow of lamplight beamed through the semi-open doorway. Before I could make any noise to let my hosts know I was awake, I caught bits and pieces of a conversation from the adjoining room. It wasn't that I tried to eavesdrop, but they were pretty engrossed in their talk.

"Now, don' worry y'rself none, mum," a male voice said. "I only he'rd rumors the king's sold'rs were in Keighley. We be a f'r piece from tha' place. Besides, Pap and t'other men be safely away right now. We 'as plenty o' friends in the area sharin' our interests. F'r sure they be keepin' a tight lip if'n need be. And we jest need t'keep quiet and mind our business."

"I worry this whole thin' will get out o' hand like it did down 'round London town." This seemed to come from the older woman who had been administering to my needs.

"'Sides, ye canna' a'ways count on pe'ple, be they friends or not," she continued. "When it comes to savin' ones own skin, pe'ple tend t'f'rget they's loyalties more of'n than not. But ye be right. Pap and t'others be safely away f'r the time bein'. These matters gotta' settle down here a bit or get resolved one way or t'other."

It seemed the room from which the voices came must be the kitchen or cooking area. This I assumed because I heard the banging and clanging of kettles and pots and the odor of food being cooked filled the cottage.

"Did ye see any sold'rs y'rself, Tad?" questioned the voice I recognized as my angel of mercy.

"Na," answered the voice which had acquired the name of Tad. "I only he'rd rumors when deliverin' cords o' wood t'Sir Winfrey's home. A friendly kitchen maid and a stable boy said they he'rd the news a couple o' days ago from a tinker passin' through the area. What 'bout our guest? That be somethin' t'be more concerned 'bout. Do we know who she be? I shouldna' brought her here wha' wi' the whole district in turmoil."

"Well, lad, you couldna' very well ha' left her in the woods to die from the cold, could ya'?" That seemed to come from the grandmotherly voice.

"No, Mum, tha' be true," he said. "I kep' my ears op'n in the village, but I didna' hear anythin' 'bout anyone lookin' for a young miss or any other missin' person. Nary a patron nor the inn owner mentioned they ha' heard o' a king's spy in the area – jest the sold'rs ov'r 'round Keighley way. She canna' be from 'round this area. Did she say anythin 'bout wha' she be doin' out in our woods?"

"She finally op'n'd her eyes f'r a few moments earlier t'day," said the girl. "I jest checked on her a short time ago, but she were still sleepin'. She were tryin' t'ask some questions, but she be really incoherent and seems t'be still in a great deal o' pain."

"Well, I gotta' few outside chores t'do a'fore we sup, Mum," said the male voice.

I heard the shuffling of feet, the scraping of a chair, the creaking and banging of a door and felt the whisper of cool air rushing through the slightly ajar door to the room I was in. I gathered the voice called Tad had gone outdoors. I closed my eyes and tried once more to assess my position and sort through the tidbits of information I had heard. Where had I been going? Try as I might, nothing came to mind. I was beginning to be worried. After hearing my hosts' conversation, my curiosity was somewhat aroused to know what kind of "interests" these people had, but I also needed to think about my own situation.

I am... Oh, my goodness... I couldn't think of my name. Slow down. Don't panic. I tried to rationalize that sometimes a blow to the head, which it seems I must have suffered, can make you forget things. With that thought, my head began pounding again. It was hard to concentrate. The throbbing started at the base of my neck and ebbed upward and downward with waves of pain in sync with my heartbeat. I must have groaned rather loudly because instantly the angel was at my side.

"How be ye feelin'? Is ye's pain bad?" she asked. The answer to this question must have been obviously painted on my face.

Looking toward the doorway and speaking into the space it occupied, she called out, "Mum, I thin' our patient could use a bit more o' ye's special concoction t'ease the pain."

The two women gently ministered to my needs. They not only fed me a brew of the pain-relieving tea, but also coaxed a little broth from the stew pot down my throat. Soon the combination of the two made me warm and groggy. I closed my eyes for just a moment, intending to ask more questions. Instead, I must have fallen asleep again.

When next I awoke, the golden sunshine was streaming in the only window in the room. It took a few minutes for my eyes to adjust to the brilliance. Then, all my senses began to awaken. The sounds of morning permeated the air, both inside and outside the cottage. From outside, I heard the shoosh-thunk-crack of wood being split and chopped as the axe penetrated tree trunks. The sound reverberated and echoed around the dwelling. From the nearby room, I could not hear any significant noise, although there were muffled pings and clangs of kitchenware being used. From the noise and the way the sunshine was drifting in, I surmised it was getting close to mid-morning.

My nostrils soon were filled with the pungent aroma of rising bread and the hint of nutmeg and other spices. Just for a moment, the wonderful smells gave me the faint feeling of familiarity. But as to where and when, I couldn't begin to guess. The cooking odors must have wafted down into my stomach for I was suddenly conscious of being hungry.

I shifted a little bit and thought I might try to sit up. Gritting my teeth and preparing myself for an onslaught of pain, I very slowly moved my body. Although I felt several sharp spasms and waves of pain, they did not seem as severe as before. The pain in my head had settled down to a dull roar. I managed to shift my position a little, but decided trying to sit up would just have to wait. I was amazed at how weak I felt and just getting resituated required all the effort I could muster.

I lay quietly, letting my body rest a bit to renew its strength. This gave me time to think on my predicament. My head still felt fuzzy and disoriented. I pondered on the two questions that seemed to be uppermost in my tired mind: Who am I and where do I belong? I just simply couldn't put a name to me. My stomach twisted in knots, both from being hungry and from the panic I felt rising within me. It was most distressing. My illusive identity seemed to be hidden deep in the recesses of my mind. I was too young and inexperienced then, and also too ill, to understand the complete workings of the brain. It too, like the rest of the body, must have time to repair itself after a severe injury.

At this moment, the effort involved in getting my mind to target on any tangible thought only increased my anxiety and made my head hurt more. Sensitive nerve endings sent a strong message that focusing on the task of thinking was too difficult for me right now. I admonished myself to take the grandmotherly woman's advice she had provided earlier and "jest rest." After several deep breaths, I was able to steady my emotions and bring them under control. I decided I wasn't doing myself any favors by becoming panic stricken. The deep breaths seemed to help reduce the panic and churning of my stomach to some extent. Once I calmed myself down, I took the opportunity to survey the lodgings I had recently acquired.

The small room was an edifice of unpretentious rusticity. Despite the soot and dust, by-products of fireplaces which cling to walls and furniture, an air of cleanliness prevailed. It looked as if the walls and the worn wooden floors had been scrubbed with a stiff brush. Warmth radiated from a crackling, roaring fire in one corner of the room in a fireplace constructed of gray clay daub and a few chunks of field stone. There was no built-in hearth, and in front of the fireplace the floor was much darker in color from stray sparks and ash escaping from the inner fire chamber throughout the years. The mesmerizing flames danced and leaped upward, changing into smoke and inviting soul and spirit to follow its wispy journey into the universe.

The most ornate article in the whole room was the carved bedstead upon which I rested. It was a comfortable, cozy and peaceful harbinger for this recuperating victim. I wondered who I had put out of this restful spot since my arrival. I slowly twisted myself just a bit so I could see the head of the bed and was awed by the carved dragon in the center of the tall, walnut headboard. The simple but beautiful etching, chiseled with care, was a display of excellent artistic workmanship. I wondered about the artist.

Although I did not remember it at the time, I had always admired the beauty of wood furniture. That was a part of my heritage that I would recall years later – how Father and Mother had taught us children the value of finely carved, handcrafted furniture and well-sculpted artwork. The lacquer on the bedstead was darkened with age, hinting it was a relic of the past. Perhaps it had been a family heirloom, passed down through several generations. I later learned that indeed this was true. It was the only piece of furniture that had been salvaged and brought from Scotland when the family emigrated south.

The rest of the room was very plain and sparsely furnished. A small, sturdy wash table was near the bed and a gray pottery bowl and ewer stood on top. In another corner was a crudely constructed chest, most likely for clothing. There were a few garments hanging on a gnarled stand in the other corner. They were dark and drab in color and looked like they could provide warmth on a cool, rainy and misty English day. Across from the bed stood a small writing table and a chair, both of crude construction. The one window in the room was high in the outside wall and was not curtained. Sunlight, creating a prism of light and dust particles in the air, came streaming through. The semi-open doorway connected the room I now occupied with the rest of the house and I wondered about the size of the cottage. I assumed at least three people lived here because I had heard that many talking.

I had been awake only a few minutes when I heard movement and saw the door being pushed ajar, almost stealthily. It was my angel, lugging a tray full of varying-sized containers. Even though the room felt warm from the fire, it must have been cooler than I thought. Swirling spirals of steam escaped from the containers as the hot contents met cool air. The girl was about my size. Both she and the older woman were of slight frames, but looked like they could easily look out for themselves.

"Mornin'. So ye be 'wake at last," the girl said. "We were beginin' t'be worried. Ye ha' been sleepin' since even'in a'fore last. It 'pears Grandmam's potion really knocked ye. I do 'ope it 'as' eased the pain."

"Surely I haven't been sleeping so long!" I said. "Wasn't it just a few hours ago you brought me tea and a bit of soup?"

Still holding the tray, the girl laughed and said, "Aye, tha' were yest'rday. Are ye feelin' better? It probably be too soon t'tell. Ye 'as a bit more color t'day. I brought ya' more broth – nothin' like Grandmam's hot soups for healin' the body."

She sat the food-laden tray on the nearby chair and pulled it closer to the bed. She helped me as I gingerly struggled to sit up without inviting the penetrating spasms of pain to invade my head and body.

"Do you have a name?" I managed to wheeze out as I carefully inched my way up into a semi-sitting position.

She didn't answer my question or even acknowledge she had heard it. Instead she fluffed and stuffed cushions and pillows around me to help prop me upright.

Then she asked, "Ya' a'right? Be ye in pain? Y'r as white as Grandmam's apron."

"I'll be fine, soon as I catch my breath," I croaked.

In my weakened condition, the laborious movement was harder than I expected. I felt totally exhausted. It was just another reminder of how fast a healthy body can deteriorate.

It was as she was turning to pick up the tray that she softly whispered: "Sarah."

"What did you say?" I asked.

"Sarah Ringold. Tha' be my name," she said.

"A very lovely name," I uttered with a little groan. I was still shifting my body, trying to settle into a position that was conducive to eating the soup and not stirring up the pain. As long as I didn't move, it was tolerable.

"Try t'eat all o' it – Grandmam says it will gi' ye strength t'make ye well," Sarah said.

The broth did taste good and I told her so. My stomach really appreciated the nourishment. It was wonderfully palatable, and despite the effort required to eat, I found I was indeed very hungry.

"I hope I'm not creating unnecessary trouble for you all," I said, recalling the conversation I heard during one of my waking moments. "And who am I putting out of bed?"

"It be Grandmam's, but she be pleased t'help. She 'as been sharin' my bed since ye came "an' tha' be workin' jest fine," Sarah said.

"As soon as I feel better, I shall be on my way home," I said. "Right now I can't think where that is. Can you tell me what happened? I guess I must have had an accident, but I

41

don't remember anything. I'm not even sure where I am or why I am here. I sort of vaguely remember a storm. After that, I only remember pain. And I am feeling a little less of that."

"We thin' y'r 'orse bolted in the storm," said Sarah. "Ye were quite a ways from here when my brother Tad found ya'. He were on his way home from a nearby village. He stayed late, waitin' out the storm a'fore he started. Else, ye mightna' ha' been so lucky. Tha' trail he found ye on be the ol' one and isna' used much any more. A few o' us make use o' it when we be in a hurry t'get home, like Tad were t'other night af'r the storm. It isna' a very good trail, and he couldna' figure out why a well-bred miss like y'rself woulda' been on it. Closer t'the village, tha' trail narrows and gets very treacherous. And down there it isna' marked so well."

"It be really quite easy t'get lost out in tha' part o' the woods unless ye know it well," Sarah continued. "Our forest is pretty far from everythin'. The trails here 'ventually wind up into the hills. Anyway, it were a bad storm and Tad didna' get home 'til way after nightfall. We don' get storms so bad usually, but it 'as been a very wet summer and we still be gettin' storms as we go into fall. The day Tad found ye, there were an unus'al 'mount o' rain. Ye were in pretty bad shape, soaked t'the skin and mumblin' deliriously when Tad brung ya' in. We got ya' dried off and into bed; then, ye passed out from fev'r and pain. Ye ha' been tha' way f'r ov'r a week."

"Grandmam was really worried 'cause ya' were in the cold and dampness f'r so long," Sarah said in continuing her story. "An' don' ye worry none. Havin' ya' here be no trouble. Grandmam says ye's lucky tha' ye' ha' a strong will. Tha' be why y'r restin' in this bed. Lyin' there in tha' heavy rain on the cold forest floor could ha' been the death o' a less healthy person."

"My horse? You still haven't mentioned what happened." I think I already knew the answer from the sketchy details she had just related.

Sarah looked toward the fireplace, her eyes fixed in a far away look as she watched the dancing flames. Then she replied very quietly.

"I be 'fraid ye's 'orse were in a lot o' pain when Tad found the two o' ye. Near dead she were and badly injured. Both front legs broke and she, like ye, were fevered from the cold an' in pain. She ha' to be put down. Later, Tad and a friend buried her near the trail an' brought y'r saddle an' gear back to our stable. I be sorry. It would seem ye and the 'orse were friends."

"Oh, poor, poor Maudie," I whispered sadly. Then, I blinked my eyes and caught my breath. How was it I could remember the name of my horse and not my own? What a truly frightening thought.

"Wha'd ye say?" asked Sarah.

I certainly did not want her to know I couldn't remember my name and could remember the name of my horse. "Nothing, nothing at all," I muttered.

By this time I had consumed most of the broth. The warmth of the soup made me feel better and took away the sharp edges of hunger that I had felt earlier. Sarah asked if I was finished. When I nodded, she took the tray and started to leave the room.

"Tell your grandmam that the soup really filled my hollow spots, and tell your mum that I appreciate being cared for the last few days," I said to the retreating figure.

Sarah turned her head and chuckled. "Grandmam and Mum be the same. Grandmam 'as cared f'r Tad and me since we were babes. Our real mum died long ago."

"And do you have a father?" I asked.

"Pap's off right now, attendin' t'some bus'ness," she answered. "He be 'ome soon 'nough an' may be ye can meet him a'fore ye be leavin'."

At the door she stopped and turned to look at me. After a few seconds, she said rather shyly, "I 'as tol' ye my name and 'bout my family. Now it be ye's turn. Do ye ha' a name or be it a secret?"

My stomach did a leap and then felt hollow again. I guess it was time to confess my ignorance, forgetfulness or whatever it might be called. "I'm sure you're going to find this rather stupid," I said cautiously. "My horse's name was Maudie and we were going to… and I live…

Again, I couldn't put a name to where we had been headed. "Try as I might, I can't remember where we were going and where we are from," I said. "And the other thing is I can't remember my own name. I don't suppose you found any papers in my clothes or on Maudie to help tell us who I am."

"No miss," she answered slowly. "Y'r clothes were pretty wet and grimy. The only thin' Tad found were some currency notes and copper coins. Grandmam washed y'r garments and put the money back when they were dried. We found nothin' t'tell us who ye be. Ya' really don' know?"

"I don't know who I am, if I have a family and who they are, or even where I was going," I said. "Strange isn't it I can remember about Maudie?"

I could hear the note of panic rising in my voice. Then I began to shake and shiver uncontrollably. I was shaking so hard my teeth were clicking and it was all I could do to keep my tongue out of their way.

"Grandmam, come quickly. I need y'r help," shouted Sarah.

44

Sitting the tray of dirty dishes back down on the chair and gently taking hold of my shoulders, she tried to comfort me. The grandmother quickly appeared, her face wrinkled with concern.

"Wha' be the matter girl?" she said to Sarah.

"She be shakin' so," Sarah answered.

The two of them helped me ease back down into the blankets, talking soothingly all the time. I heard the words, "jest rest," "deep breaths" "jest ya' relax there lass" and the shaking finally subsided. My head was throbbing again like the rhythmic beating of a big drum. I felt what little energy I had possessed draining completely away. I wanted nothing more than to "jest rest" for a while and let the panic and fear of not knowing who I was go away. Sarah explained to the grandmother our conversation once they got me settled down.

"I didna' know wha' t'do f'r her. Wha' are we goin' t'do Mum? How can we help her?" Sarah was totally rattled, trying not only to comfort me, but herself as well. "Ye be a'right," she said as she patted my arm and squeezed my hand. I thought that was more for her than me.

"Now, now, don' neither of ya' worry none." The grandmother spoke in a gentle and reassuring voice. "Sometimes accidents cause a person na' ta' 'member thin's f'r a time. But as healin' begins, the head gets lots better. Everythin' comes back, crisp and clear as a win'er day. Now ya' jest rest there lass and I be bringin' ya' more o' me special tea. Thin's be better by and by. Jest be a good patient an' let y'r body get well. The rest will come 'bout ov'r' time. Ye still be a pretty sick lass. The fever 'as broke a bit and no doubt ye be on the mend soon enough."

Grandmam left the room, returning shortly with her famous tea. Sarah stayed a little longer, prattling about how much better I'd be after a short nap. All the while, with my head aching fiercely, I searched my cloudy mind for some clue as to my identity. While we waited for the tea to work, we chatted about things I could recall. She quizzed me on several number facts, asked questions about English history and what kind of stories I had read. From my answers, she decided I was very educated and came from a family of means.

"Lots of people can read and write," I said, noting that didn't really give credence to her idea that I came from a family of means.

"Tha' be true," she said. "I know sev'ral servin' girls who read very well, and it be a blessin' f'r their fam'lies," Sarah said. "But I don' know many people wi' such nice clothes as ye were wearin'."

It still frightened me that I could recite such trivial things like numbers, places and things, but not remember the details that counted and mattered about my personal life. It bothered me that I could name my horse and not know any other facts about me or my family. Perhaps, like the grandmother said, I just needed more time for my body to repair itself.

"I be leavin' ya' for a while," Sarah said. "Ye snuggle in there and jest rest yer body. And if'n ye wan' and feel up t'a it, I ha' a couple o' books I could read to ye later," Sarah said.

She picked up the tray of dishes and left. A few seconds later the door swung closed, giving me leave to rest and recuperate.

My bewildered mind returned to the nagging thought of who I was and where I was. Was I really lost to my family? Did I have a family and would they be searching for me? I hoped I did, and deep down I felt I did. I hoped the premonition was true. Would they know where to look? Had I left word with anyone where I was going? Sarah said her cottage was nearer the regular trail to the village and quite a ways from the path I had traveled. In fact, I assessed we were not near any place I had been or knew about. And what hills was she talking about?

Perhaps I had run away from my family. I wished my fuzzy brain would allow me to recall such an important detail. I remembered once reading about a lad who ran away from home. When he was found dead in a strange town, people didn't seem to care. Thinking about that story made me feel even sadder because I couldn't remember my own story. I squeezed my eyes tightly shut and tried to swallow the big lump in my throat. A warm tear slid down my cheek.

By this time, the warm herbal tea had relaxed me and I could feel myself drifting. It's all right, I thought. For the moment, it doesn't matter who I am or where I am going. Thanks to the generosity of this kind and loving family, I had a chance for life. And even in my nebulous state, I could feel the overwhelming pull of adventure. It seemed for the moment I had tempted fate, but I had survived. I was ready to rekindle and tend to the fires of my preordained life – whatever that might be – just as soon as I regained my strength, and my memory. For the time being, I would just let the tea take over and do its work. I closed my eyes and drifted into a much needed, health-reviving sleep.

CHAPTER FOUR

Alarming News

The Ringold cottage was a pleasant environment for recuperating. At first I was a pampered guest, but day by day my strength and the use of weak limbs slowly returned. The fever broke and the pain subsided enough for me to get out of bed and hobble around to take meals with the family. My days continued – one after another as my stay moved from weeks to months, still with no signs of recalling my previous life. At first I just bided my time, but as my health and strength improved I was able to help out when needed for what I began considering my new family. I still had a few deep bruises, a foot that was healing and occasional headaches which made me feel nauseated. The main ailment that constantly nagged me was my loss of memory.

I hoped I would soon regain my memory and continue on with my life, whatever that had been. Later, as fate stepped in, returning home wasn't an option because there were too many other important things to consider. By the time I regained my memory, I had already become involved in the political and religious tidewaters that flourished and created havoc all over the British Islands. My family would never have understood my loyalty to strangers. And when all was said and done, it was destiny that took the planning out of my hands. Two things happened to seal my future.

First, there was Tad. I had been kind of afraid of him at first. He seemed so gruff and unconcerned about me. From a distance, I sensed his interest was more about when I would leave than how I was really feeling. I remembered the conversation about how he should never have brought me to this cottage and wondered if he still felt that way. Later I discovered his concern was much more than I could have imagined. Despite his gruffness, even at our first meeting I liked him. He had poked his head through the open doorway and asked if I felt better. Then he came in and introduced himself.

"I hope ye 'as found 'commodations here most pleasin'," he said with a twinkle in his eye. "I be Tad and the one who found ye out on the ol' trail. I canna' for the life o' me figure why ye'd be there."

"Indeed, this is the grandest bed to rest in and you have all been so kind," I answered. "I can't begin to tell you how much I appreciate the care and concern you all have given me. And I do have so many questions. Am I ever going to get my memory back? It is so confusing not knowing for sure where I am or who I am."

And like Grandmam, he put his hand on my shoulder and said, "Jest rest. We be talkin' later."

I had felt an attraction to Tad even then. What was not to like about this young man with his unruly reddish-brown hair, greenish-brown eyes, more freckles than his sister and a smile that wrinkled his face? He still seemed a bit suspicious of me, but even that had dimmed. Right from my first vision of him, Tad had stolen my heart. I felt like I had acquired much more than just a new friend. I couldn't really put into words how I felt about him at this point. We just seemed compatible and enjoyed each other's company. I felt comfortable when he was around. I liked his sense of humor, and once we had gotten past the initial amenities, he made me laugh. I would forget my troubles as I listened to his stories. I wondered if I already had a suitor or was promised to someone. I hoped not.

I'm not sure how Tad felt about me. I wondered if he considered me anything more than an inconvenient houseguest. I couldn't begin to tell him about my feelings until I had regained my memory. I sensed the concern and interest Tad took in me would eventually hinge on the type of person he thought I was. He could not see who or what I was in my real life. That was a disadvantage for any kind of relationship beyond being friends for now. I just knew when his green eyes met mine and he smiled, I melted inside.

I appreciated Tad's effort in searching for information about me during the first couple of weeks I was still lying abed and recuperating. He made numerous trips into nearby villages and eagerly sought out the gossip at local inns but found no one who could help with the mystery of my identity. People had not heard of any spies in the area, although I wasn't so sure he had not ruled the idea out even if I didn't fit the role. Many of the tavern keepers had all kinds of stories to relate about people looking for young lads; however, no one seemed to be trying to find a girl who had been riding a chestnut mare.

I am quite certain Tad never offered much information. He was only a listener, but I can imagine he certainly asked questions to prompt any loose-lipped traveler or tinker. Did that imply I must have been in discord with my family? Still, deep inside, I hoped there was a loving, caring family somewhere, waiting for me to come home. But where were they? Was I so lost they didn't know where to look?

Years later I would discover my family had indeed led a desperate search for me. I heard they had sent out runners to all of the villages near our home and on to many of the estates I was known to have visited. Eventually the web of searching spread out, but their concerns did not reach the tavern in the nearby village where Tad spent time until it was much too late. By then, the fingers of fate had sealed my destiny.

Both Tad and Sarah stopped often at Grandmam's room to see how I was doing. Tad told me he was twenty, just a couple of years older than his sister. Although she had much responsibility in the cottage, it seemed we must be about the same age.

In my mind, it seemed Tad was already a man when I first met him. I guess I found that unusual and couldn't really think why. He was already providing some support for his family, meeting their daily need. His thin, lithe body was well-accustomed to hard work. He called himself a woodcutter and I got the impression he was probably more at home in the woods chopping trees and hunting food for the table than he was here at the cottage. He said he and their father eked out a living from the trapping and wood gathering, taking both the furs and wood stacks to be sold in nearby villages.

I liked Tad's being a vibrant force in his family, taking responsibility when his father was away. When Pap was at home, Tad was constantly with him. They were either cutting wood to sell or off on what I now assumed was church work. Pap and Tad were both very involved in helping to promote their faith and both spent a lot of time with their church interests.

It was apparent this family loved the father, and the goodness of this man was praised by Sarah, Grandmam and Tad. In asking about Pap several times since I had joined the family for meals, they would just say: "He be afoot and 'bout some Godly business." This comment didn't make much sense until I got to know the family better. By then, I had already become involved and the fingers of fate were tightening. I officially met Pap after I had been at the cottage about three weeks. He must have snuck in during the night. When he stopped into Grandmam's room, he didn't seem surprised to see me. Thus, I knew he had been informed about my mishap.

"I'm pleased to meet you, Mr. Ringold," I said. "I hope I have not caused your family too much inconvenience. This isn't exactly how I thought I would spend my days, although I can't tell you what I might have been doing. My past and future seem to be in limbo."

"Now, lass, it be jest fine. My family be 'appy takin' care o' ye. From now on, jest call me Pap. Not sure who Mr. Ringold be – I thin' tha' would ha' been me father," the man said jokingly. "Friends 'as a'ways called me Pap, and since ye be a guest, and I hope a friend, ye must do the same."

I immediately liked Pap Ringold. He was a tall wiry man, boasting a thick crown of reddish-brown hair in tight ringlets. It was obvious that Sarah's auburn curls and Tad's unruly red hair had been inherited from their father. He had a short cropped beard and his eyes were like a gentle green spring field – one that might be filled with sheep. (Where did that come from?) I think Pap was even thinner than his son, but I could tell he was not a weak man. His children bragged about his wielding an axe. They claimed he could down enough trees in a day's time to keep the family well fed and comfortable.

But he didn't seem to spend much time in the woods these days.

In the short time I had known Pap and his family, my curiosity was aroused when I thought about the "Godly business," heard bits and pieces of conversation at various times and noticed Pap's excessive absences. I wondered what he could be up to, especially when food and warm clothing were frequently found on the doorstep. Perhaps Pap was a minister or disciple of their religion. I had asked Sarah, only to receive a more puzzling answer. "He be much more valuable to God's work than as a min'ster o' the faith," she had said. The family didn't offer much information and I decided he must be involved in some kind of secret activities. At this point I felt that was no concern of mine. I only hoped for his and my sake that his activities were not something to bring the law down on us all. And even if that happened, I felt like I owed the family some loyalty no matter what they were involved in. With my memory loss, I was certainly beholden to them for giving me their help and friendship. It seemed a fair exchange – after all, they didn't know anything about me.

It was Pap who gave me a name. My memory was not cooperating, despite the fact my body was healing and I was feeling stronger every day. Would I be in this state of nothingness forever? The thought terrified me. How awful it would be to go through life not knowing who you are or where you had come from. I tried not to let the despondency I felt interfere with our daily routine, but it required great effort on my part. Pap had come in one afternoon and noticed how troubled and impatient I was. He did his best to cheer me up, wisely telling me my body and mind were still mending and I just needed to give it time.

"But ye do need a name. We need t'call ye somethin' – tha' is 'til ya' can 'member y'r own name. Now wha' shall ye be?" he said.

I smiled at him, thinking what a kind and thoughtful man he was. "I really don't know sir," I answered. "It is pretty hard to name someone you don't know anything about."

"Well, ye know lass, we gi' names t'babies all the time and we f'r sure don' know how they be a turnin' out," he said. "With ye's curly hair, we could jest call ya Curly. Or 'ow 'bout Missy? No, I thin' a good name be Lucky. I thin' ye be pretty lucky t'ha' my Tad find ye. And from wha' I hear, ye is lucky to'be 'live. How do ye like the name Lucky?"

"It is kind of an odd name for a girl, but I do like it sir," I said. "I think it sounds like a good name, because I am lucky all of you have taken such good care of me. I hope I won't be a burden much longer."

"Now, Lucky, don' worry 'bout it," he said. "Tha' be why God 'as left his servants here on earth – offerin' help t'others. And ye certainly qualify right now. Some day, it may be ye can repay the favor."

I didn't really intend to get involved with the Ringolds. I only wanted to get well and be on my way, with the thought of finding my family and having them reimburse the Ringold's for their generosity, if they were able to do so. I suppose I could have left once I regained my strength, although I doubted they would have let me go. It wasn't as if I was incapable of caring for myself and needed physically to be tended. I still limped a little on my bad foot. But the real problem was where would I go since I wasn't really sure where I was? I couldn't force myself to say the words "I'm leaving," even though I knew their protest would be long and loud. They all made me feel warm, secure and temporarily happy as I continued the healing process. My memory had not allowed me much of a peek into my past. Every so often a smell, a kind word or some action would give me a feeling of something I had experienced before. But there was nothing tangible.

Right from the beginning, I felt at home in the Ringold cottage. Something about this family attracted me, pulled me into their midst. I wanted, and needed, to be part of their lives. I really had grown to think of Grandmam as my own grandmother and Sarah as my sister. As for Tad, I was still trying to figure out where he could fit into my life. I only knew if I left, I would greatly miss him. I only hoped I hadn't become a burden to the family. Grandmam had been so kind to let me use her room. Once I was able to be up and about, I offered to let Grandmam have her room back.

"I can move in with Sarah, if that is alright?" I said. "Or, I can just sleep out in the big room on some cushions until I get my memory back."

"I won' here o' 'ny sech thin," Sarah said. "It be pleasurable t'share my bed wi' my new sister."

The cottage was not large by any means, but the family assured me it was adequate and suitable for their needs and a guest. It was a quaint and simple habitat nestled deep in the woods with a limited view of small mountains and hills peeking through bare branches. I'm not so sure the hilly slopes could be seen in spring and summer once the trees leafed out. The exterior of the cottage was a combination of fieldstone and rough-cut timber, topped with a thatched roof. Three chimneys protruded from the fireplaces providing warmth for the family – small ones for the sleeping rooms and a large one in the great room. The large great room was the main living quarters for the family, providing space for cooking, eating and a comfortable gathering area. Leading off the room were two sleeping rooms, one for Grandmam and the one Sarah and I were to share. A short, narrow stairway led into a loft where Pap and Tad shared a large room. Since Pap was away a great deal of the time, Grandmam had been left in charge of Tad and Sarah.

I guess my biggest surprise about the family was their emphasis on religion, which somewhere in my mind brought a wave of recognition. But like many thoughts I had these days, who knew where the ideas came from or when I would be able to regain my past.

"I think I might be Catholic – at least that is something that comes into my mind," I told Grandmam. "Odd. Isn't it surprising I can remember such simple things as that but I can't remember so many other things, like who I am?"

And as usual, Grandmam would "tsk, tsk" at my ideas and tell me to give it time. When I asked about their beliefs, Grandman said they were neither Catholic nor Anglican, but were one of the new religious groups springing up all over Europe.

"We call ourselves Puritans," she said simply. "It serves our needs and provides what guidance we need f'r a God who loves us."

I searched my mind to see if I had any feelings about previous experiences with the Ringold's religious practices, but nothing rang of familiarity. As I thought more on it, I had a nagging suspicion this group of people was not one I had known or would have been associated with in the past. But again, there was nothing tangible to keep me from getting involved. I told myself not to be silly and place judgment before I really knew about my past life. I wasn't sure I had truly made a faith commitment, although I would think a strong dedication to faith would have been almost instinctive.

If indeed I was Catholic, I think studying a catechism would have been demanded of me. But I could not recall if the idea was something I knew or just surmised.

In the few weeks I had been bedfast, I had not been so aware of the Ringold's faith. I had only experienced their genuine kindness. But once I was able to hobble around and get out into the family's main room, I soon realized religion was a key ingredient in their daily lives. They spent a great many of their evenings reading their testaments by candlelight. "Thanks and praise" was a part of their daily conversations. Sarah very patiently explained the concepts and the family's views on their religion to me. I began to understand their beliefs and how they viewed God. As my days of recuperating and growing stronger continued, I began to accept their way of life. I felt comfortable joining in their prayers and testament readings.

"Our teachin's be cent'red on emphasizin' the righteousness o' God and his power t'control and direct everythin' in our universe," Sarah explained. "We believe life be preordained and God 'as a'ready determined wha' we be and how we live. It be up t'us t'follow His ways. It were God who brought ya' t'our doorstep. Tha' be wha' we firmly believe. An' it be our pleasure to help ye get well, 'cause tha' be wha' God 'as expected o' us."

When I asked about where they worshipped, Sarah said "We don' ha' a church. When we w'rship God, it be simple and na 'laborate. We don' need formal'ty or 'dornments like in the Roman church. The folk in the village don' care much f'r us so we 'old our weekly meetin's secretively when we can at some member's 'ouse or t'other places. An' a lot o' our worship be a private matter wi' jest ourselves and God."

I never felt like an outsider during my time with the Ringolds. It was almost as if I belonged to this family. I loved Grandmam and how she had taken me in. But who wouldn't? She was what I had always thought a grandmother should be. She was warm, understanding and caring, but she could be stern if need be. I loved teasing Grandmam – it always made me feel good and brought a faint memory of someone else I had loved to tease. They had all accepted me and I them and their way of life. It suited my needs for the moment – the quiet, simple life of hard work, friendship and prayer.

It was the very beginning of fall when I had come to the Ringolds. Now winter was edging ever closer. Pap had returned home and was determined to get as much wood stacked as possible for his upcoming deliveries – almost as if he had some kind of premonition he would not be around for the woodcutting much longer. After all the Ringolds had done for me, I was happy to help with stacking wood in the many piles around the cottage. Sarah and I were the same size, so I borrowed one of her house dresses when I was lending a hand with household chores. And when I helped with wood gathering or outside chores, I wore my riding clothes. Grandmam frowned at wearing pants, but they must have been fashionable in my world.

For several weeks Tad and Pap had been cutting up downed trees into fire-sized logs in the nearby forest. It was Sarah's and my task to load the cart with wood, which was pulled back to the cottage area by Willie, one of the work horses. Then Sarah and I would arrange the stacks in cords and bundles for delivery. It was hard work, but necessary. And it gave me time to think of other things besides not remembering who I was. We all fell into bed at night completely exhausted from our labor.

It was about this time that the second alteration in my destiny occurred. Everything changed when a dead soldier was found on the old trail between the village and the Ringold cottage. It was the same trail I had been found on. We had just come in for an afternoon bite to eat, after having spent the entire morning in the nearby oak and birch forests just beyond a couple of other buildings bordering the cottage. It was pleasant to have time to sit and rest after the hard work. Grandmam always kept us well-fed when we came in from our wood gathering. Suddenly we heard the sound of hoof beats in the yard. We all jumped at the pounding on the door and the man didn't wait to be invited in. He just came rushing into the kitchen, quite excited and agitated about something.

"Sorry t'bother ya' there, Pap. There be a real 'mergency up t'a the cave. Seems there 'as been a death. A king's man were found on the ol' trail. Ya' better come quickly. Decisions need t'be made."

All this the man wheezed out in the hoarse voice of one who had taken only minutes to ride from the village, despite the distance. He was a large man and his rosy nose and pink cheeks were more likely from his taste for ale than his energetic ride. His ruddy complexion was not so much from the cold as having spent his life within the confines of the local pub. The room fairly reeked with the odor of a barley keg.

The visitor took a few deep breaths; then, he continued. "It were ol' man Visner. He foun' the body this mornin' on his way t'market. Said he took the sh'rtcut 'cause his wife wan'ed some herbals right 'way from the 'pothecary. She were makin' a medicinal concoct f'r the young'uns sniffles. Visner said Mary, the little one, were pretty sickly right now an' the missus was fear'in for the child's life. So, he were in a

60

hurry and took the ol' trail, the fas'es' way possible down t'a the village."

"Hey, slow down there a minute. Ye 'as ha' a 'ard ride. Looks like t'me ya' could use a stiff drink o' ale and a minute t'catch ye's breath," Pap said as he poured a cup of the brownish liquid and handed it over to McMann. "Does ye know how the sold'r died? Did ya' get a chance t'talk to anyone? Be there some kind o' mischief goin' on?"

McMann downed the liquid in one gulp. Suddenly, he became aware of me, the stranger in their midst. "Oh, a... a... a...," he sputtered. "I be sorry. I hope it be a'right, the news I mean."

"Jeb McMann, this be our new friend Lucky," Pap said. "She 'as been stayin' wi' us 'cause o' a bad accident out on the trail 'while back and 'asna' regained her memory. Jeb here be an ol' friend o' the family."

I noticed the strained looks on the faces around me. What were they afraid of? I didn't think anything could be that bad, or could it? The worst thoughts passed through my mind – criminals, tax dodgers or traitors? What did it all mean? I would never have suspected them of doing anything wrong, but with McMann eyeing me and stuttering, I knew something was not quite as it should be. I thought I knew these people, but it would appear I didn't know everything about them. For a brief moment I had a fleeting thought of religious lectures, but then it vanished. Perhaps it was just remembering brief conversations with the family about Pap being on "church" business that gave me cause to worry.

My history lessons came to mind and I wondered if the family might somehow be connected with the religious controversy that plagued our land. How did I know so much about this when I couldn't remember my name? Why was I so aware of the religious upheaval in England unless my family, and perhaps I myself, had been a part of it? As on many occasions in the past few weeks, I had the feeling that there must have been someone in my past opposing these people. More puzzlement. Had I been for or against them? I shivered at the thought of what I would find in my past once I regained my memory. Pap noticed the shiver and the perplexed and frightened look that passed across my brow.

"Now, it be nothin' t'worry 'bout. Jest a bit o' misunderstandin'," Pap said, trying to mask the tension in the room.

McMann continued his story. "Well, Visner saw the body and stopped t'see if'n the man needed help. But recken the sold'r were be'ond help. Anyways, Visner got his herbals and stopped jest long 'nough to tell Dep'ty Farqhuar 'ow he knew right away it were a king's man 'cause despite the mud and dirt, he had on a spiffy' sold'rin' uniform with shiny buttons and those a'paulet thin's tha' hang off'n the shoulder. Good thin' I were standin' in the street when the news be told. I were jest heartsick and frightened all at the same time. And others he'rd the news same as me."

"The gossipers be havin' a heyday speculatin' on this one," Pap said. "It seems they a'ways ha' plenty t'talk 'bout wi'out givin' them this kind o' situation. Some o' them folk jest have no love for us Puritans."

"Ya bet," McMann answered. "I offered right away t'gi' the dep'ty a 'and in gettin' t'the body, but he said he 'as a couple o' good lads for tha' kind o' work. Soon as I see'd them leav'n, I followed. Near as I could tell, they didna' find the cave, ev'n though the body werena' far from it. But tha' ain't sayin' the king's men won' find it when they come. And ye can be sure they be here soon 'nough. I heard the dep'ty say he be reportin' the 'ncident right away t'the capt'n o' the guards. Then tha' whole bunch will be here, thicker 'n flies."

McMann stopped to catch his breath and then continued on before we could interrupt him. "I followed them back t'the village, at a safe distance o' course, and waited t'see wha' they be doin' next. A couple o' locals 'appened t'catch Farqhuar an' I he'rd them askin' if'n they'd be an investigation. He tol' them he didna' see 'ny wounds an' it looked like the poor lad jest took sick and died. But ye know how loose-tongued some o' them locals can be. I he'rd one rather unpleasant lady at the inn say 'f'r sure them Puritan folk up in yond'r hills were 'sponsible.'"

"I can jest hear them talkin'," Pap said. "On more than one a'casion I 'as he'rd them complainin' 'bout us Puritans bein' up t'a no good, prowlin' the countryside all times o' day or night and disturbin' pe'ple. I 'as ha' to control my temper more n' once."

"We don' hurt 'ny one," McMann said. "Jest mindin' our own bus'ness an' worshippin' God the way we wan'. Tha' be more n' some o' 'em busy bodies do. We prob'ly do more f'r our fellowman than most o' them town folk ever thin' o' doin'. 'Nyways, I don' know wha' the dead man be doin' or if'n he knew 'bout the meetin' place. But it sure don' look good there by the cave n' all. And where there be one o' them sold'rs, ye can be sure they be more."

"Tad and I be ready t'go with ye in jest a moment," Pap said. "I thin' we need t'a be walkin' t'the cave rather than takin' 'orses. Why don' ye put y'r 'orse in the pen with t'others right now and gi' him a good drink. By the time ye are finished with tha' task ol' friend, we be ready to go."

"Do ye thin' ya' might'n need more hands?" Sarah asked. "Lucky and I could both come 'long and do some scoutin' if'n need be."

Was this all in the name of religion? From what I had seen of Jeb since he rushed in the door, he just didn't seem to fit in the same mold as the Ringolds. I was somewhat mystified as to what was really going on. Of course, I had my suspicions. It would seem the soldier was found in a hilly ravine, not far from where I had met my fate. This was the first I had heard about the cave and I gathered it was a meeting place for the Puritans. The Ringolds were connected in some way. Perhaps the soldier had lost his way. I could easily sympathize with him, having been in the same predicament recently myself. And if he was ill he could have easily been delirious and disoriented. Whatever the reason for his death, it seems fate would step in, bringing me closer to my future and the Ringolds.

"I certainly would be happy to come along if there's anything I can do," I said. "If your family is in danger, then I feel obligated to help after all the care and help you have given me."

"Now, go on wi' the lot o' ye," Grandmam said, trying to make light of a situation seeming to warrant worry. "T'is nothin' t'get y'rselves worked up 'bout. Jest a sold'r pass'n thru and he got lost. Look at Lucky there. She got lost jest the same as the sold'r. She be lucky we found her a'fore she died. Ya' be jest a bunch o' ol' women, shakin' at ev'ry gust o' wind an' hidin' from ev'ry shadow."

"Nonetheless, Grandmam, we need t'get t'a the cave and make sure ev'rythin' is a'right. It be crucial nothin' be amiss up there right now," Pap said getting up and making his way toward the coat hooks by the door. As he put on his coat and cap, he said, "Ya' ladies can pack a lunch and a few warm garme'ts f'r our friends. They be a leavin' t'night. We may ha' to finish our 'rangements whilst our friends be on their way t'the coast."

Then he turned to me and said, "Lucky, since ye be here and there be ev'ry indication we could find trouble at our doorstep, ya' mightn' na' want t'stick 'round. Na' sure where ya' could go since ye canna' 'member where home is, but we can help get ye t'a safe place. Ya' 'as been a lot o' help since ye came and we 'as ev'n considered ye a part o' our family. If'n if'n ya'do stay wi' us, be forewarned."

"We be hones' folk and wan' t'let ye know where thin's stand," he went on to say. "I don' know how y'r 'legiance be t'ward the king and his views o' religion. An' may be ya' don' 'member or don' know how ya' feel. But I guess ye should know 'bout our view. I know ye 'as a'ready 'cepted us and our faith somewha' and ye seem t'know we kind o' ha' our own priorities in worshippin' God. Us Ringolds 'as gone beyond jest worship and if'n ya 'asna' figured out a'ready, ya should know wha' we be a'doin'."

"Pap, watch wha' ye be sayin'." Tad said. "Ya' be a scarin' her and it may be she don' need t'be involved in our bus'ness."

"We owe ya' the truth, Lucky." Pap said despite the warning from Tad. "F'r many o' our fellow Puritans it 'as become very dangerous f'r them t'stay here in England. So, we help them leave. I guess ye might'n as well know we be part o' the movement t'help Puritans harassed by the courts and the king escape from England. My own pa and gram were sech victims o' the king and his policies. My pa ga' his life f'r his beliefs and I guess I will too, if'n tha' be wha' the Lord 'as in store f'r me. The cave be a stoppin'-off point. Us and some t'other families here in the woods, includin' Jeb, help get folks t'a the coast and off t'Holland, the Americas or any other destination where they can feel safe and worship as they see fit. If'n ya' thin' ye 'as t'leave, we'd much 'preciate y'r not mentionin' our activities t'anyone else. It mightn' put the lot o' us in a bit o' danger."

Tad really seemed upset his father was telling me about their involvement. "We don' know anythin' 'bout her," Tad said, his voice rising to indicate his anger with his father. "Much as I like Lucky and her bein' 'round, I don' thin' ye should be tellin' her our life story. Wha' if'n Lucky is one o' the king's spies? I know ye don' thin' so, but jest wha' if?"

Tad grabbed his coat, cap and a matchlock pistol with a bag of powder from the shelf above the doorway. He turned to me as he started out the door. "Ha' ya' been playin' wi' us, or be ye really a lost soul tha' 'as 'nveigled y'r way t'our hearts?" he snarled at me. "Perhaps our Lucky is jest fakin' a memory loss t'catch us! Couldna' tha' be true, Lucky?"

"Tad, I be 'shamed o' ye," said Sarah as she grabbed my hand in friendship.

"I doubt tha' be true," Pap said in defense of me. "I 'as a'ways been a good judge o' character and I thin' our Lucky 'as ha' the misfortune of findin' us an' tha' be it."

Pap, too, grabbed a pistol and powder bag from the shelf. He was just behind Tad and the two were ready to leave when Sarah said, "Wait. I wan' t'come and help wi' wha'ev'r I can. I know those woods ever bit as good as Tad."

I was still recovering from Tad's bruising comments and his obvious distrust of me. I was crushed and stunned. It took me a few minutes to reconnect to the situation. How could he feel that way? I thought he was my friend.

"Do let me come along and help," I said as I searched for words to defend myself.

"You've been so good to me and the only way I can repay you is to give you a hand with whatever problems you might encounter. I could easily lead a king's man astray – well, I'd probably get lost again, but it sounds like that could be helpful for you."

"I am sorry Tad if you feel you can't trust me," I said in a voice just a bit higher pitched than usual. I was feeling a bit of anger myself. "I am no spy, or at least I don't think I am. I'm almost certain I wouldn't have the least idea of how to be one."

"Calm down the two o' ye," Pap said to Tad and me. Tad just shrugged and went out the door. Trying to console me, Pap said, "Tad sometimes doesna' see the whole story."

"I guess at this point in time I'm not sure what I believe or what my convictions are," I said. "But it doesn't feel wrong to want to help, and I think I have always followed my heart. It would seem so since I am here and not with my family. I, too, feel like I have become part of your family and the least I can do is offer my loyalty and support. And if it is wrong, I'll worry about consequences later."

"We really can be a big help t'ya' Pap, and Grandmam can easily get thin's ready here," Sarah said.

"A'right ya' two," Pap said. "We might'n jest need a couple pair o' 'xtra hands. Never know wha' we be gettin' into. Hope I won' be sorry in the end. An' I hope ye won' be regrettin' y'r decision Lucky."

He tossed Sarah a pistol and powder pouch from the shelf. As he pulled yet another weapon and powder bag from the shelf he said to me, "Do ye thin' ye know how t'use one o' these?"

"I think I may have used some kind of musket or pistol in the past – maybe for hunting? I'm not sure how I know that. It's just one of those feelings that come over me every so often. Handling a weapon doesn't seem an uncomfortable notion," I answered.

Pap nodded his head in approval and gave me the pistol and powder. Sarah grabbed a cloak from the hook and I already had on my riding suit. I wasn't sure I wanted to be saddled with the bulkiness of a heavy cloak, but Sarah insisted I would be warmer with it. So I, too, donned the garment. We strapped the pistols and powder packs around our waists and I followed Sarah out the door.

"Ha' the pouches ready when we get back," Pap said to Grandmam. "Canna' tell ya' how long we might'n be. If'n we ha' na' trouble it shouldna' be very long. We may ha' ample time t'spare or we may be on the run like in other 'casions. If'n anyone comes 'round askin' f'r us, jest tell them we be out scoutin' f'r wood. Be ready t'leave at a moment's notice if'n need be."

Jeb had returned to the cottage from taking care of his horse. He impatiently inquired as to whether they could "move out an' get up t'a the cave or were we jest goin' to stand 'round and talk the whole day?"

Pap told him we were ready and I and Sarah would be joining them for a couple of extra pair of hands and bodies. Jeb gave me a suspicious look.

"Be ye sure 'bout this?" Jeb said.

"Don' worry," Pap told Jeb and Tad. "I thin' we ha' got a good, loyal friend here willin' t'sacrifice her good name t'help us. I feel safe with Lucky 'long."

Jeb and Tad exchanged glances. Turning to Tad he spread his hands open, shrugged his shoulders and nodded his head as if to say "a'right?" Tad still seemed miffed that I was coming along, although he said nothing.

"I guess ye could look at it eith'r way," Pap went on to say. "If'n indeed Lucky be a spy, and I don' thin' tha" be true, we 'as got her 'long and know wha' she be a doin'. And if'n she wan's to help us as I thin', then good for us wi' another pair o' willin' and helpin' hands."

Jeb nodded and shrugged his shoulders as if to indicate that it wasn't his choice, but if that was what Pap wanted, so be it. I still felt betrayed that Tad didn't trust me, but I guess I could see his point of view. After all, they were the ones who had much to lose. And so Sarah and I followed Tad, with Pap bringing up the rear.

Without wasting any more time, we headed out. We walked just behind the cottage and out-buildings, following our wood-gathering path for a short distance. Then we turned onto a slightly worn path. I had never been in this part of the woods before, but Pap told me it would eventually take us to the trail that had first brought me to the Ringold's home and to their kind generosity.

Despite the seriousness of the situation, stirring in me was the feeling of adventure – a feeling that did not seem new or outlandish. I suspected the idea of adventure might be why I was in the Ringold's care. If I had been looking for adventure, it would appear I landed on its doorstep. As I followed Sarah, I felt sure I was more than just following a trail to help some other Puritan folk. I sensed this latest venture would become my trail of destiny.

CHAPTER FIVE

The Cave

We followed the poorly defined path at a brisk walk. Jeb kept us going at a pretty rapid pace as we continued to wind in and out of the woods to the ravine and cave in the hill. No attempt at any conversation was made. I think we were all either too stunned or lost in our own thoughts, plus just keeping up with Jeb was in itself a difficult task. I had thought I was in good shape after moving wood for a couple of weeks, but I guess my body was still recuperating. And I was sorely puzzled and hurt at Tad's disapproval. I wondered how he could feel that way about me. He didn't even apologize. He had just turned away, muttering the whole time about "puttin' our lives in danger" and "why would Pap have so much trust in this skinny girl." I wondered what kind of life experiences had made him so distrustful.

We seemed to be avoiding the trail as we continued our brisk walk around patches of wet ground, brown leaves, pine needles, tall dead weeds and brushy thickets. Once I had adjusted to the silent pace, I had time to contemplate my new-found friends' dilemma. My thoughts turned to the dead soldier. Was he lost like I had been? Did he die because of fever and chills? What had prompted him to come up the trail? The men seemed to think he had somehow left the nearby village and found the trail. Was he so far gone in his fever that he didn't have any clue about where he was going? Or, was it that he knew about my friends and was hoping to catch them going against the king? I kind of figured that because the area was wild and overgrown, the evidence of him being in this spot could go either way. I understood how a stranger could easily become lost in the overgrowth, or even at this time of the year when you could see sky and bare limbs above.

I considered the possibility that the dead man was some kind of spy and had been in the area for a variety of reasons, including the business of my friends. I think it would be difficult to track anyone or anything in this part of the forest unless you knew where you were going or what you were looking for. I certainly would not have been able to find my way back to the cottage. We had done way too much zigzagging for me to visually eye any landmarks.

My mind was in a whirl as I tried to digest the information Pap had provided before we left the cottage. Now that I thought about it, the actions of the Ringolds all became very comprehensible. It certainly explained the many comments about Pap's activities and his being away from home for days on end. And there were also the mysterious gifts of clothing and food (and I suspected gold and copper coins) that I had seen deposited on the doorstep a couple of times in the past few weeks. Knowing the kindness of these people, it only seemed inevitable they would help others. I kind of admired the dedication to their faith.

We had been slowly skirting a path for a short time when I suddenly became aware of my shortness in breath. The path, which was already undefined, had gradually become a steep, rocky incline. At this point the strenuous activity of just keeping up with the others caused my wandering mind to reunite with my body's stress signals – acute pains in my legs and rib cage. My wan strength was being sapped and my concentration demanded the attention of both body and mind for the moment. The seriousness of this situation in which I had most recently involved myself would have to wait and be reflected upon later. By then, it would be much too late for consideration.

Winding our way cautiously through the small but rocky crags and crevices, we reached the top within a few minutes. I stopped for a moment to catch my breath and take in the view from the ridge. We were high enough that the vista should have encompassed quite a distance, but with the thick forest there was not much to see except an endless array of leafless ash, scraggly pines and bronzed-leaf oaks. Closer I could see the intermingling of yellow grass tufts, dead leaves, low shrubbery thickets and sparsely scattered gray rock. Above, an azure blue sky and white puffy clouds greatly accentuated the grayish stones surrounding us.

We had reached the actual trail and I could see the downward path at this point. It seemed much friendlier and more defined. We continued winding our way around a few dangerous crags, small hillocks and rocky ledges. Tad told me this was the treacherous old trail, but it was still easier going than the path above had been. Ahead, I could see the forest was actually thinning and becoming sparser. I thought Skipton must be at the end, but when I inquired Pap said the trail led into the small berg of Colne. He said Skipton was a good distance beyond.

We came upon a massive gray-granite mound that rose right up into the cloud puffs. The top elevation was smoothly rounded, then broadened out at the base into abrupt jagged, rocky spurs. I might have given this rocky hummock no more consideration than the rest, but Jeb stopped and cautiously turned off the trail at the end of one of the rocky outcroppings. Tad followed and the two held up their hands for us to stop. They listened and stealthily moved forward, their heads bobbing left to right and left again. You could almost see their ears lift upwards as they strained to discern any unnatural noises.

"Looks t'be clear," Tad whispered and motioned for us to follow.

Pap, Sarah and I followed close on Tad's heels. After we left the path, we followed along the base of the stone uprising that had now become shadowed with deep crags and crevices. Not more than a couple dozen paces beyond the rocky outcroppings stood a large boulder. Jeb and Tad suddenly disappeared around the boulder and was swallowed up in one of the shadowy crevices abundant around the giant hill of rock.

Listening and looking around in all directions as Jeb and Tad had done, the three of us rounded the large boulder and saw the shadowy space in the rocks where the other two had disappeared. Sarah, Pap and I squeezed through the opening. I reckoned Jeb must have had to inhale and grow in height a couple of inches in order to ease his larger frame into the narrow space. Once inside, I looked around at the high vaulted, but small, rocky foyer. From what I could see, it seemed to be a deep cave. On one side was a natural arched entryway leading into a much larger chamber. Overhead, the fading daylight faintly shimmered down from a small hole at the very apex of the high vaulted ceiling.

"Ye go 'head," Tad said to all of us. "I can jest watch here a bit, even though it appeared t'be safe a'fore we entered."

It took my eyes a few moments to adjust to the semi-darkness of the cavern. Although I had never in my whole life been in a cave before, it seemed as though I had not forgotten my geography lessons. It wasn't like some caves I had seen drawn in books in our library showing formations hanging from the ceiling and rising up from the floor. This cave seemed to be more of just a hollow space with a few thick shapes. The majority of those had erupted from the floor. There were only a few formations from the ceiling and I was awed by their spiraling, grotesque configurations formed from the dripping of water throughout the past eons of years.

A shaft of light from the foyer wafted through into the large cavity and created spectrums of odd colors reflecting off the asymmetrical shapes. In the distance, the constant drip-drip-dripping of water could be heard, echoing around and bouncing off the chamber walls. The eerie lighting from daylight peeking through in various places and the grotesque configurations made me shiver – like "death had crossed over my back." Now, where had I heard that before? I shrugged. It didn't seem important right now, even if I could remember.

I thought again about the dead soldier. He could have never accidentally found this cave and I began to doubt he had heard of it. I kind of felt Grandmam might have been right when she accused Pap of looking for ghosts where none existed. Most likely the man's death would be reported to his commander as an illness and considered of little consequence. Surely there would not be much inquiry conducted. How naïve I was at that stage in my life.

Sarah and I continued to follow Pap as he threaded his way around several large rock formations. We turned into another shadowy crevice, one I didn't even see until we were actually turning into it. We entered the room-sized chamber where limited light from several long torches near the back bounced off the cavern's formations, creating ethereal shapes and shadows. Pap whistled, or rather I should say he made sounds similar to an owl's hoot.

Three hoots he gave and then he said, "It jest be me, Pap Ringold. How be ye Albert? Ev'rythin' a'right?"

Two bodies slowly emerged from the dark shadows and stepped into the dim light. An older man, in rumpled and dirty traveling clothes stepped forward, followed by a woman, who appeared to be about the same age. She was nervously clutching her shawl and trying to tuck loose strands of hair back into the bonnet on her head. Even in the dim light I could tell the pair had come from a life of comfort and were fairly well to do. Their attire, although not elaborate in detail, was very fine brocade and velvet cloth. Most likely, these folks had once been titled and owned land. I was trying to take it all in and understand why they were hidden away here in the dark. Surely, they could easily have just boarded a ship somewhere and traveled to another part of the world. Again, my naivety kept me from seeing the whole picture.

The man I assumed was Albert spoke in the English of the educated as he and the woman slowly inched their way toward the opening. "Everything seems to be fine now, although I thought I heard commotion late in the afternoon yesterday. We carefully listened and watched, scarcely daring to breathe, but as nothing happened, we didn't think much about it. These large caves can give you cause for worry with all the sounds echoing throughout the chambers."

Albert said he had gone out toward evening for a bit of fresh air. Pap looked at him with concern. Albert went on to say he had been most careful to make sure he heard or saw nothing.

"That's when I saw the body. It really frightened me," Albert said. "I could see he was a king's man, and as he appeared dead, I thought the best plan was to just get back inside the cave and into our hiding place as quickly as possible. I didn't see anyone else, but that's not to say there weren't any others. Mistress Frost has been very nervous and anxious ever since I told her. I couldn't decide whether to risk going clear out of the cave and pull him inside or to just leave him. After it got darker I went out to see if he was still there. He was and I thought it safer not to bother with him last night."

Albert continued his story, talking in a soft whisper as if he were afraid the cavern walls had ears. "When I went out to drag the body in this morning, it was a good thing I was being overly cautious. It was then I saw three men just loading the body on horses and heading down the hill. They were quite busy with their task and didn't see me. I quietly eased myself back inside, with my heart beating so loudly I was sure they would hear it. After a half hour or so, I peeked out once more and saw nothing. Other than the dead man and the men who came to take him away, I did not see anything else suspicious. But both Mrs. Frost and I have been extremely nervous this whole day. Thank goodness you've come. We prayed hard you would hear the news and come to fetch us."

"The men takin' the sold'r away, be they king's men?" Pap asked.

"No, just young men pretty shabbily dressed. I can't think they had anything to do with the king or his soldiers," Albert said.

"Mos' likely tha' be true. I thin' we be safe 'nough f'r the time bein'," Pap said. "Our frien' Jeb were in the village and knows the dept'y 'as been notified 'bout the death. I thin' it were his men ye seen. I don' know if'n the dept'y be turnin' the man ov'r to the captain o' the sold'rs right away or jest how it w'rks. But t'is certain t'be a 'vestigation, so we need t'get ye out o' here a'fore the dept'y or the sold'rs can study up on wha' 'appened. Most o' the 'rangements for ye's journey are done; jest a couple o' details yet. Jeb be takin' care o' those final plans. But we can get ye on the way."

"How soon will we be leaving," asked Albert, raising his voice. "We've been in this unpleasant place for a couple of days and Mistress Frost is feeling a bit sickly from all the moisture and the cold. I know the Lord and you will take care of us. I trust in that, but I think its imperative we move on. I never felt safe here and feel less so now. Traveling about the countryside should be safer than staying here."

"Don' know 'bout tha', but we'll ha' ye on y'r way jest soon as we can," said Pap. "I do 'gree, we must get ye out o' here right o' way."

"So ya know 'bout the king's man," said Jeb. He and Tad had gotten in on the last bit of Albert's conversation.

"He were dead, then, when ye saw him?" Jeb continued to question Albert. "Be ya' sure no one seen ya'?"

"Aye, dead he was and as far as I could tell there wasn't anyone else around except those three young men," said Albert. "The rock at the entrance pretty well shields one from the pathway. Do you think there'll be more soldiers? Have any of you heard anything else about the man or his fellow comrades? I wondered what the fellow was doing here. It just doesn't seem a very likely place for one soldier to be wandering around all alone."

"Aye, I were a bit worried when I he'rd the news," Jeb said. "I be sure it were the dep'ty's men who took the body back t'a the village, but the local regent 'as t'be notified and mayhap by now he a'ready knows."

About that time Albert noticed Sarah and me. He looked us over carefully; then asked Pap who his help was. Pap introduced his daughter Sarah and me as a valuable friend of the family who had come to help out in whatever way might be needed.

"I thought it might'n be nice t'ha' a few spare hands jest in case we 'as t'split up. An' it should be nice for ye t'ha' a couple o' women 'long so ye doesna' feel so overwhelmed by all us men," Pap said to Mistress Frost. Sarah and I rushed over and gave her a hug. She seemed to relax a little, seeing our concern and sympathy for her situation.

Pap talked about the plans already in place to get the couple safely onto the next leg of their journey. He said several stops would be made along the way in order to provide safety for the couple before reaching the coast and boarding the ship to take them out of England.

"Right now, though, we be takin' ye t'a 'bandoned cabin near our cottage where ye be restin' for a few hours. We'll be settin' out 'bout midnight," Pap told them. "Hope ye don' mind travelin' by horse ma'am, but tha' can get us t'the next point a'fore daybreak. In jest 'bout a week, I hope ye be headed to 'merica."

"Praise the Lord for all the help," said Albert. "The missus and I are really at your mercy here, Pap, so whatever needs to be done and by whatever means of travel you can arrange, we are grateful. It is by far better than what the king and his loyal ministers would have provided for us or demanded of us. We can't thank you and all the others enough for the help and dedication you provide for many of us. How about you? Do you intend to eventually join us in America?"

"I thin' God likes me here where I can help t'others," Pap said. "Bu', not t'say we might'n have t'board a ship sometime.

Ye can set the way f'r the rest o' us when it comes time t'join ye. Tad and Jeb are watchin' t'make sure we can get safely away. Hopefully, we be a leavin' soon."

"We're ready," Albert said. "I can't wait to get out of here."

"Will ye be up for the walk then Mistress Frost?" Pap asked. "Daylight's beginnin' t'fade and we should be takin' off soon as we can. The trail be pretty treacherous and gruelin' and we be needin' t'move 'bout fast. We don' want t'a be walkin' af'r dark if'n we can help it. But if'n tha' be the case, hopefully we can be up in the north for'st where it isna' so dense."

"I'll manage," Mrs. Frost said. "I've got my traveling clothes on and it can't be as bad as waiting here in the semi-darkness for who knows what kind of trouble. I've always been able to do a lot of walking, so I'll do my best to keep up."

Jeb came back and reported he and Tad had not seen a "lick o' trouble. Do ya thin' we be gettin' up the trail t'ye's place safely wi' no trouble?" Jeb asked. "Mayhap, we should be a splittin' up."

"I thin' we be a'right. I don' 'spect to run into 'ny difficulties," answered Pap. "Jeb, soon's we get t'my place, ye be takin' care o' final travel 'rangements liken' ye a'ways do." To the Frosts, he said, "Ye 'as all y'r baggage t'gether? Sarah and Lucky, help the Frosts wi' their belongin's. Watch y'r step there, Mistress."

"We don't have much. We're traveling light – it's much easier that way," Albert said.

We followed him. He picked up a small satchel, leaving a shoulder pouch and a small cloth knapsack for Sarah and me. I thought how hard it must be for these people to leave everything behind and go onto a life filled with danger at every turn. It meant putting a lot of faith in God. But, after my days with the Ringolds, I could see how that might be the only way to practice freely a faith filled with guidance and comfort. Later, when I expressed these thoughts to Sarah, she laughed at my inexperience.

"Both Mistress Frost and her husband were each wearin' several layers o' clothin', wi' jewels and coins sewn 'nside t'save space in they's travel bags and t'make sure tha' some o' their valuables would reach the final destination," Sarah said.

Meantime, we needed to get back up the hill and Pap gave the order to follow him as quietly as possible. Jeb had preceded him by a few minutes and had gone ahead to make sure the coast was clear. We had just emerged from the shadows and were heading into the larger cavern when Tad rushed towards us. He waved for us to stop, shushing us with his finger to his lips.

"Pap! I thin' there be trouble!" Tad uttered a hysterical whisper. "Looks like some o' the king's men be snoopin' 'round a'ready. I saw at least three, though I canna' be cert'n. Mayhap they be more a'hind some o' the rocks and bushes. I thought I heard talkin' a wee bit ago, then I actually saw them lurkin' 'round ou'side the cave. Canna' be sure they even know it is a cave. Ya' don' thin' they be here from Skipton this soon, do ya'?"

"They must ha' a'ready been here on maneuvers," Pap said. "They canna' ha' gotten here from Skipton yet – even if'n the dep'ty didna' waste any time lettin' the captain know."

"Prob'ly some o' ye's friends," Tad snarled as he turned and looked at me. "How did ya' get messages t'them. Were it a'fore I found ye?"

"Tad, we don' ha' the time t'argue or be rude t'our friends right now," his father admonished. "Get back to y'r post. Jest watch and lis'en. Stay calm and 'bove all, don' do 'nythin' foolish. We can jest stay way back 'nside the cave 'til ye thin' we be safe. Gi' a whistle soon as it be clear and we can make a run for it. We be cuttin' through the for'st. It be tougher goin', but there be better nat'ral coverage than goin' the trail."

I couldn't believe what Tad was saying to me. I felt as though I owed everyone an explanation for my being here. I only wished I could tell him why I was included in his family and where my travels were to take me. But I could not remember. I prayed to God that he would keep us safe as we continued aiding the Frosts on their journey for religious freedom.

"Do ya' need me and Lucky t'come watch wi' ya'?" Sarah asked.

"Na'. Neither o' ye shouldna' be here in the firs' place. I don' know why Pap pampers ye so and lets ye get into predicaments 'nyway. Jeb be out there watchin'. He and I be takin' care o' it," Tad said gruffly.

It would seem Tad had not changed his opinion of me and I felt badly. What could I do to convince him I wasn't putting any of us in greater danger than we already were? Fate. That seemed to sum it all up.

After looking around, Pap said he had an idea. "Ya know Tad, I thin' may be the girls could get out into the larger part o' the cavern. It would surely be a lot easier 'xplainin' wha' we be doin' here if'n sold'rs find the openin' o' the cave. Af'r all, we jest brought the girls up f'r a bit o' explorin'. Wha' do ya thin'?"

"Well, it jest might'n work," Tad said. "Ya' two wait 'til I get back out t'a the entrance with Jeb, then ye come out into

82

the main chamber. Mind ya', don' be talkin' or makin' noise. We don' need to 'tract the men's 'tention."

He quietly turned and went back to his post at the cave opening. After a few minutes Sarah and I wound our way through the shadows one more time to the main cavern, neither of us saying a word. Through the ceiling hole, I could see daylight was dimming. I wondered why the soldiers had come here so late in the day. The coincidence of them just happening by this time of day was too ridiculous even for my naïve mind. It had fleetingly crossed my mind several times why the deputy from the village didn't know about the cave? He surely must have known about it – especially if he had lived in this area all his life.

Time is a rudimentary element, especially when one is waiting for an event to happen, or in our case to not happen. Sarah and I, along with Tad and Jeb, peered into the darkness, listening and waiting. It seemed like we waited an eon, when in actuality it was only a half-hour. The chirping of crickets, the whirring of moths (or even some bigger, flying critter) and the stirring of leaves could be faintly heard as sounds filtered through the openings and then echoed from wall to wall. The wind made a slight whistling noise as it blew across the uneven surfaces of the rocky hill over top. I heard a humming sound like human voices, very muffled. I thought the men must be very close to the cave opening if we could hear voices. Sarah heard the sounds, too, and we grabbed each other's hands.

Pap must have heard something back in his corner of the cave, because he cautiously came slowly out of the shadows, almost scaring us. He placed his finger on his lips and walked silently closer to the entrance where Tad and Jeb were watching. Because of the accoutrements of the opening, it provided a good vantage point to see what was going on around it without actually being seen.

I focused on listening and really couldn't make out anything significant. The voice sounds became blurred and intermixed with the wind coming through the cave openings. I wondered if I had actually heard the voices or only imagined them. But it seemed Sarah was on the alert also and was feeling the same anticipation I was.

"Sarah," I whispered. "Should we get our pistols out? I don't want to be caught off guard."

She nodded and quietly pulled her weapon out of the pouch she had been concealing underneath her cloak. I too, pulled my pistol out. Watching her silent directions, I stuffed the powder deep into the weapon and made it ready for firing, if the need arose. This action seemed familiar and I again had the feeling this was something I had done in the past. The weapon felt familiar in my hand.

Pap came back to report it was impossible to see anything. "Darkness be settin' in, bu' we do ha' some moonlight to help us get back up the hill. I don' understand why they 'as na' gone back t'a the village and connected up wi' their unit," he said softly. "I canna' figure why they be here. This don' look good."

"Are they on the trail or in the woods around the cave?" I asked softly.

"It be jest shadows out there," he whispered. "Tad still thin's there are only three men and he isna' sure they know 'bout the cave. He thin's they would be in here out o' the cold if'n they knew 'bout it."

Tad came back to the large cavern. "I thin' the three men 'as 'parently started down the trail and mos' likely be headin' t'ward the village," he said. "I canna' see 'nythin' o' them. I thin' we be safe 'nough f'r now t'leave the cave. I thin' we should leave quietly, one at a time."

"Sounds good – we 'as t'fend f'r ourselves. We need t'get the Frosts out firs'," Pap said. "I want ye all t'go up the trail until ye reach the big granite boulder. It be jest a short distance and the trail be pretty level – ye can see a far piece until ye get t'a the rock. At tha' point, turn left through the woods. If'n ye's lucky, ya might'n be able t'see a faint path there as we ha' used tha' shortcut a few times. It be 'ard goin', 'specially in the dark." Raising his head and looking upward, he said, "Thank thee Lord for an evenin' tha' provides some light from the moon and a few stars." He lowered his head and said to the rest of us, "Go as quietly an' swiftly as ye can. Ye shouldna' have any trouble findin' the 'bandoned cabin. As soon as I leave wi' the Frost, Jeb ye and Sarah follow. Tad, ye be las' and take care o' Lucky."

Pap and the Frosts carefully, one by one, left the cave. We all held our breaths as they adjusted their eyes to the darkness and started back up the trail. I worried about us all going out onto the trail and asked Tad if he were sure the soldiers had really gone back to the village

"I thin' so. Don' worry none – Pap 'as been taking care o' people like the Frosts f'r a long time an' 'as 'ncountered many a situation," Tad said. "Bu' he jest seems to 'ha an ear for knowin' where danger be lurkin'."

How had I come to be in such a dangerous situation I thought to myself? Blaming what seemed to be my craving for adventure was only partly why I was with the Ringolds in this damp, dark cave. Again the words destiny and fate crossed my mind as we waited our turn to leave the cave in search of safety.

CHAPTER SIX

Fateful Deeds

*J*eb and Tad kept a watchful eye, both up the trail and down. Tad perched himself into a cozy niche just behind the big boulder where he could advantageously watch and not easily be seen. No movements were noted, nor were there any unusual sounds – neither from those making their way back up the mountain path nor from the soldiers that had been seen earlier.

Pap had told us to wait a short time between each departure. Sarah and I, still inside the cave, counted the ticking of minutes with the continual plunk of the water in the background. Eventually, Jeb came into the main cavern and told Sarah it was time for the two of them to leave. I gave Sarah a hug and told her I would see her soon.

"Be ye a'right with this 'rangement," Jeb said to Tad. "Lucky kin go wi' me if ye'd rather ha' Sarah by y'r side."

"No, I wan' Lucky wi' me," Tad said. "Tha' way I know where she be and if'n she be up t'trouble."

Waiting until it was our turn was hard. I had asked Tad if I could come out to the opening and wait with him there, but he insisted I sit tight where I was. I tried not to let the cave noises bother me. Even though there was a bit of shadowy light coming from the hole in the ceiling, it didn't do much to make me feel secure. Then Tad became impatient and could stand the suspense no longer. He came back to where I was waiting.

"I be goin' out for a quick look," he whispered. "Stay very quiet and ye can come up t'a the cave 'ntrance where I 'as been sittin'. If'n I run into sold'rs and you hear a shot or any sounds o' confrontation, get out o' here fas' as ya' can. Get y'rself up there to the big rock and turn into the for'st like Pap tol' us. Hurry 'long and try to find Jeb if'n ye can. Ye shouldna' get lost easily if'n ye follow Pap's directions. Anyway, I be right back."

The wait for Tad's return seemed endless. I peeked out once, but from my vantage point I could see nothing but darkness and shadows. Even with the moonlight Pap had talked about, the steep and treacherous trail would not be easy to follow for either us or the soldiers. I was glad not to have to travel it without a guide familiar to the land – or at least I hoped not. I kept my eyes peeled to the rocks in front of me, almost becoming hypnotized. I was somewhat relived to know we had taken time to make our weapons ready for firing earlier. Suddenly, a tall shadow appeared near the opening of the cave. My heart almost stopped beating and I raised my pistol in preparation to shoot. Tad must have seen me in the frame of the cave opening. It was then I heard the low hoot.

"It's me! Don' shoot f'r goodness sake," he whispered.

I breathed a sigh of relief. "Thank goodness it is you! When I saw the shadow, I almost fainted. It's a good thing you hooted first. I'm not sure what I would have done if you hadn't given a signal."

Tad eyed the pistol I was still holding.

"Do ya' really know how to shoot tha' thin'," he asked. When I answered "Yes," he seemed to be even more suspicious of me and why I was here with his family. I was a bit upset Tad didn't seem to be the least bit concerned about the danger he had placed the two of us in.

"Are we safe enough to leave, or do we need to wait?" I asked.

"It looks t'a be clear 'nough and safe f'r the momen'," he said. He turned and motioned me to follow him.

"We might jest as well go. It 'pears tha' ev'rythin' be a'right. Stay close behin' me an' don' make 'ny noise. I thin' Pap and t'others 'as gotten up the trail safely since we didna' hear anythin'. An' we can thank God there be a bit o' moonlight– don' know if'n tha' be good or bad," Tad whispered as we quietly exited out of the cave and began making our way up the trail.

I had just thought to myself the whole episode had been an unnecessary worry. It would seem nothing would mar the delivery of the two Puritans to their destination. But I was wrong. Tad and I had no more than gotten out of the cave and onto the trail by the rocky hillocks when I saw the shadows from behind us. I yelled at Tad who jumped, grabbed me and shoved me behind the nearest rock. I couldn't see where he had gotten to as I ducked into what I thought was safety. I saw a flash of fired gunpowder with its metal projectile searching for a target. It felt close and I scrambled to get behind another rocky hillock.

I thought I was safe and took a few seconds for my eyes to adjust to the dark. I twisted quietly, looking for any signs of Tad. I turned my head toward the forest just in time to see a raised hand with the thick end of a bludgeon slowly coming down towards me. As my assailant lunged wildly at me he tripped, but not before the flaying butt of his gun found me. I ducked, trying to avoid the blow, but I wasn't fast enough. The widest part of the weapon hit me squarely on the head.

I was dazed and must have blanked out for a few seconds. When I came to, I shook my head and tried to focus. I wondered where Tad was. Then I saw my assailant lying almost at my fingertips. My head spun violently, but even in my dazed state and the semi-darkness of the night I could see he wasn't moving. I reached out and touched his head. My hand came away sticky. Blood! He must have struck his head on the nearby rock abutment when he tripped and fell. I released a quiet sigh of relief. I was shaking at the close call, but felt I was out of danger for the moment. I was just about ready to holler for Tad when I saw the faint shadow of another soldier. The second man must have heard the movements of either me or his friend. He turned and I could see the shadow heading straight toward me. He was frantically whispering the name of his buddy. I was afraid to move, fearing any noise would only draw him to my hiding place. What was I to do? Where in the world was Tad? I needed his help. The soldier was still threshing through the shrubs and stumbling over the rocks, but I had no doubt he would find me.

My pistol had been in my hand when I went down. Where was it now that I needed it? I obviously must have dropped it when I was hit. In the dim light of the moon, I saw a small dark shadow near my fingertips. I slowly inched my body forward, daring not to breathe, as I reached for the shadow. I wrapped my fingers around the pistol and picked it up just in time to see the soldier standing near the rock I was hiding behind. He was barely the length of a man away. He saw me at exactly the same time I saw him and raised his bludgeon, striking out at me. I felt the cold rush of air as his weapon sliced through the air, missing me by only inches. I did manage to slide out of the scope of his swing, but he twirled on me, breathing hard. I could feel his rage as he raised the weapon to strike at me again. He didn't intend to miss this time. Again I shifted, twisted around and moved closer to tall grasses and a rocky ledge. I hoped it would provide the needed cover. But he spotted me. Despite the darkness, moonlight reflected off the metal on his weapon and I could see he was frantically stuffing powder down the shaft of the musket. The firing end was pointed directly at me.

In a fuzzy region of my brain it registered my life was in danger and I didn't have any time to waste. I thanked God my weapon had been primed and ready for use, and my response was to aim it at my assailant. It just seemed natural to release the firing lever. The shot threw me back against the rock where I had been crouched down in hiding and I dropped my weapon. The deafening sound at that close range echoed and reverberated around the hillside. I was dazed and for a moment I wasn't sure what I had done. All this happened in a matter of minutes. In the dark I couldn't tell if I had killed the soldier or not, but he was no longer looming over me. I struggled to my feet, still dazed from the blow to my head, weak from my accident weeks earlier and now the jolting of the pistol as it fired. I felt sick to my stomach. Quietly and still crouching low to the ground, I inched my way up the shadowy trail.

"Tad! Tad, where are you?" I frantically shouted in a whisper. Panic was creeping into my voice when I heard the faint groan. "Here! I be ov'r here," he said soflty.

I headed in a crouching crawl toward the direction of his voice. I found him a few feet away, lying on the ground behind a large rock. Like me, he seemed stunned and sort of disoriented. "Are you all right? Looks like it will be my turn to take care of you."

"I thin' I was jest grazed a bit. I feel a bit o' blood," he said as he brushed his fingers across the side of his head. "Help me up. I be fine. Sorry, wasna' much help. Wha' 'appened? I heard two shots. The first one got me. I saw one o' 'em swingin' his weapon in the air. Where be the shootin' comin' from? Did ya' see three men?"

"It was me. Mine was the second shot," I whispered back. "I don't know if that fellow is dead, but we haven't got time to wait around and see. I don't think I missed and I don't know if there are any more of them or not. For sure two of them are lying on the ground near where I was hiding."

Tad stood up and cautiously looked around, then motioned for me to follow him. We didn't waste any time starting up the trail. He grabbed my arm and pulled me along, moving as fast as we could go. We only looked back to see if trouble was following us when we reached the rock and turned on the path going to the cabin. As we turned into the forest we didn't see anything but heard the thrashing of someone rushing through the thickets. We assumed it was the third soldier, struggling along the dark trail. From the panic in his voice we knew he was looking for his friends.

"George, Darwin, where are you? I heard some firing. Answer me, George, Darwin... Oh my God! Darwin, answer me. George! He's been shot!"

It sounded at this point, as if there was only one of them still able to even follow us and for the moment he was more concerned about his fellow companions than with us. The moonlight and the few stars made it a bit easier to find our way in the full darkness of night. Once we followed the forest path for a short distance, we could no longer hear the soldier's commotion. Tad gave a couple of loud hoots, but there was no answer.

"Hopefully Pap and t'others got clean away an' are close t'the cabin by now," Tad said in a whisper.

"Do you think there were any other soldiers? Do you think we'll be followed tonight?" I continued to whisper as I trembled from the aftershock of my murderous deed.

"Ev'n if they be able t'follow us, I doubt it seriously right now. Af'r all, it be dark and the sold'r didna' see us back there. 'Member, our house be off'n the main trail and Pap will ha' carefully cov'red 'is tracks. An', we must do the same," Tad said as he broke off a fairly large pine branch and proceeded to sweep the forest floor behind us as we went. "Wi' the hole ye most cert'nly left in one o' them, I can a'most be sure t'other fellow prob'bly won' try t'follow us t'night. Least I hope not. But ye realize now, there be trouble a brewin' f'r all o' us."

"Oh Tad, I'm so sorry. I never stopped to think about consequences. I thought the soldier was going to kill me and I just followed my natural inclination to protect myself. It'll be all right, won't it? I hope no one suffers because of me," I muttered dismally. "I just did what I thought I had to do to save myself!"

By this time I had really worked myself into a state. What harm had my deed done to my new friends? I had only wanted to help them!

"Hey Lucky, don' fret so," Tad said, trying to console me. "Y'r right. Ye did wha' you ha' t'do. Pap and I both would ha' done the same. 'Sides, ye might'n ha' saved all our lives. I wouldna' be s'prised to learn those men knew lots more 'bout us than we care to ha' them know. So, don' get worried. An' one thin' f'r sure – this clears up my idea tha' ye mightna' be a spy."

My goodness, I thought. Was he apologizing? Still, I truly was devastated at my deed and his admittance didn't seem to be so important at this time.

"I really feel terribly guilty," I said, trying to make myself feel better. "How could I have done this to people who have been so kind? Will your God forgive me?"

"Lucky, take it easy!" he said, as he put his arm around me. I began shaking and he gently rubbed my back, trying to help me calm down. "Ya' know, Pap were right – ye be a good person and one o' us now. We take care o' each other. For the momen', though, we best get up the trail a'fore we run into 'ny more trouble or tha' confused sold'r comes t'his senses."

Still feeling very shaky, I followed Tad down a hill and up into another unfamiliar part of the forest. He had given me a branch to use and we each made wide sweeps as we continued our trek on a short, faint path. I observed it must have once been a trail, but more recently used from the Ringolds hiking over to the cave at various times. It was even more strenuous following Tad home than it had been going to the cave. This whole venture was a strain on an already weakened body. My head ached again, presumably from the last blow and I was beginning to tire. I was thankful Sarah had made me wear the heavy cloak because I was beginning to feel the dampness and chill of the night air. My body felt stiff and the cold only made me shiver and ache more.

We finally reached a small clearing. There stood a building, surrounded by forest. From its rustic appearance I could see the affects from many years of wet weather. The roof had collapsed at one end. The windows were boarded up and it looked like it might just completely disintegrate with a brisk wind. Tad whistled and Pap came out of the open doorway.

"What took ya' so long," he asked.

"There be some trouble. Are t'others here?" Tad asked.

"We kind o' figured ya' ha' trouble 'cause ye be so late. I sent Jeb, Sarah and the Frosts on t'our cottage where they would be warmer. We may ha' a change o' plans t'night. Wha' kind o' trouble ye be talkin'? Ye can tell me 'bout it as we walk back t'the cottage. Do ye thin' they be followin' ye?"

"I don' thin' so. We ha' been mos' careful," Tad said. "And I thin' ye definitely be changin' plans when I tell ya' the news. Leavin' the cave we be attacked by the three sold'rs we seen earlier. At least we 'sume they be the same. Two o' them might'n be badly injured, or maybe dead. We don' know f'r sure. The third be lookin' af'r his friends when we got away."

"Wha' do ya' mean?" Pap asked, a note of panic rising in his voice.

"We were 'tacked when we left the cave," Tad said. "They shot f'rst and one o' them grazed me head. And from wha' Lucky says, I reckon she be lucky t'ha' walked away."

"Let me see y'r head," Pap said to Tad. "Ha' Grandmam clean tha' spot up and get a poultice on it t'night."

Then to me, he said, "Be ye a'right?"

I could see the concern and the deep care in his eyes and knew that he would protect me with every ounce of his life once he heard the story. I felt somewhat comforted.

"One of them tripped while he was trying to attack me with the end of his weapon. He did manage to knock me down before he went over himself. He hit my head with the butt of his musket and I think I sort of fainted for a moment. When I came to, another of the men was coming right at me, trying to hit me with the end of his weapon. He missed, but he just kept coming at me as he began filling his musket. I guess I did the only thing that came to mind. I shot at him with the pistol you gave me. I don't know whether I killed him or just injured him. We didn't wait around to see."

"Oh my dear Lord," Pap said, raising his eyes skyward. "Oh, protect these two an' gi' 'em strength t'bear they's burdens." And then to us, "Come on, we as' got t'get t'the cottage an' make plans f'r leavin' t'night. Ye hurry on 'head there Tad and let Grandmam take care o' tha' wound right away. Tell t'others wha' 'appened af'r they left the cave and why ye 'as taken so long. Lucky an' I be followin' close a'hind, soon's I make sure ev'ry thin' is right in the cabin."

The welcoming lights at the Ringold cottage gave me the feeling of having come home. The door opened as we approached and Grandmam and Sarah were there, with open arms to greet me and Pap. I was never so happy to see two people in my life, or for that matter the roomful of people I had spent a good share of the day and evening with. I heard a gasp from Mistress Frost and an "Oh, no!" as I managed to drag myself into the kitchen where I sank to the floor. Grandmam returned to taking care of Tad, but stopped just a minute to put a warm cloth on my head where some blood had gathered from my latest conflict. I just sat there kind of dazed and caught tidbits of the conversation as Pap told the Frosts he would have them safely on their way by midnight. I was so tired. I felt like I was floating for a moment in an empty space of swirling thoughts, while my weary body collected itself. I took a couple of deep breaths. Suddenly, it was as if a heavy cloud had lifted. My head cleared and the fuzziness I had felt for weeks seem to instantly disappear. All at once I knew who I was!

"Catherine," I managed to utter.

They all turned to stare at me. Pap was the one who spoke. "Wha' was tha' ye said, Lucky?"

"Catherine. Catherine Grafton, that's who I am," I said. "My father is Thomas Grafton."

"Well, lawsy me!" Grandmam chuckled as she said, "Ye's memory 'as come back, jest like I said. It seems tha' last blow t'y'r head must ha' knocked some sense into it. I ha' he'rd tell how tha' can 'appen. Well, well, so you be Catherine Grafton. Wha' a 'portant soundin' name tha' be!"

"Well, Catherine Grafton, it 'pears tha' ye, 'long wi' the rest o' us, are in a heap o' trouble," Pap said. For all his outward calmness, he was pacing the floor and his tenseness was evident in his walk. "The king's men will most likely not be here a'fore t'morrow at the very soonest. But there be the poss'bility more men may be near the cave than we saw, or they ha' a unit in the village tha' might'n be lookin' for they's comrades."

"I am so sorry," I muttered. "I only wanted to help, and now look at the mess I've caused. When I think about it, I guess I have always been one to act impulsively and never consider the consequences. I just remembered something... my Father was always berating me for those kinds of actions. Please tell me what I can do to help. Should I go to the deputy in the town and tell him what I did? I really and truly didn't mean to cause you folks more trouble than I already have."

I looked at the Frosts. "I am truly sorry. I hope this doesn't make your plans of getting to the coast more complicated."

"Don't fret miss. Pap here will get us all where we need to go. He and the Lord will take care of us, just like he has hundreds of other people." Albert said.

"Listen to me, Lucky, well, 'er Catherine. Ye knows Lucky be how I a'ways thin' o' ye," Pap said. "The trouble really be ours – I thin' those sold'rs didna' jest happen near tha' part o' the trail. I don thin' they knew 'bout the cave but they been on t'us an' were lookin' f'r evidence o' our activities. Ye did wha' you ha' t'do. An' as f'r givin' y'rself up, I thin' ye be safer in our comp'ny. I don' thin' the dept'y or the sold'rs would treat ya' very fairly. Jest sit back while we get on wi' our plans. Don' be too hard on y'rself. Any o' us would ha' done wha' ye did."

"I tried t'tell her that very same thin'," Tad said to Pap.

Pap questioned both Tad and me thoroughly about what had happened and whether we felt sure we had not been followed. We both reassured him that we felt almost positive we had gotten "clean away."

"We were most cautious," Tad told his father. "Both o' us used the pine limbs and tried t'dust tha' ol' path best we could. So, if'n indeed sold'rs come, I thin' they will ha' trouble findin' any footprints. Course tha' isna' t'say they won' find the cottage if'n they discover tha' ol' path. It don' be marked very good, but ya never know 'bout sold'rs – especially if'n ye thin' they be on t'us."

We had been too busy getting away from the soldiers and I hadn't seriously considered all the consequences of the last few hours. Now, as I sat there on the floor the overwhelming reality of my deed sunk in. I began to shake and tremble. Indeed, I was in serious trouble, well, for that matter we all were. Shooting soldiers, even if they are only wounded, was not looked upon kindly by the law.

"The man was at such a close range, there is no doubt in my mind that I didn't shoot him," I mumbled more to myself than the others. "I have always been good at shooting, probably better than my brothers. I can now remember some of those hunt outings with Father, his London friends and my brothers. I rarely missed the birds and beasts we sought."

Jeb, who had been sitting and quietly thinking over the situation, now spoke. "I thin' the girl should go wi' the Frosts. I don' thin' she be safe if'n the sold'rs come. Matter o' fact, I really don' thin' it safe f'r 'ny o' ye up here 'ny more. I wouldna' be a bit s'prised t'find this whole woods swarmin' wi' sold'rs come midday t'morrow. As f'r me, I don' thin' I be suspect at the momen'. Course I may be goin' on a visit meself once all the 'rangements be made through our contacts. I don' thin' we should tell anyone 'bout this. It be jest our secret."

"Ye may be right Jeb 'bout the sold'rs knowin' wha' we be doin'," returned Pap. "We ha' lived up 'ere a long time and 'as been lucky we ha' not seen much danger. We jest a'ways took our chances. But times are a changin' an' the sold'rs mayna' be as forgivin' as in the pas'. I be a thin'in' it would be good for the young'uns t'get away, 'specially Lucky here. The sold'rs these days might'n be a bit more 'spicious o' a stranger 'mongst us. Sorry ye 'as gotten involved Lucky, but we be takin' care o' ya'. I 'spect tha' now ya' know ye's name, ev'rythin' else will fall into place soon. What say you there, lass, do ye want t'leave and try t'find ye's way home? I canna' tell ya' where ye live or how t'get there. P'rhaps ye won' be able t'find y'r way 'less'n ye goes t'Skipton or ov'r t'Leeds. We 'ave never been ov'r tha' way, so I canna' tell ye much 'bout how ye be getting' there. An' if'n truth be known, both be a f'r piece from where we be."

I knew this was just a beginning. Skipton seemed a name I was familiar with. Though, from the way Pap talked, I must have really gotten lost if my adventurous destination was to that location. I faintly remember Father, the boys and me going into Skipton from Grafton Manor and it hadn't seemed like such a long trip – maybe half a morning. All I could really recall at this point was thinking a day filled with adventure would be fun. But it certainly had proved to be more than I might have wished or bargained for. I wasn't at all sure how this one might end, or whether I would able to continue with my life. I certainly had altered my fate, in only a matter of minutes! I could feel the fear of the deed welling up inside me like a hard, gnarling fist.

"I can't go home, not yet. I'm still not remembering everything," I said sadly. "I can't tell you the name of my village, nor do I remember a lot of details yet. I guess they'll come in time."

I put my head in my hands and tried to shake some thoughts into it. "I can picture my family and it seems my father was very strict. I can't go home because my father w... w... w... would never understand my involvement. Everything seems clear now as far as who I am. My memory has given me back my identity, and all the problems that went with it. Father and I were always at odds with each other as I recall. And I don't think I even said good-bye to him the day I left. I think the answer for now must be to accompany the Frosts on their journey. I see no other alternative. Is that okay Mr. and Mistress Frost if I accompany you?"

Albert nodded and said, "If ye think that is the only choice ye can make or want to make, we would be glad for the company."

"As I think on it, I recall my father was a very proper lawyer. He would most likely not accept any excuses," I said as the picture of the stern man crossed my mind. "I may have killed a man to save my own neck, but from what I can tell you of my father, he would not approve. I have no doubt he would see his duty would be to turn me over to the authorities. I can't even be certain he could justify defending my case.

100

"Father's code of strict adherence to God's laws and the king's laws would prevail," I added. "He has no sympathy for weakness. Father does not accept such a trait in anyone, especially his own family."

"Oh Lucky, I mean Catherine, I mean Lucky... surely you be unfair in the judgment o' ye's father. He canna' be such a 'ard man. Surely he mus' love ya'. And, ye only did wha' you ha' to do; af'r all, it sounds like t'me ye's very life were in danger," spoke up Sarah who had been busily pouring mugs of Grandman's hot tea for everyone to enjoy and to "get their bearin's." Sarah's concern was sincere and made me almost forget the seriousness of the situation. Then, the fear returned.

"I have always been taught to revere life, and look at the mess I have made," I said, surprised such a thought had come to me. "Father always told us to seek an intelligent solution to problems rather than using force or violence. He would do just as I have said – I have no doubt about that."

"Now, lass, ye be 'xaggeratin'," said Grandmam as she walked over and patted my shoulder. "Ye should try t'get back t'y'r family. 'Xplainin' the circumstances probably wouldna' do a bit o' harm. Y'r ma'am is probably heartsick ye 'asna' returned by now. I surely would be if'n my chil'r'n 'ere didna' come home. And ye's brothers, surely they be a missin' ya'. Course, may be y'r family thin' ye's dead by now. Still, ye should return home, only t'let them know ye be livin'. Don' ya thin' ye owe them tha' courtesy?"

"I probably should, if I could remember where home is," I answered. "But even if I did return, I know my father's reaction. I'm sure he would not be sympathetic toward my behavior. Yes, I know Mother and my sister will miss me and be concerned. And my favorite, Nathan – by now, he'll be off at school. It seems odd these things are coming back to me. But, I think the best thing for me is to leave and send back a message once we get to our destination. Perhaps then they can forgive my misdeeds."

I only hoped this would be true and my family would not be bitter towards what I thought to be the best action for all concerned.

"Well, lass, if ye's sure tha' be wha' ya' wan', though bein' a father, I don' know as I 'gree," Pap said setting his mug on the table. He came over to where I was sitting and helped me onto my feet. He gave me a hug.

"May be, we don' ha' t'make a decision yet," Pap said. "We might'n be much luckier than we thin', since the king's men won' know right away who did the shootin'. Soon or later they be figurin' out it were someone further up the trail. And tha' would be us. Caution never hurts. I 'as a plan tha' may jest take us from the trouble here and gi' us time t'thin' 'bout wha' we can do. We be a leavin' yet t'night and gettin' as f'r as we kin."

"Sarah, Tad, Lucky – best get y'rselves ready," Pap said. "We canna' waste much time. An' we be a travelin' light, only takin' a couple changes o' clothes. Tha' way the dep'ty and the sold'rs will thin' we be comin' back. We might'n sometime. But I'm thin'in' we be gone f'r quite a long spell. Once we get the Frosts on their way, I don' thin' we be helpin' 'ny one else f'r 'while. Jeb, ya' can pass tha' word 'bout if'n ye be 'round."

"I be 'greein' wi' ye there," Jeb said. "I can let ev'ry one 'nvolved know we be slippin' away and won' be 'round f'r a bit. I be a stoppin' in the village a bit f'r catchin' up wi' contacts and 'earin' the latest news. I 'ope there won' be 'ny problems wi' tha' task. I'f'n I 'ear or see 'nythin,' I be gettin' some sort o' signal t'ya'.

"Well, if'n ye be 'round f'r a bit af'r we finish wi' gettin' the Frosts t'the coast, could ye keep an eye on our place? May be ye could ride up 'ere, too, a'fore ye catch up wi' us at the next point o' rest," Pap said. "But don' go gettin' y'rself into further trouble on our 'count; if'n it don' look good t'come up this way. And if'n ye decides t'move on af'r, well I wish ye luck."

"Same to ye all. I best be gettin' on me way and get thin's 'ranged," Jeb said. "Hope t'see ya' at the next contact point. Be careful, all o' ye."

Jeb left and we heard him ride out a few minutes later after he had retrieved his horse from the pen. While waiting for him to leave, we sat there, staring into space. We all needed a minute to digest the events and to get our thoughts organized.

Grandmam started putting food into leather pouches to take on the journey. It was then Pap turned to her and said. "I don' know as ye be in je'pardy 'ere but may be ye should come 'long. 'Ow 'bout a visit t'see ye's brother Artie ov'r on the coast? Canna' thin' they'd hurt an ol' woman. But ye never know. Now I ponder on our situation, I would feel less concerned if'n ye were goin' wi' us."

"Oh, go on wi' ye there, I don' fright'n eas'ly," she said. "But t'would be nice t'visit Artie. It surely 'as been a good while since las' we saw 'im. As for restin', why this ol' body can keep up wi' the rest o' ye!"

Grandmam chuckled as she left the room to gather up her belongings. Pap picked up the food bags, grabbed a pile of coverlets from a chest in the room and headed out the door. By this time, Sarah, Tad and I had put together our few meager belongings in shoulder pouches. We grabbed warm cloaks and coats from the hooks and followed Pap. Grandmam was the last out the door, blowing out the lanterns, making sure the fires in each of the fireplaces were nearly out and quietly saying goodbye to her domain. We followed Pap to the horse pen where four horses stood waiting for us – almost as if they knew their family was in trouble.

"Seven of us are going to ride four horses?" I inquired. "Won't that make travel rather slow and tedious?"

"Don' worry. It be a'right," Pap said. "For a bit we ha' t'double up, but these horses be used to 'ard work and 'eavy loads. 'Opefully there be 'xtras at one o' the contact points."

I should have offered to help with saddling the animals, but once more the enormity of the damaging deed overwhelmed me. I leaned against the fence to keep from sinking to the ground. My knees felt like jelly and my stomach just kept churning and twisting into one giant knot. Get hold of yourself, I admonished. I tried to think about what lay ahead for all of us. I hoped Tad still had his gun. I'm not sure where the one I used had gotten to. I hadn't given it any thought until now. I supposed I had left it lying with the soldiers where I had dropped it after the scuffle (if indeed that is what one calls a killing). I was sure Pap and Sarah still had their weapons. I was thankful I didn't have one; I had done enough damage for one night.

I tried to focus on the whole situation at a single glance in my mind's eye – to do a quick evaluation of the episode in a few seconds. My life had changed forever! So many thoughts and questions plummeted into my mind. I felt fuzzy-headed once more. Why were the king's men there already? It must be like Pap had said – the Ringold's operation had already been discovered and the local regent's office knew about it. Most likely spies had reported the family or maybe the soldiers had been cautiously investigating illegal activity in general in the village and up along the trail. I was still puzzled by the fact the local deputy didn't seem to know about the cave. I never would have found it, but surely the locals would have known about it. There would be time to worry about these things later, along with trying to remember where I lived and what my purpose had been.

I spoke up. "Seems like there's going to be a few of us roaming the woods tonight. Is this going to be a problem? I mean...we aren't in any real danger are we?"

Although Tad had assured me we wouldn't see any soldiers, I really was concerned they would find us all sneaking through the woods. The thought of running into more trouble in the middle of the night seemed too threatening for comfort and could only indicate we were guilty.

"Don' worry," answered Pap. "We be goin' separate routes and be meetin' up later. Tad knows where t'go – Lucky, Sarah and Grandmam, ye go with him. Ye ha' t'double up a bit for now. The Frosts be goin' with me."

Tad and Pap finished saddling the horses. Pap made sure his guests were situated comfortably on their horse. Then, packing the Frost's and his extra travel bags, one of the food pouches and two of the coverlets around his saddle, he climbed on the loaded horse. There was barely room for him. Wishing us luck and telling us he would see us at the rendezvous point, he and the Frosts head south of the cottage and toward the village trail.

"Will they be goin' through the village?" I asked. "It doesn't seem like it would be safe."

"Na, they be jest goin' down the trail a bit and then ridin' through the for'st. It isna' so hilly there an' na' so thick," Tad answered. "They be safe 'nough."

Tad helped Sarah on one of the remaining two horses with Grandmam behind her. He handed them their knapsacks, a food pouch and two coverlets. Helping me on our horse, he handed me our travel and food pouches and the rest of the coverlets. Then he climbed on the animal, situating himself for a long ride. The four of us headed quietly beyond the cabin into the thick wooded area, one we hadn't seen yet this night.

Now I, Catherine Grafton, would leave what had been a safe haven for the past couple of months and ride into the winds of destiny. My mind was filled with thoughts of the whole event. How would it all end? This certainly was not the future I had envisioned for myself. The excitement of adventure had now been replaced with a fear I had never known. It was frightening to realize a whole life can be altered in just a moment, never to be the same again. Was I to forever be earmarked as a criminal against the king? Where should I go? Firmly in my mind was the nagging fact my father would never welcome me back into his home, if the true story were to be told. Could I go back and not tell the story? What would I tell them about where I had been?

I thought about my decision to not go home. I supposed I could have returned and told a lie, but in clear consciousness I wasn't sure I could live with the idea. Keeping such a secret would be very difficult. Somehow, I felt I couldn't live with the untrue tale very too long. I was convinced Father would never have condoned my impulsive behavior to aid the Puritans' escape. Even if a small token of sympathy might be elicited from him because I had felt the need to protect myself, he would have considered the whole episode foolish folly and highly unethical. I could already envision him decreeing I would never see the Ringold family again. I wasn't sure I could live with such a decision. It seemed more terrifying than any of the rest – never to see Tad again. I could not, nor did I want to even consider the idea. Even with Tad's attitude toward me, which had changed under the circumstances, I felt a bonding with him, and his whole family. I guess subconsciously my choice was made. At least for now, I would go to the coast with the Ringolds and accept the family's protection. Once we reached the coast and saw the Frosts safely boarded on the ship and out to sea, then I might know what the fates held in store for me.

And so we rode, Grandmam, Tad, Sarah and I, through the woods and into a destiny only God could foretell.

CHAPTER SEVEN

Journey into the Night

Midnight. The journey had begun. My future, at best, was in the hands of God. At worst, it rested on the valuable knowledge of the Ringolds to successfully defy the odds of discovery – both in their Puritan pilgrimage activities and in my escape from the king's gaol. What had started out in the beginning as a promiscuous and light-hearted adventure had now become a full-fledged flight into a new world of unknown danger. I now knew my identity, and could not even acknowledge the fact. In my mind's eye, I could see no possibility of returning home. Don't look back, I told myself. Concentrate on the future. I continued to process and solidify this thought. I told myself the pages of my previous life had now closed and I was on the verge of a new chapter as I rode further and further away in the arms of my new family. It was both exciting and terrifying. I rode with Tad, Sarah and Grandmam through the night toward a new life.

An opalescent moon guided our way through unfamiliar woods filled with dark shadows and on past a few villages and small sleepy hamlets whose names were never mentioned. Even now, after all these years, I can still recall how terribly frightened I was. I clung to Tad, feeling the warmth emanating from his body to mine. That closeness gave me comfort and eased my fears. He was an able rider and the horse bore the burden of both of us as we moved swiftly through the night. If it hadn't been for Sarah and Grandmam right behind us, it could almost have seemed a pleasant dream. In reality, it was a nightmare. Had I really killed the soldier? It all seemed so vague, like a bad taste in my mouth that wouldn't go away. It was self defense, I quickly protested to myself. Still, it was the very kind of behavior Father would have severely criticized. For that matter, I was inwardly chastising myself for such spontaneous actions. I should never have been here in the first place. It was the very kind of behavior which had often been the basis of trouble for me in the past, although much less seriously than now. Where would I be if I had not taken the shot? I shivered with the thought I could have been the one left lying on the ground instead of the soldier.

"Be ye a'right?" asked Tad. "Are ye cold?"

"I'm doing just fine. I am a bit cold. Mind if I snuggle closer?" I asked.

"Sure, snuggle in," he said. With that, he seemed to pick up the pace a bit, motioning to Sarah and Grandmam to do the same.

I was feeling a bit better from the warmth of Tad. But what I really wanted was to just close my eyes and awaken in the cheerfulness of the Ringold cottage with the aromatic smells of Grandmam's stewed rabbit cooking in a big pot in the fire pit. I wanted to feel the warmth of the fire coming from the big fireplace and to be sharing the task of setting the table with Sarah. I could almost taste the hot, tantalizing food and see us cheerfully gathering around and placing the meal on crockery dinnerware as we sat around the roughly hewed wooden table. And I wanted to take part in Tad's teasing as he came in from his outside chores. I wanted all this desperately, with no dead soldier hanging over my shoulder, threatening my very existence.

The damp fall air chilled our very bones, and maybe even our souls, as we rode. My soul felt the gloomy chill – the deep, cold and evil-lurking shadows, not only in the night but in the outer reaches of my mind. I clung tightly to Tad's waist as he deftly led our animal through the forest. Although we had our ears attuned to the night sounds, surprisingly, even those were limited. It was as if God's evening creatures sensed the urgency and secretiveness of our flight through the midnight hours and kept their nocturnal musings down to a soft whisper. None of us spoke. For the time being, we each seemed lost in our own little worlds of terror, studying and deciding how best to handle our part in the whole situation. I was tired, both physically and mentally. I think we were all trying to absorb the events of the day and evening, the swiftness of the journey and the danger upon which we had embarked. I blinked back the welling tears in my eyes as I faced the reality of where we were and what we were doing.

Snuggling closer to Tad, I felt myself relaxing. I didn't have to think about where we were going and it was comforting to know Tad was leading us away from the trouble smoldering at the cave. I laid my head against his back and felt the monotonous movement of the horse. I let my thoughts wander where they might – about what had happened and what we would experience as we road toward the ocean.

I had never been to the ocean and had no concept of the distance or the time it would take. I had gathered from Pap's comments there would be a number of stops. He also had said if all went well, the Frosts would be boarding their ship in a week's time. Beyond that, I was both curious and afraid of the complications of the journey – where we would stay, the unique countryside along the way and the potential dangers we would encounter. I only hoped the horses would hold out until we could properly rest them. Tad said they were hard working animals, but still...

The long ride gave me time to think about my life and how it had changed. My memory had returned, and the past flashed by in a whirling kaleidoscope as I recalled my family and events. I called to mind the day Maudie and I first met, both determined each of us would be the stronger of the two in this new relationship. It had been such a pleasant day and a great birthday surprise. Even now, I considered her one of my best gifts ever. She had been a constant companion, and I could tell her secrets I would never dream of telling a person. Now, poor Maudie was dead due to my foolishness and the desire to have one last adventure. My father had been right. I could see I had been wild and irresponsible. But no matter, the situation "couldna' be changed" as the Ringolds would say.

How kind these people had been to a total stranger. I felt beholden to them and sad all at the same time because my actions placed them in such jeopardy. Eventually I would come to understand the Ringold's danger was of their doing. I had probably saved their lives through the death of the two soldiers – if indeed they were dead. Because of the Ringold's involvement in the movement to aid fellow Puritans in escaping from the powers of the King and church politics, they would have eventually had to flee their home or stand trial and face the consequences of gaol. But at this point, I still didn't know all the circumstances. Despite my many adventures, I was very naïve and inexperienced in ways of the world. I did not fully understand the injustice experienced by these people who only wanted to worship God in a way different from the Church of England. When we went to the cave, the short, simple explanations offered by Pap had been adequate. I still had lots of questions and felt the Ringolds owed me more information on their activities than I had already received. It was my curious nature and I wanted to know all I could about the situation. I never meant to get so involved, and now I was in too deep. In my innocence, the possibility of excitement and a new adventure had enticed me to join them – just to see what was going on. Now two soldiers were most likely dead and my debt to them had been paid in blood.

The few weeks spent with Tad and his family had convinced me they all were eagerly accepting the challenge of this terrifying adventure with the greatest of pleasure. And, I too, would have been a more eager participant in this midnight flight had I not been partially the cause for the journey. The closeness of Tad became a soothing, tension-relieving antidote for me, which I sorely needed at this time. My senses were heightened by his closeness and the warmth emanating from his body. My feelings for Tad had not yet formulated to the word love, but I guess I was open to the possibility. There had been something special in how I felt about him, right from the first moment my eyes met his. As for Tad's feelings toward me, I really didn't know. Although no words were spoken by either of us as we rode, I sensed, or hoped, my feelings were shared.

"Tad, there are so many unanswered questions." I spoke softly so my voice wouldn't carry into the night. "Will we have a chance to talk, just you and me? What's this whole thing about? I don't understand it all. I am involved and it's because I have offered my loyalty to you and your family. Do you think the soldiers really knew about Pap? And why didn't the deputy know about the cave? I am puzzled and feel bad all at the same time because I have led us into new danger. And mostly, I want to know if there will be time for us to get to know each other better – I mean more than just as Sarah's brother... Well, I mean if you would like to become friends. Do you think that's possible?"

He whispered back, "Ye cert'nly be full o' questions. Oh Lucky... oh, ah, be it a'right t'call ye Lucky? Tha' be 'ow I 'as come t'thin' o' ye and am in the 'abit of callin' ye by tha' name. I be so sorry ye 'as gotten mixed into this fracas. I don' ev'n know all the details m'self. I be sort o' new at helpin' Pap. I 'as ha' to worry 'bout wha' be goin' on. He 'as done all the plannin' in the past an' I 'as helped wi' some o' the travelin.' The Frosts be my firs' all-out eff'rt to aid the Puritan's in they's plight. All's I know is we 'as been helpin' people most o' our lives t'fight f'r wha' we, and they, believe in. I, too, wan' t'find time f'r us t'know each other better, now tha' you 'as your memory back. I know we didna' ha' a very good start. Guess tha' were partly my fault 'cause I 'as been so worried 'bout wha' we be doin' and 'ow it be a comin' out t'our favor. When we reach the meetin' place, Pap most likely should ha' news and answers for ye. Don' worry on it; f'r now we jest ha' t'be getting' t'Pap safely t'morrow."

The questions still nagged at my already troubled mind, but for now I would just cling close to Tad and let him and the horse take us to wherever we needed to go. My inner conscious echoed the foolhardiness and the misfortunes of my actions, both before and after the accident. The only thing I could actually feel really good about in this whole adventure so far was my growing friendship with Tad and the entire Ringold family. Just knowing Tad might care for me made this whole venture worth every bit of the trouble I now found myself in. This was my fate – God had led me to this place and time. My destiny was in his hands.

I thought about fate and how the future is determined. Does only God know the answer? In the Grafton household, God was not the master of our destiny. Our future was defined by the goals each person worked and strived for in their lives. It was a concept Father had drilled into our young minds practically from birth and was always urging us to choose activities to make us responsible citizens of England. I always supposed he was right, although by my very nature I questioned the idea and had difficulty accepting it. Brother David was an avid believer in the idea of life being what you make of it through your own hard work. But if this idea were true, why did I feel I had no control over my actions. On many occasions I tried to follow the rules and guidelines set for us. But I think my fate was controlled by something greater than Father and me. I think fate possessed me to ride out into the countryside and challenge the rules. Things just seemed to happen to me without any rhyme or reason. And, I might add, those happenings were not always to my benefit. What about the whole logic of fate and who was responsible? I was on the verge of what many philosophers in the past had contemplated. Could I control my fate and destiny or was it really, as the Ringold's believed, preordained and in the hands of God?

A long ago memory of a sunny spring day suddenly came into mind.

* * *

It was a day to be treasured forever as we basked in the warmth of the sunshine streaming down to earth in golden rays. Our favorite of all governesses, Anna, promised us a picnic after our daily lesson. We had all piled onto the pony cart, laughing and joking all the way to the small wooded copse near Kimble's tenant section. Even little Mary had been allowed to come along and David seemed very easy and light-hearted that day. Anna had conspired with Molly and brought a wonderful basket filled with our favorite foods, including delicious berry tarts and meat pies. After devouring our meal, we turned to enjoying Mother Nature at her best.

The small oak timber and the shallow pond nearby are still vivid in my memory. The trees were smiling with the warmth of the April sun, just beginning to fill out. Specks of yellow-green danced in the breeze amidst the dark umber colored trunks and branches. It had been a perfect spot in which to frolic and play. I remember the boys and I spent some time trying to catch frogs, but we weren't very successful. The frogs had come out to sun themselves on the flat rocks. The minute we reached for them, they turned and jumped into the pond. I guess they thought it was a secure haven from the mischievous intruders into their world of peace and quiet. They were right – we weren't quick enough and the water was too cold for our fingers or for wading to catch them. We all agreed come summer, when the water was much warmer, they would be begging for mercy.

Anna and Mary lolled under a large oak tree quite near the pond. Anna was reading a book and nonchalantly keeping an eye on us three rowdy youngsters. Mary had snuggled up next to Anna with her favorite doll and was deep in an afternoon slumber. We had finally given up on the frogs and gyrated toward the coverlet Anna had spread out under the giant oak. The three of us flopped down, taking advantage of the quiet moment, the warmth of the spring sun and the puffs of clouds floating above us in a sea of azure blue. Anna reached into the basket beside her and handed each of us a pastry Mollie had provided for an afternoon treat.

It was Nathan who started the conversation. He had finished his tart and stretched out on the coverlet on his back. He reached out, plucked a stem of grass from near the edge of the coverlet and placed it between his teeth. He then tucked his arms under his head and looked up at the sky. He closed his eyes momentarily; then, a big smile spread across his face as if a pleasant thought came to mind, or he knew a secret that no one else knew. He took the stem out of his mouth and using it as a pointer, he told us to look at the clouds overhead.

"Right up there is a wild elephant and he is growing a trunk – just like the elephant in one of our lesson books," he said. "Do you see the trunk beginning to form? And look over there. See the dragon chasing the mouse?"

I turned and stared up at the white shapes adrift in the blue ocean of air. Some of the puffs were splitting, others joining to make new and unique formations.

"I can sort of see some shapes, though I gotta' admit Nathe' ole' boy, I don't see the elephant or the mouse," I said. "But you're right. That big cloud does sort of make you think of a dragon."

"Look at those clouds hanging over the pond," continued Nathan. "Looks like the head of a horse, or better yet, one of those striped horses living in savannahs of Africa!"

"What a silly dreamer you are, Nathan – they are just clouds. I don't see any shapes other that cloudy puffs," David sternly chided, taking all the fun out of the moment.

"It's a good dream," commented Anna, closing her book and joining our skyward gazing.

"Maybe so," David spoke authoritatively, becoming a clone of our father. "Father says daydreamers never amount to anything. They are too feckless and not in charge of their lives. He says we must very carefully obey all the rules and learn all we can in order to be masters of our future."

"Daydreamers are very important and necessary in our society," Anna told David. "They make the world a wonderful place for new thoughts and new inventions. They are the people who write the books and the music we so enjoy. How sad the world would be without the dreamers. The world we live in, David, needs both kinds of people – the realists like yourself and the dreamers like Nathan and Catherine. Wouldn't you agree?"

"Oh, I suppose you may be right," David answered begrudgingly. He would never concede a point if it contradicted with what he believed was expected of him.

"Besides," Anna said rather flippantly. "I believe our fate is already signed and sealed from our birth. God has already decided what each of his creatures shall be and shall do in the universe. Oh sure, he provides us with opportunities for good or bad deeds, but I believe we are all part of his scheme for life from one generation to the next."

"You mean no matter what a person does with his life, no matter how hard he works and tries to do what is expected, life is planned out for him?" From his tone of incredulity, I knew David could hardly believe what he was being told. This concept was too liberal and unrealistic for him to even conceive. "I am the only person responsible for me – not you, not Father, not even God. Just me! You work hard for whatever you want in life, and you get it!"

"Take care, David! Don't make God angry with your words." Nathan the dreamer admonished. "God takes care of us all and gives each of us a life to fulfill. I think as part of his plan he gave us all dreams. Some people just don't use them." It was obvious Nathan believed Anna's theory.

"That's a wonderful thought, Nathan." Then Anna turned to David and sadly said, "Do you really think hard work is the answer? Life can be very mean and cruel. Sometimes things just happen and you have no control over them. What about people who are very poor, or very ill? Do you think they planned their life that way? They too work hard and have dreams just like you and me. You see, there are all kinds of beliefs in this world. Maybe you're right, maybe I'm right. Who knows? I think we have no control over our destiny – the future for each of us has been written in God's great books of life. But you are just children. Remember my words when you are older and wiser and life has dealt with you, be it fairly or unfairly."

As I grew older and reflected on people who had influenced my concepts of life, I often wondered what had become of Anna. She had seemed, despite her gaiety during playtimes and the strictness and discipline in her schoolroom, a most unhappy person. Of course, this was the perception of a very young girl. She wasn't with us very along and I was almost sure she left our schoolroom because she didn't think like Father had wanted us to think. He didn't need another dreamer in our household. In my young eyes, Anna had certainly seemed very worldly and wise. I learned a lot about life from Anna, although I think Nathan and she were more kindred souls than any of the rest of us.

As I thought about Anna, I suddenly realized at the time she would have been teaching our lessons she would have probably been just about my age. I often wondered what tragedies had occurred in her life to make her so cynical. I had to laugh at the oddity of the situation. Here I was, thinking about Anna, a philosopher of preordained fate, and myself, traveling in the night to an unknown destiny. Was our future really predestined? A few months ago I would have said I wasn't so sure I believed all Anna told us. But I did believe in dreams and how things sometimes just happen to people, be it fate or circumstances. Often a true destiny emerges as the result of tragedy or despair. I can remember thinking about people our family knew and how often they had become a different person than the one they dreamed about becoming as a result of life's events. And so, whether it was predestination by God or just my luck, fate had brought me to this time and this place. Here I am. And, I guess you could say it was from my choices. Maybe life is a combination of both Anna's beliefs and Father's.

* * *

I was brought back to the moment as I felt the pain and stiffness in my aching body. It seemed like we had been riding for days and weeks, but actual travel time had only been about four hours. We had stopped once for a couple of minutes. It had been hard getting back on the animals since none of us were used to riding long distances for hours on end. I wasn't totally uncomfortable riding behind Tad, but I certainly was not used to riding behind someone. I had always been the one leading the horse, well sort of. Maudie usually had a mind of her own once I got her going in the direction I wanted. Thus sitting as I was, I could feel the stiffness settling in, adding to the tiredness I already felt in both my mind and body. I was thankful I did not have to be responsible for guiding and keeping a horse going at an even pace. I had been able to just sit here on the animal, with my arms around Tad's waist and not even have to think, if I didn't want to. I wished I could quiet my mind – it seemed cluttered with random thoughts.

I was beginning to feel the effects of rolling around on the rocks by the cave and the jolting bounce of the ride. I tried not to move other than with the movements of the horse, and in actuality, that was easy. Because of both Tad's and my experiences in riding, practically since birth, we seemed to be in tune with the horse's easy gait through the countryside. I must have dozed off though, for just a minute. I awoke with a start, as one often does from a catnap, embarrassed and a little bit disoriented.

"I'm sorry," I muttered to Tad as I shook my head, trying to shake away the dogged tiredness that I felt throughout my whole body. It is amazing, I thought, about how much torture and abuse one can put the body through and it still continues to function. "I only shut my eyes for a second – to just rest for a moment while my whirling mind slowed down."

"My poor Lucky. Be ye a'right?" he asked. "It 'as been a very long ordeal and sur'ly ye are utt'rly 'xhausted."

I liked his concern and he did not know how true his statement was. In all the years of my young life, I cannot remember ever feeling as drained, exhausted and tired as I was at that moment, well except for the days after my accident.

"I thin' we should stop," he continued on without giving me a chance to answer. Tad gave a low whistle and slowed his stead down so Sarah and Grandmam were abreast of us. "We be stoppin' for jest a bit. Surely ye could use it Grandmam. How 'bout ye Sarah? An' I truly thin' Lucky needs a little time t'rest. Ev'n I be gettin' a bit tired. Pap didna' 'xpect us t'ride clear to Crawfords Point wi'out stoppin'. He suggested we might'n stop off 'bout half way."

I tried to say, "I'm really fine. There is no..."

Tad flung his hands in the air and interrupted me. "Now who couldna' keep her head from bobbin' jest a few minutes ago?"

I just smiled – it was useless to protest.

"We be ridin' jest a'might f'rth'r," he went on to say. "There be a nice ol', out-o'-the-way dairy jest a short distance from here – owned by a good Puritan frien'. We can stop there and rest. We won' be meetin' Pap 'til 'bout mid day. Tha' be when he said we should prob'ly meet up. Pap and the Frosts 'as jest 'bout as far t'go as we do. They jest be goin' a diff'ren' route. And for sure the Frosts would be needin' a rest. Af'r all, they be no more used t'this kind o' travel than are the rest o' ye."

"Speak f'r y'rself there, Tad. Jest how of'n do ya' go 'bout at the mid point o' night, ridin' through woods and towns you don' even know and tryin' to find ye's way wi'out breakin' ye's neck?" Sarah pointedly directed this question at her brother.

"Well, I 'as done so a couple o' times lately and I didna' break anythin'," Tad retorted. "O' course tha' were wi' Pap and guess tha' doesna' make me an 'xpert, but I at least 'as SOME 'xperience!"

The brotherly/sisterly squabble brought back memories of my own siblings and the rhetorical clashes that had ensued on more than one occasion. My thoughts turned to my own family, and in my mind I spoke to them. "David, Nathan and Mary, will I ever see you again? I wonder what strange destiny awaits all of us. Oh, Mother, I'm so sorry. And Father? Oh, how disappointed you would most likely be with me."

All these thoughts rushed swiftly through my tired, wandering mind. I felt cold again; for a brief second, it felt like my heart had stopped. Had I made the right choice? Had I been unnecessarily hard on myself? Would Father have welcomed me back, knowing the deed I had done? The decision was made, and I closed my eyes. I nodded, signaling to myself it was the end of the discussion. I did not want to think about them right now. I had enough to think about and future problems to encounter without clouding my judgment with sentiment. I needed to stay with this moment. Later, there would be time for thinking and perhaps even contacting my parents. Only time would tell.

My thoughts were interrupted as Tad continued on. "As I were sayin', there be a small dairy jest a bit f'rth'r. The man'ger won' be 'xpectin' us in the wee hours o' the mornin', but we most likely be more than welcome. We be takin' a short time t'ha' a bite and rest a bit. Be patient jest a might longer – I know wha' I be 'bout. How be ye a'doin', Sarah? Grandmam? Be this journey too hard on either o' ye?"

Sarah just gave him a disgruntled look. "I can do anythin' ye can do."

Grandman gave him the same look. "Go on wi' ya' thar young'n. I can out las' ya' any day o' the week," she said. "Af'r all them years o' 'ard work and them years ye's Grandpap and me fought jest t'stay 'live. Them were ter'ble days o' fightin' when the ol' king were 'live and we seen friends an' family die'n f'r naught. Ya' thin' a little mi'night ride be too much f'r me? Why lad this ride be easier 'n bak'n a meat pie!"

And so, on we rode into the night. The sky was filled with a bevy of stars and I could feel them smiling down on us, encouraging us to stay strong. Maybe it was God's way of talking to me. I felt a limited sense of security in the cold, gray predawn. And as I had done in the weeks and days since

I left Grafton Manor, I wondered again where this adventure would lead.

CHAPTER EIGHT

Yuker's Dairy Farm

We had not gone a far distance when we found ourselves following a slightly grass-covered, but deeply rutted pathway. The long lane was bordered by dark, short and tall ballooning shapes. Later, I noticed the hedge consisted of lilac bushes, no longer in bloom nor with many leaves at this time of year. It again reminded me that it had been early fall when this whole adventure had begun.

We were greeted by several buildings of various shapes and sizes that were probably filled with hay, oats and plenty of milking cows. The buildings stood at the end of the lane and were a welcoming sight for weary eyes and tired bodies. The dairy awaited us, offering a much needed rest. I hated to admit it, but I was thinking that a little time to catch a few winks would be heavenly. In the dark I could not easily make out the details of the cottage itself, although in its shadowy form it appeared to be a low, rambling building. Near as I could make out, the dairy was nestled at the edge of the forest we had been following for almost the whole of our ride. As we rounded the corner of the first building, a faint glow from shuttered lamp light winked at us.

We had just pulled the reins up to stop the horses when the top part of a Dutch-style door flew open. Encompassed in the framework of the doorway was a burly, middle-aged man, about as tall as he appeared to be wide. A deep, resonant voice greeted us with gusto and just a hint of jocularity, and definitely fit the overall stature of the man clad in homespun work clothes covered with a well-soiled leather apron. Underneath his leather tam wisps of graying hair poked out around his face. A full, graying beard covered his chin and fell about half-way down his chest. This, I assumed, was our host.

"Well, if'n it isna' Tad Ringold." the man bellowed out in surprised recognition. "Wha' brings ye t'my humble dwellin' here at the end o' the world in the wee hours o' the mornin'? Wha'ev'r be the reason, ye is welcome, most welcome. It 'as been a long while since I ha' seen them lean bones. Looks like ye's gotten a bit tall'r and thinn'r since last ye stood at my doorstep. Be that possible?"

"Aye, it 'as been a while," Tad answered. "I thin' last time were 'bout a couple o' years ago when Pap and I were passin' through ye's part o' the world. I s'pose I 'as grown. Grandmam be a'ways complainin' tha' I ha' outgrown' my clothes, so it must be true."

By this time Tad had dismounted and was walking towards the man who came out of the barn with a wooden bucket full of milk. The dairy man set the container on the ground and wiped his brow.

"Greetin's my friend," said Tad, holding out his hand. Yuker wiped his hand on his apron and grabbed and shook Tad's hand with gusto. Tad tried to get quick introductions out but the dairy owner didn't give him a chance – he totally monopolized the entire conversation.

"Ye must come in and rest a spell," said Yuker as he put his arm around Tad's shoulder, not giving him time to get in any other words. "How be Pap? Be he stayin' clear o' trouble these days? Knowin' him as I do, I mos' likely doubt it, huh? Know'n ye all like I do, I'll bet there be some errand o' great 'portance and ye be offerin' ministerin' to folk who don' do anythin' 'sept put they's faith in God. So ye and y'r frien's here been out ridin' all night, is it? Did ye come all the way from ye's part o' the woods? 'Tis certainly a long ride and ye must come in, ha' a bite to eat and rest a bit. Come, come... Let us go ov'r yond'r there into my livin' quarters."

This Yuker said as he turned and motioned Grandmam, Sarah, and me to follow. Sarah and I slowly eased weary, muscle-tightened bodies off tired horses. It took a minute for the ground to stop moving and to get my legs straightened out from riding behind Tad on the horse. I was so stiff I could hardly move and I imagined Grandmam would have to feel that way too. Although, that lady had a strong constitution and would never have let anyone know she was aching. It had to be hard on her old body – traveling and being scrunched up on a horse throughout the night. But as usual, she never had a word of complaint nor even uttered a groan as Sarah helped her down. Finally, Tad managed to get a turn in the conversation and introduced us all to our host.

"It be good to see ye 'gain," Tad said. "I do hope y'r 'ospital'ty 'xtends to us wayfa'rs afar from 'ome on a cold ev'ning'. We could use a bit o' rest if'n tha' be fine wi' thee. Go on 'nside there with Yuker," Tad directed me, Sarah and Grandmam. He turned to Yuker and said, "A'right ifn' I take our 'orses ov'r to yond'r stable?"

"Aye lad, tha' be fine. Ye be findin' everythin' ya' need there. Be sure and gi' them animals a good rubbin' and a bag o' oats," Yuker directed. "Take ye's time and join us soon as ye can. I ha' a hot fire goin', a big chunk o' tasty cheese, fresh bread, a cup o' hot grog t'warm ye's toes and plenty o' room f'r ye t'rest a might."

"There be no real need for ye to fix up anythin," Tad said. "Grandmam made us up some o' her foodstuffs we can eat, but we sure would 'preciate bein' able t'jest rest a short time. We praise God for ye's gen'ros'ty. Wi'out kind folk like ye, our mission would be much more difficult."

"T'is my pleasure. I only do wha' God 'xpects o' me," Yuker said. "As for ye's food, ye jest save it for later. Ye might'n be needin' it f'rth'r down the road in a day or two."

"I could come and help with the horses if you'd like, Tad," I said. He answered he didn't need help and that I should follow Yuker.

I found it most interesting that Yuker didn't seem the least bit surprised by our interruption of his night's sleep. But then I observed he had come from the barn and I wondered if he had been expecting us or was only alert most evenings for wayfaring strangers to stop in. By now it was going on about 4 a.m. and I realized that his work routine would have begun at this hour. He would be up, taking care of his livestock and milking the cows. From the barn, I had heard their rowdy utterances and recalled my own home where those same sounds were regularly heard. I couldn't see any animals. I just heard their complaints.

Yuker swept us into his home and we entered into a cozy room that contained more paraphernalia than I had ever seen congregated into one spot. Every corner of the room, along with all the spaces in between, was filled with books, musical instruments, and every kind of curio and gadget you could imagine. He must have been collecting these things a long time, and taking them all in made me dizzy. My curiosity was really piqued to know what kind of man was offering us hospitality. I assumed his wife would have helped him accumulate these things. I thought it odd she wasn't up and about to greet us. Perhaps she was a sound sleeper and not affected by all the noise and commotion we were making. Or, perhaps his hospitality to such groups as us did not include his wife.

It was the dancing, leaping orange and yellow flames in the fireplace along one wall which attracted our attention and beckoned us to gather close and warm ourselves. In front of the large fieldstone construction, similar to the fireplace in the Ringold cottage, were several benches. We sat down on the stationery seats, all too tired to ask questions or even converse with one another. All we wanted to do was sit on a seat that wasn't moving for a bit. After that a few hours of sleep would do much to rest our tired, aching bodies.

Yuker proved to be a charming host, preparing a nourishing bite to eat in no time at all.

While we supped on his food, he kept up the chatter. Tad and he talked about some interesting visits when he and Pap had stopped. Yuker asked about our journey, and Tad explained a few of the details, or at least as much as he dared tell without including Yuker as an unwilling accomplice to our crimes of murder and tyranny. Finally, Yuker led us each to a soft, warm place in which to catch some much needed rest. I had trouble settling down and the few hours went too rapidly. Long after everyone else had fallen asleep, my mind kept bouncing and jostling as if I were still riding. I finally drifted into a light slumber, but not before hearing the creaks and groans of the house and the snapping and crackling of the fire.

As I watched Yuker carry out his duties as a host, I wondered about his life. I had always been greatly interested in people. Even as a youngster, I always wanted to know more about people than they sometimes wanted or were willing to share. I was the one that always questioned the people we met, the governesses, tenants on the farm, and even the market people. I wanted to know all about their families and what they wanted out of life. David was like that to some extent and when I think back, I guess I was more like David than I cared to admit. He thought I went too far and was often embarrassed by my prying questions when he was with me. He called me a "pesky, nosy interloper."

There was a time in my life, when I was about thirteen, I kept a journal, interviewing and writing down things I had heard members of the household or estate say. Although Nathan was the dreamer and the real writer in the family, I liked to dabble in writing down lists and ideas. But mostly, I would just sit and listen to stories about people and wonder what it would be like to be in their shoes. Often, I was envious of people that had led adventurous lives and I would have given anything to do the same thing. Maybe, I was more of a dreamer than Nathan – at least, he could look at life realistically if need be. I always wanted the adventure that was just out of reach. I would tell Father or anyone who would listen that I couldn't wait to be grown up so that I could get out into the world and do something exciting. Well, I certainly had gotten out into the world, and look where it had gotten me – dead men left in my wake and me running away from soldiers in the dead of the night into unknown countryside.

My wandering thoughts eventually returned to Yuker. What an odd name, I thought to myself. Was it his first name or his family name? Tad had not explained, other than just "This is Yuker." The man's robust and muscled body gave evidence to many years of hard work and lifting heavy loads. But, the surroundings of his home let us glimpse into his soul – that of a gentle man who most likely was highly educated.

Later, when I had a chance, I asked Tad about him. It seems that Yuker's mother had been a member of a very elite Irish family and his father had been an educated laborer on her family's estate. The two had fallen in love and because a marriage would not have received family blessings, they ran away together to England. A very kind, old uncle of Yuker's father took the couple under his wing and in turn, they learned about raising cows and helping to run the dairy.

"We'd been tol' Yuker were 'bout thirteen or fourteen when his moth'r and fath'r were both killed in a mob uprisin' in a small village ne'r here," Tad told me when I inquired. "It seems tha' sold'rs got into a row wi' a few villag'rs. His par'nts, who were merely passin' by, sudd'nly found theyselves in the midst o' a riotin' mob. They were killed, 'long wi' many village Puritans. The dairy bus'ness became Yuker's way o' life, but he were able to study and get an ed'cation through a compromisin' friend and landlord. 'Ventually, Yuker 'nherited the dairy from the old landlord when he died. Yuker isna' a wealthy man, but he doesna' wan' f'r much."

"Did he ever marry?" I asked, since I had not seen any sign of a wife.

"No," Tad had continued. "There were a girl once. She were the delight and love o' his life as I understand it. But they nev'r married. Seems her par'nts were lookin' at social status and wantin' a marriage o' prestige for their dau'ter. Yuker, though he be a gen'le man, would not suit. I of'n thin' he nev'r got ov'r his love f'r the girl. But it don' mean Yuker

131

be a bitt'r man. Much to the contra'y. He loves life and pe'ple and jest 'cepts life for wha' God ha' gi'v'n him."

How sad was Tad's story. I told him so, and he agreed. The story made me think about Tad and my feelings for him. I only hoped those feelings would continue to grow and the fellow I wanted would not get away. I definitely knew that I would not accept Yuker's fate. But maybe he had been a fighter, too, and his destiny was not to be with the woman he loved. It did not surprise me that considering the death of his parents and the circumstances of Yuker's life, he would be helping Puritans in their escape from the king's men.

Yuker awoke us about 8 a.m., after we had captured a few hours of sleep. The welcoming rest had not been nearly long enough and in the midst of friends, I felt utterly and totally isolated and completely exhausted after the long, grueling ordeal of the previous day. This time we walked down the lane, past the lilac shrubs and back out onto a different pathway than we had followed before. We had gotten a much later start than I think Tad had anticipated. He seemed extremely anxious to lengthen the distance between us and the Ringold home. With this decision, I certainly did not disagree. At Yuker's insistence, some cheese, bread and vegetables had been added to our food pouches. He had even given Tad a few extra pouches of grain for the animals. Yuker had thought it best for us to follow the forest trail around the nearby village rather than go through it. Both he and Tad had agreed the fewer people we encountered, the safer we would be.

"When ye get near the village, walk close t'the woods quietly and quickly," Yuker said.

"Once ye is past, get on y'r horses and stay 'long the woods jest ploddin' at a steady pace. Don' 'tract no 'tention for a short ways. Kind o' use ye's judgment, but after a short time, ye can put a little speed on as ye move on t'ward y'r next destination. Ye never know how fast news can travel, 'specially bad news. I nev'r 'as been a great lov'r o' them red-coated, saber-'appy varmints that pacify the king."

We all thanked Yuker for his kind hospitality as Tad and Sarah gathered up the reins of our trust-worthy animals. It seemed the short rest had been good for them and they were ready for the journey.

"Ye take care o' y'rself there, Mist'r," Grandmam said as she placed her hand on Yuker's shoulder. "We pray one day we won' need help from folks like ye and the un'rgroun' routes f'r our fellow worshipp'rs. Wi'out ye's kindness and help from t'other folk, Pap wouldna' be so successful. Thank ye for bein' here to gi' us help and 'couragement."

"I pray f'r ye and all our help'rs," Yuker said. "It 'as been a long, 'ard road f'r many o' us t'w'rship God as'n we please. I promise ye, there will come a day when all pe'ple may love an' 'on'r God in they's own way."

Those comments were all Yuker had made about our plight during the visit. I doubt he had given any thought or concern his own safety might be jeopardized in this dairy hide-away. Both he and Tad agreed the dairy would probably not even be given consideration by any inquirer of the king. I thought the same thing weeks ago, but my recent experience had given me cause to have other thoughts! If a king's man was in search of someone, I rather suspected they left no stones unturned in their attempt to carry out justice.

We left Yuker's safe harbor of warmth and friendship, following the worn and traveled forest path on foot as the dairy man had suggested. We followed Tad in a brisk pace, an entourage of four and two horses. I asked how much further to Crawfords Point. Tad answered we had about a half-day's journey.

Sarah and Grandmam were doing their best to keep up with Tad's vigorous pace. I was surprised they both seemed eager and ready for any new adventure the day and the journey might offer. As for me, in the past I would have been ready for any new experience. My enthusiasm had been curbed by the happenings of the last couple months, and most especially by the last twenty-four hours. I admired Sarah's courage and energy in our current situation. I had only known her a few months but I was aware of how vulnerable she could be despite her toughness and her protests. Perhaps she was an echo of my own ego.

"Are you planning to walk the whole way?" I asked Tad as I huffed and puffed along beside him. "If so, I doubt we'll be anywhere close before night fall. And, we will be exhausted before noon if we keep up this pace for any length of time. Before my accident I could have easily kept up this pace, now I don't think I've got the stamina. And no matter how much Grandmam protests, I hardly doubt she can keep up this pace for long."

Tad laughed. "No miss, we don' plan t'walk the whole way. We jest needed t'get through this thick forest area. Yuker said it isna' far and once we pass the village we can get back on our 'orses and on down the trail."

It had been an exhausting journey thus far. I took comfort in the fact Tad had taken on the responsibility of leading and guiding us. He also was showing bravery when, he too, was probably as scared and worried as the rest of us. I was proud of him and this increased my feelings for him. He was much like his father and I could see the gentle side of both of them as they carried out their daily duties. My heart gave a slight lurch. Just for a moment I felt a terrible nagging sadness, the likes of which I had never experienced before as the thought of never seeing Tad again crossed my mind. I only hoped and prayed God would include Tad as an integral part of my destiny.

On leaving the dairy we encountered a damp mist in the air, created from the mixture of morning sun, heavy dew and the cold ground. The mist soon lifted as the sun's rays penetrated and warmed the earth. It could have been a glorious day but for our errand. The forest began to thin a bit but still provided good cover as we walked along the outskirts of the village. We could see smoke from chimneys in homes along the outer edge of the small berg. A church bell sang loudly into the morning air, and the thunder of carriage and wagon cart wheels echoed and bounced off the surrounding hills as the conveyances lumbered into the village from the main roadway. In the distance we could see a cottage nestled at the base of a small hillock and surrounded by a pasture full of grasses ablaze with the colors of fall. Although no smoke was rising from its chimney and we saw no one about, I wondered if there might be people inside the cottage watching us wind our way along the forest path.

We next passed a dilapidated stable attached to a weathered cottage whose sagging roof gave evidence of abandonment. It was isolated and secluded from the rest of the village by a small grove of pine trees – a good place to hide if the need arose. My, but I had become devious. A few months ago I would not have given much thought to that idea or to the place. As far as we could see to the right was a hilly meadow, speckled with trees and shrubs. To the left, more forest which began to thicken just outside the village. Its dark, heavy shadows would either become our protector or our demise.

As we reached the outskirts of the village, Tad signaled for us to mount up. We rode silently and slowly for a short distance. Then he motioned us to pick up speed. With a half-day's journey still ahead of us and a late morning start, we didn't have time to dally. The animals, as well as ourselves, would be tired before long. But the short rest we had taken gave us all a limited supply of renewed energy. We continued to wind our way around and through what I called the "never-ending forest," onward toward the rendezvous point. The rest of the morning's venture was uneventful – only the steady plip-plop, plip-plop of the horses, bringing us ever nearer to Pap.

The journey, perhaps under less strained circumstances, would not have seemed such a long trek. In my more adventurous days, I would have eagerly looked at the scenery and placed it in my picture memory to share with Nathan at a later date. We had often shared our adventures and brought back vivid stories of what we saw, heard and did.

But now exhausted and bone-weary, I wasn't interested in seeing where we had been or where we were going. I just wanted it to end in a safe place. The miles and hours had somehow become distorted out of perspective. Had we really only been traveling less than a day? My tired mind seemed to sway from lucid to hallucinatory thoughts – from the welcoming closeness of our destination to a ridiculous paranoia that we had been riding around in circles throughout the same forest for hours. Could this be true? Had Tad become disoriented and gotten us lost? Of course he had not – Tad knew about these trails and had been going along them for years with Pap. I would imagine he could wind his way through the thicket blindfolded.

I scolded myself – where is your trust and confidence? You are really overwrought! How absurd to have misgivings about Tad! It was this interminable woodland that was providing my misgivings. Perhaps this was the same forest we had been following from the Ringold's home. Tad told me this part of the country was known for its unlimited arborous, wooded sylvans. And I vaguely remembered from my early geography lessons there was a section in the midlands which was almost primordial woods.

As the morning hours began disappearing into mid day, I became ever more apprehensive and anxious. Would Pap have heard any news along the way, or would Jeb have been able to get any message to him in case there had been unknown dangers? I wondered about how this would have happened. I could not visually conceive any way for Jeb and Pap to make contact to receive news. It would be a far piece for Jeb to ride at a fast pace in order to catch up with Pap. Tad said Pap and the Frosts would be traveling about the same distance, but had we all gone out of our way to get where we wanted to be? What was in store for all of us now as we neared our destination and rendezvous with Pap at Crawfords Point? Would we all be able to go back to our homes and resume our previous life? Not me for sure, and I hardly doubted the Ringolds could go back now either. I was sure their helping other Puritans would just be a matter of relocating for them.

I pondered my biggest question of all – where would the venture take Tad and me? Would there be a forever for us? I had a dream and the thought of it not coming true scared me more than anything else at the moment. This journey had made me realize how important Tad was to my future life. I only wanted the opportunity to tell him so and hear his response. While we had been riding, when I wasn't thinking about my fear and involvement with the soldiers' death, I even fantasized we would become husband and wife with a household full of children and love all around. Where we would live, though, I could not even dream about. Whoa, I thought to myself. What foolishness was in my head! First things first – I had to let Tad get around to letting me know if he even cared for me before I could think about planning a wedding and lifetime together.

The adventure of my life was widening in scope. Not only did I have to be concerned about my destiny with killing a soldier, I now had another facet to be concerned about – my future destiny as it related to Tad Ringold.

CHAPTER NINE

Crawfords Point

We arrived at Crawfords Point by mid afternoon. It had been a long grueling ride from the dairy, stopping only for human and animal necessities. I was impressed with Tad's management of our journey and getting us to our destination. For his age, he seemed far wiser and more knowledgeable about the world than I, even though I was sure my education had been more extensive. I didn't know a lot about him. He never talked much about himself, especially his life as a youngster. What I knew about him I liked and I hoped, as we became closer friends, he might share those stories of his youth.

We had finally ridden out of the heavily forested hillocks and began following a fertile, agricultural and pastoral area with small knolls and tiny rivulets. I wondered if a few of these streams would eventually lead to the ocean. Sarah and Grandmam followed closely behind Tad and me as we made our way along a swampy green stream. We continued to ride along the shallow stream for a short distance as it meandered through marshy grasses and eventually led us to the hamlet of Crawfords Point. In another day and age it might have been narrower and deeper, but years of erosion had caused the channel to widen. Nearer to the village, the channel had completely eroded away and the stream branched off in two different directions.

When I asked Tad about the village, he said he had never been to this spot before. It was a new route Jeb and Pap had found recently. Tad said the three of them talked about it and decided to give it a try because it seemed a safe meeting point and not on the way to anywhere. He thought the hamlet was at least three days from the coast, maybe more. In later years I was never able to retrace our path and find the little village marked on any charts or mappings near or along the English sea coast. Crawfords Point was one of those out-of-the-way places that sprang up overnight due to a landlord's prosperity and disappeared in a similar way and circumstance.

We were greeted by deteriorated dwellings that were a conglomerate of crumbling stone, splintered wood and sagging thatch roofs. It was an area which hinted at abandonment long ago. From our observations of the dwellings we could see so far, it was apparent no one lived in Crawfords Point any longer. Of course, I rationalized there may have been more to the little burg than we could see from our current view.

Tad led us down the deserted roadway and we turned into what appeared to be the remnants of a miller's shop. Despite the dilapidation and deterioration of the village dwellings, the mill had faired better than its neighbors. At least the building was still standing sturdy and strong, almost as if it had reckoned with the forces of time and won. On one side of the weathered wood and river rock construction stood the mighty water wheel. Once it had been a force of energy for a productive enterprise. Now, it stood latent and still. The giant wheel was a misshapen form of rotted wood and rusty iron, overgrown with moss and fungus. Very little of the wheel itself was visible due to the entanglement of weeds and shrubs surrounding it. The wheel had become part of the stream and a small paludal marsh, providing a refuge for monstrous and prolific weeds.

As we wound our way toward the half-open sagging doorway of the mill, the building did not emit friendly vibrations to me or the rest of us tired and weary travelers. Some buildings permeate their personality and character and I have always had a keen sense about whether a dwelling was warm and welcoming or whether it was an unfriendly space. The mill seemed to threaten my very existence. Perhaps the feeling was due to the uncertainty of what was ahead of us. But this was the rendezvous point and we must go in. Maybe the answers I sought to my questions would be here.

"Where ya' been? Wha' took ye so long? Ye be a might later than I 'xpected," Pap said, the worry and concern at our tardiness vividly apparent.

"We stopped at Yuker's t'rest a bit and stayed a might too long," Tad answered. "Where be the Frosts? Be there 'ny problem gettin' here?"

"How be our ol' friend?" Pap inquired, ignoring Tad's questions.

"Good. Yuker's good. Same as I 'member him," Tad said.

"Tha' be good news," Pap said. "We need to get ye's horses out o' sight. The Frosts be safe and restin' at 'nother place – it were a 'ard journey f'r 'em. I 'asna' he'rd from Jeb, but soon's he gets here we be movin' on t'ward the new location. It be safer. I jest don' feel comf'rt'ble here. Don' know why. Mayhap I be nervous 'cause o' ev'rythin' tha' 'as 'appened."

Pap's words pretty much echoed my own sentiment. After we all had carefully lowered our weary bodies down from the horses and made the legs work again, Sarah and Grandmam followed Pap inside the mill. Pap told us to take the horses to a building behind which looked like it had once been a horse barn or stable. I offered to help Tad take care of the horses. Trying not to leave much of a trail, we led them carefully around back of the mill to a tumbled-down, makeshift shed. It was scarcely visible through the tall, dry brush and weeds. We unsaddled the animals and brushed down their lathered coats as best we could with our hands. We patted them and thanked them for their hard work of plodding down the trails to get us safely here. Then we penned them in the portals of the stable, latching the sagging gates to hold them in. There was an ample amount of hay on the floor and grain in a trough in the corner of each pen which thoroughly puzzled me. Where had these fresh supplies come from?

More questions and still no answers! But I hoped soon there would be explanations for more than just about the comforts for the horses and the incident at the cave. Once we made sure the animals' needs were filled, Tad and I returned to the main door of the mill. Inside the building the dust, dirt and grime had seeped into every nook and cranny, an accumulation and tribute to its longevity. The remains of a bin and grist wheel stood near the middle of the room. On the floor were parts and pieces of the complex wheel, all scattered about in various assemblages.

Tad and I had barely gotten inside before our sense of security was shattered with the thundering approach of hooves. We stopped our conversation in mid-air. Panic-stricken looks passed between us and the air became laden with electric tension. Pap was a fast thinker, ready for action. I suppose his many years of being in dangerous predicaments had conditioned his reflexes to the point of instant responsiveness.

"Quick ev'r'one, move into tha' room ov'r yond'r," Pap whispered. I had not even noticed the doorway before, but now I could see a dark, shadowy opening leading off the main room. "I be greetin' our vis'tor, whoev'r it be. I hope it be Jeb arrivin'. Like ye four, he be long overdue. But if'n it isna' Jeb, we canna' be too cautious. Shoo... shoo...grab y'r thin's. Don' leave anythin' lyin' 'round and don' make any noise!"

We all scrambled as quietly as we could – picking up our belongings and slipping into the shadowy darkness. I glanced back to see Pap on one side of the door with his pistol ready for action. Tad shoved me on into the room and pulled his own pistol out of the holder he had hidden under his coat. He took up the space on the other side of the half-open door.

Afternoon sunlight was trying to peek through a small and very dirty window high on one wall of the room. Filtered gray clouds and shadows from the tall dead bushes created an opaque curtain across the opening creating a dim light. Once our eyes adjusted, I could faintly make out a door which most likely led outside. It was barred with a board and wooden latch. It was comforting to see the door; although, I wondered when the last time it had been opened. It might have been shut for such a long time that the weathering process had swelled and sealed it shut for all eternity. Thus, I decided we probably couldn't consider it a way to escape.

I looked around to see what might be available for defending oneself if the need arose. What few items I could see around the room in the dim light weren't going to be of much use. Along one wall was a cot. Covering the wood and hemp construction was a deteriorated ticking coverlet with large patches of straw protruding here and there. In the center of the room was a roughly hued bench, covered with dust like everything else in the building. A small table with shards of broken pottery from what might have been an old oil lamp stood in another corner. The pieces didn't look big enough to be of danger to anyone.

I whispered to Sarah and Grandmam to sit and rest themselves on the bench. Sarah used the hem of her skirt to wipe the bench off and erase the years of collected dust. I hovered near the door, just barely out of sight in the shadows. By this time Pap had motioned Tad to wait with us women. My heart kind of lurched a bit when he silently came into the room. I was happy to see him with his pistol ready. It was comforting to know we were not stuck here without some means of protection. I took another quick look around the room to see if there was a loose board or anything I could use in case I needed to defend myself. I found nothing which gave me a feeling of vulnerability. I hoped and prayed nothing would go amiss this time and I, nor any of us, would have the need to defend or protect ourselves.

From our hiding place in the gray shadows at the back of the building, we heard the sound of faintly creaking boards and the stealthily concealed footsteps of the intruder. Except for these sounds, the stillness in the building was deafening. I think we all stopped breathing and were silently waiting for the explosion of action. Suddenly, I heard the door open with a ghastly thud. It sent shivers down my spine. I heard Sarah gasp as her breath caught and stopped in the middle of a whispered inhalation. I'm sure our eyes were as wide as silver coins. The tension increased as we all held our breath. After a brief moment of intense silence and the eerie creaking of more boards, we heard an angry cry from Pap.

"Jeb! Jeb, it be me, Pap! My God man, what be ye 'bout! Ya' sure gi' us all the scare o' our lives. Where ya' been and why be ye so late?" Pap suddenly lowered his voice as he asked, "Be ye 'lone? Ye 'asna' been followed 'as ye? Ya' 'asna' brought trouble wi ye?"

"Well now, Pap, I guess I got ye," Jeb burst into a hearty, robust laugh. He really seemed to be enjoying the situation and the joke he had pulled on Pap. "I were jest testin' ye's skills. Wouldna' wan' ya' t'get rusty in ye's ol' age. I do believe I be quite 'lone, or at least I 'ope I be. I 'as much news to tell. Where be t'others? They 'all be 'ere? None o' ye ha' 'ny trouble 'long the way?"

"We all be 'counted f'r," Pap answered, sighing with disgust. "Now jest 'old the news 'til we can all hear it. I jest be checkin' 'round outside, or ha' ye a'ready done so?"

"Deed so. Been watchin' for a bit," Jeb answered.

"Well ye must ha' seen Tad and the ladies ride in then – they ha'na' been here more'n a few minutes," Pap said. It was almost as if Pap was testing Jeb's loyalty.

"No, sorry I didna'," Jeb replied.

"Jest when did ya 'rive, if'n ye ha' been watchin' a bit?" asked Pap, becoming somewhat irritated by Jeb's answers.

"Well, if'n truth be known, I jest rode up and I 'as been checkin' a'hind me ev'r since I came down the roadway," Jeb said. "I be most sure I 'asna' been followed. I 'as been 'xtra careful the whole journey. Ye know me Pap, I don' take chances."

We heard a little shuffling, then creaking boards, and finally the sounds of footsteps of someone re-entering the mill.

"Well, it does 'pear we be in no danger f'r the moment," Pap said. "But ye know, Jeb, we canna' be too careful. We 'as a lot o' lives t'be responsible f'r right now and I don' like tha' ya' be taken' it so lightly."

"Truly Pap, I 'as been mos' careful. I know ye's concerned. But 'member, I be in this, too, so there be no need t'worry. I don' take chances or put us at risk," Jeb said as a sort of apology.

"It's a'right. Ye can all come on out now." Pap hollered over his shoulder to the four of us waiting impatiently for his words.

It only took us a moment to gather anxiously around to hear what news Jeb had brought.

"What kind o' bad news be ya' bringin' us, ol' man?" asked Grandmam.

I hadn't noticed before, but I suddenly sensed she did not like this man nor did she trust him. He had seemed helpful enough to me in the past, but I had only seen him on a couple of occasions, both of which he had manipulated to his own advantage. Right from the first, I had gathered he was the town gossip and spy for the soldier's activities, but I did not know for sure what he really did. I carefully took stock of the man.

At a glance, he did seem like someone you might not put a lot of trust and faith in. He was carelessly thrown together, despite his costume – a brightly colored frock coat, ruffled blouse, and feathered hat. Father would have called him a "dandy." He had worn this same outfit both times I had seen him and it was not what one would call traveling clothes. Previously, I had not taken much notice of him. Now, however, he appeared unshaven and rough in appearance. He had been traveling, and of course one doesn't always look their best under those circumstances. Just so, he gave me an uneasy feeling. He never really looked at any of us when he spoke – mostly, he studied his shoes. Maybe it was because of his manner of dress, or maybe it was just the hint of discomfort

146

I felt when he was around, but I, too, felt distrustful of him. It was obvious Pap considered him a dear, trusted friend.

After a few moments of trying to control the irritation Grandmam's question and voice tone had stirred in him, Jeb answered. "Well, it should please ya' t'know Ma'am I might'n be a bringin' news tha' ain' so good t'the ears."

"What kind o' bad news? I be sure them sold'rs cain't ha' got on t'us and our trail so soon," Grandmam challenged.

"It would 'pear, Grandmam, they jest may be on our trail af'r all," Jeb answered cautiously. "An' wha' I thin' it means is they a'ready 'as been figurin' out wha' we be doin' and they ain' so 'appy 'bout it. I be confiden' tha' if'n they are comin' af'r us, we be a good half-day or more 'head o' them."

"Jest wha' do ya' mean, Jeb? Why might'n the sold'rs be followin' us?" Pap questioned Jeb with a cool calm I was sure he did not feel.

"Do ye thin' we be safe 'nough here?" asked Sarah. "And wha' 'bout our frien's, be they safe in their hidin' place?"

"I don' thin' we are in desp'rate trouble or 'nythin' like tha' f'r right now," Jeb told us. "I know I got a good start on 'em and I be pos'tive they didna' see me leave. 'Sides, they didna' know f'r sure wha' they be lookin' f'r. Let me tell wha' 'as 'appened since I left ye t'other evenin'." Then he began to tell his story.

* * *

"I headed back down t'our village from ya's place, taken' the faster path ev'n though I knowed it not be quite as safe. I were careful, stayin' jest off'n the trail and makin' as little noise as I could. I didna' see 'nyone or 'nythin' and the night noises were pretty much wha' they should ha' been f'r tha'

147

time o' night. I won'ered as I passed near the caves wha' 'appened t'the sold'rs."

"When I got down t'the village, I wen' straight t'McGrew's tavern. Be there any news t'hear, McGrew's would be the place. And sure 'nough, there were plenty a'goin' on – all the way from local gossip 'bout who be stealin' chick'ns from Sir Henry Cooper t'a scand'lous tidbit 'bout our schoolmast'r. Some say he were a spendin' more time than need be in the comp'ny o' a married lady. I wish tha' lad good luck and ha' fun."

"I mean, "wha' a shame," he said contritely noticing the disapproving look Grandmam gave him. "Sounds like he be a courtin' trouble and deserves ev'r bit o' punishment comin' t'him. 'Nyways, I were there barely 'alf-'our, visitin' wi' the locals and eyein' tha' crowd o' sold'rs gath'red in one corner. Didna' seem much o' anythin' were 'apenin' wi' them. They jest be visitin' 'mongst theyselves. They were laughin' heart'ly at the jokes they be tellin' and swillin' down ale like they ha'na' a concern in the world. One fellow were spoutin' some 'ome-grown po'try and verse. He werena' too bad eith'r. I ain' no judge, but he did make it sound sweet as music the way words come rollin' out o' his mouth. The crowd o' sold'rs seemed t'a be enjoyin' his words, too."

"I ha' a'most become hypnotized when suddenly the tav'rn door swung op'n wide an' a sold'r come runnin' in. The lad were greatly disheveled in his 'pearance and as wild-eyed as any tomcat I ever seen." Jeb gave a sneering laugh as he continued on with his story. "He looked sort o' like he might'n ha' spent his ev'nin' rollin' 'round a moun'ain and beatin' his way through thickets. Anyways, the sold'r came rushin' in, talkin' wild and rantin' hysterically. He were gaspin' loudly and tryin' t'catch his breath all at the same time."

'Captain Doudry, Captain Doudry!' shouted the lad, yelling almost incoherently. 'I need help! There's trouble up the hill.'

'What ye be hollering about," Doudry said as he stood up. 'What kind of trouble be ye talking?'

'I was up on the old trail looking for Petrie and Morgen,' the excited soldier told Doudry. 'I kept hollering and hollering and wondering why they didn't answer. They told me they were goin' t'be on the hill all day. They didn't come back t'night. So I went looking for them. Then I found them. They are both dead. They' been killed. I need help to get 'em back down here to the post.'

"Af'r tha' I was only able t'hear snatches and pieces o' the conversation, but gath'red he be tha' survivor o' the cave. It were shortly after tha' the whole group left and I he'rd mention o' curfew and comp'ny headquarters. Then nothin' much 'appened and I went up t'a my room ov'r the cobbl'r's shop by the tavern. I were sure if'n there be any commotion I would most cert'nly 'ear it. Though, by tha' time, I were dead tired and ha' also takin' my share o' McGrew's ale."

"The sun were barely peekin' ov'r the h'rizon when I he'rd the ruckus the next mornin'. I got slowly off'n my cot and op'ned the shutt'rs jest wide 'nough to take a peek. From wha' I could see through tired, squinty eyes and und'rstand through the fogginess tha' clouded my brain, a comp'ny o' sold'rs were gatherin' in the street. They were donnin' they's milit'ry coats and hats and reportin' t'a their capt'n. A few men were holdin' the reins o' horses, waitin' f'r t'others to get on those animals. Some were mounted wi' impatient looks, sayin' 'we be ready, let us move 'em out and go.' The comp'ny o' 'bout 25 men were talkin' 'mongst theyselves, but the sounds were real muffled so's I wasna' able to catch much o' wha' they be a sayin'. The capt'n then gi' orders f'r mountin' up wi'in the half-hour. Tha' be when ol' Jeb decided he better be a dressin' and gettin' his bones up the trail, puttin' a lot o' space a'tween him and the village.

"I did manage to get out o' town 'head o' the sold'rs, but barely. I were ready to ride up the back trail when I he'rd the final order t'mount up. I 'gain circl'd 'round the cave and stayed jest off'n the trail. I wan'ed t'stay a moment and see wha' they might'n discov'r, but decided the safes' thin' was goin' straight t'a ye's place so I'd be there if'n the sold'rs rode tha' far. I reckon it were 'bout mid mornin' when a couple o' sold'rs come a ridin' in. They didn't seem to be in much of a hurry and were taking a good look 'round as they rode up t'ward the cottage. Then they began t'ask questions."

'Ye has a pretty good stack of wood here,' said the younger of the two men as he eyed the area. 'Burn a lot do ye?'

'Tha' be true 'n we sell a lot,' Jeb answered. 'Wha' can I do f'r ye?'

'We be looking for a couple of our fellows and saw the smoke. We thought there must be a nearby cottage and it appears we have found it. Is this your cottage?' said the older man as he eyed the area. 'Are you the only one in this area?'

'Yeah, this be my place. There be more folk f'rth'r on up the trail – closer to the hills and bluffs there. Be there a problem?' Jeb asked. 'Does ye's sold'rs go wanderin' 'bout of'n an'get theyselves lost?'

'Mind if we look around a bit?" said the older man ignoring Jeb's comments. 'Our men were supposed to be on one of the trails – thought might be they had gotten up this way. Ye has not seen anything of them, then? Ya know Stanley, I don't think I believe him. Didn't we see ye down at McGrew's last evening?'

'Aye, most likely ye did,' answered Jeb before the man called Stanley could answer. 'I stop down there quite a bit for a good pint o' ale and some good comp'ny. An', yes indeedy, I were there for a couple o' 'ours last evenin' a'fore comin' up'ome 'ere.'

'How do ye get up here?' one of the soldiers asked.

'Why on my 'orse and on tha' trail down yond'r – the one ye jest came up,' Jeb answered, pointing in the direction of the well-used trail which was a direct route to the village.

'Well now, I know for a fact there are two trails. Don't ye think they are both a bit tricky – especially in the dark and with a head and bellyfull of ale. I don't think ye came here last night at all. I think ye spent the night in the village and came up here this morning. I think I saw ye a bit earlier down in the village, just before we left. Is that not so?'

'No, I don' thin' so,' Jeb lied. 'I been here a good while, elsewise ye'd not ha' seen my smoke.'

"I lit a fire, thinkin' tha' would jest 'sure them ye were 'bout," Jeb said as he returned to his story telling. "Mayhaps they mightn' ha' not come ridin' in a'tall if'n it ha'na' been f'r the smoke. I may ha' done more damage than good. I thought at firs' they didna' know the place 'xisted. Bu' af'r talkin' wi' them a bit, I thin' they knew 'bout ye's place and they would ha' been knockin' at ye's door even if'n there were no smoke. But now it be done. Canna' worry none 'bout wha's a'hind."

"The two were jest full o' questions and thin'in' I ha' no right t'be at ye's cottage. While we were talkin' they were all the while lookin' 'round. One thin' led t'nother and I tol' them all 'bout ye and the family, Pap," Jeb said. "I tol' them ye ha' gone away on some fam'ly bus'ness, and tha' ever'one wen' 'long with ya'. Tol' them tha' bein' sech a close friend o' the fam'ly and all, I off'r'd t'come up and keep an eye on thin's.

I even tol' them I helped out here sometimes wi' the stackin' and wood gatherin.' But they still werena' satisfied."

'That y'r horse," one soldier inquired. 'Why do ye have such a large pen for only one horse?'

'The fam'ly 'as four 'orses and they all took one f'r travelin' t'take care o' fam'ly bus'ness out t'the coast,' Jeb answered. 'And of'n they 'as ov'rnight guests. We be on the trail up t'the moun'an and pe'ple come and spend a couple o' days f'r huntin' an' we be a restin' point f'r those who live f'rth'r up. The big cart ov'r there takes a couple o' big 'orses to pull it ov'r t'a area villages where wood be deliv'r'd.'

'He's prob'ly nothin' but a 'drunken frothblower and can't be relied upon to tell the right time of day, let alone the truth,' said the younger soldier. 'I say there old man, I don't think ye are telling the truth. What be ye doing up here? Tell me again about ye's friends. Are ye stealing from them old man?'

'And why would I be a doin' tha'?' I asked them. 'Wha' would be my point? I tell ye my frien's 'as gone t'the coast. I jest came up here t'make sure all be well. An' since I be here, I built a fire so's I could fix me a bite t'eat when I get done stackin' more wood f'r Pap.'

'So, has ye been out wooding today?' asked the older soldier. 'Where do ye go for the wood – anywhere near the old trail?'

'Na, I ain' been out t'day," Jeb answered. 'An' as f'r where we be woodin', we try na' t'chop an area dry so we go all ov'r the woods 'ere. Sometimes we do get ov'r by the ol' trail. But tha' be a far piece to tote the wood. More of'n, we go further up 'long this trail. It be easier f'r getting wood down t'the villages below.'

"The two continued to be rude, makin' fun o' me an ya's family," Jeb said as he went on with his story. "They were havin' a good time elbowin' each other. I surely didna' like either o' those men. I put up wi' them 'cause I 'oped they might'n share some news wi' me, but the pair o' them were a couple o' closed-lip varmi'ts. They kept right on a' questionin' me – ev'n got a bit rough. But mind ya', it were all f'r the cause so's I tol'rat'd tha' little roughin' up I got. They continued to ask questions. I stuck t'a my story, ev'n though I don' thin' they thought it quite right. By this time 'nother couple o' sold'rs rode in and took a long look 'round. I guess they's curiosity were satisfied 'cause 'ventually the whole lot o' them rode off wi'out so much as an apology or 'nythin.'"

"I hung 'bout the cottage until mid day wi' no further sight or action from the sold'rs. I ev'n walked 'bout the area a bit wi' an axe jest in case they left a'hind 'ny straggl'rs doin' some spyin' on ol' Jeb. Bu' nothin' unusual were 'bout. Tha' be when I decided it be best t'catch me 'orse and get on ov'r this way. I would ha' been here sooner if'n they ha'na kept me so long an' askin' so many questions. I got here fast as I could 'cause I felt awfully uneasy 'bout how they be actin'. So, here I am and late 'cause I kind o' back tracked a bit so's if'n 'ny soldr's were a'hind me, I 'ope I confused 'em. I canna' be sure o' tha' now, can I? They were 'ighly 'spicious, o' tha' I ha' no doubt. And I thin' tha' 'spicion were a'ready in their 'eads. Else, why would they ha' questioned me and roughed me up like they did?"

* * *

While Jeb finished his diaglogue, Grandmam eyed him with disbelief. "Ya' don' look too roughed up t'me," she said. "Ya' look the same as ev'r, jest a raggedy ol' man! I wouldna'

153

put it past ya' t'ha' led the whole king's guard right t'our door jest t'save y'r own skin."

"Now Grandmam," Pap cautioned. "Jeb here be as dedicated to our cause as we be and he wouldna' no more jeopardize us than we would him. Ain' that so Jeb?" I think Pap was questioning Jeb only for our benefit. Pap sincerely trusted Jeb, despite the fact that some of us lacked confidence in the man. I wasn't sure how Tad felt, but he was most respectful due to Pap's friendship.

"I be sorry Grandmam, if'n you don' thin so 'ighly o' me," Jeb said, not only to her but to the rest of us as well. "Truly, I do care 'bout wha' 'appens to ye. I canna' be sure 'em sold'rs didna' follow me 'ere. But tha' ain' t'say somewhere's 'long the way they might'n ha' picked up my trail or learned 'bout our bus'ness. Mayhap someone in the village snitched. Ye knows there are plenty o' folk there who take great pleasure in seein' all us Puritans hangin' from the gallows. An' these sold'rs be smart men. They might'n ha' jest put the pieces t'gether from various conversations with villag'rs. I were very careful, Pap. I took all the precautions o' coverin' my trail and back-trackin' so's they canna' find us easily."

"Jeb, don' ye fret," Pap said. "Ye knows well as I tha' they ha' been on t'our activities f'r a while now. It may be tha' no 'mount of precautions will ha' made a bit o' difference."

"Do ye thin' we should be a movin' on f'r the night, or be we safe 'nough 'ere?" Tad seemed to be the only one concerned at the moment about the immediate future – or at least the only one who had taken the time to presently consider it.

"Say," interrupted Jeb, completely ignoring Tad's question. "Where be our precious cargo? Did ye dump 'em somewhere 'long the way or ha' ye sent 'em safely on t'reach they's destination?"

At least someone else besides myself seemed concerned about the absence of the Frosts. I, too, had wondered where they were, but things had happened so fast since we had arrived there hadn't been time to ponder their plight. From Jeb's question, I assumed this was not the usual procedure for transferring those seeking shelter.

"Now Jeb, don' worry none," Pap said. "The Frosts be safe and in good 'ands. Matter o' fact, if'n we feel safe 'nough, we need be gettin' out t'where I left them. I 'as changed our meetin' place. I were able t'make contact wi' some ol' frien's, Tom and Millie Miller, who I didna' know were livin' out this way 'til a short time ago. Since we got here early this mornin', we stopped out there and they be delighted t'see us. Ol' Tom warned me na' t'spend too much time here at the mill. He said we would be most welcome at their farm. So tha' be where I left the Frosts and came here t'wait for ye all. I know Millie will ha' a hot meal and warm beds 'waitin' for all o' us when we get ov'r t'the farm."

"So, ye ha' been able t'make a couple o' new contacts," said Jeb. "We certainly needed them 'long this way, wha' wi' Devin getting' caught by king's men and the Bossard's both takin' sick wi' t'flu and dyin'. Thought we'd be 'ard put t'find someone in this stretch a'tween us 'n' the coast."

Jeb had been leisurely leaning against the mill bin as he spoke, but now straightened up and headed toward the door. He stood there a brief moment, looking out into the waning afternoon light.

"I be a bit nervous and won'er if'n we don' wan' to get t'ye's frien's 'ome directly?" Jeb said. "I thin' we need to be a wipin' up all evidence o' meetin' 'ere and leave."

He then went out the door, only to return moments later with a couple of shaggy pieces of dead brush that had been growing near the wheel. He busily began scattering the footprints by swishing the brush around the room.

"I be much inclined to 'gree wi' ye," Pap spoke up. "I know a couple more 'orses ov'r in Ol' Tom's stable won' be makin' a bit o' difference. He 'as got a real riff-raff o' varieties 'nyhow. And we should be safe there, or at least he seemed t'thin' so. They be far 'nough out o' the way and they also 'as a 'specially good spot f'r 'hidin', if'n there be a need."

"Pap, do ye wan' me to move the 'orses, then?" asked Tad, as he too started toward the door. "They be in a good place right now; tha' is, ifn' no one finds them. I 'sume it must ha' been ye's new acquaintance, Ol' Tom, who left us grain and fresh hay. Do you thin tha' stuff in the shed be a problem if'n anyone would come a wanderin' this way?"

"We be needin' the 'orses t'get out t'Ol' Toms. It be a f'r piece from here," Pap said. "We 'as t'go back the way ye came, 'long the stream and then a bit south. It may seem a bit out o' the way, but I don' thin' 'nyone can find us there. An' yes, we need to mess up the stable area. Precious though the grain may be, dump it outside 'round in the weeds. May be some critters will enjoy the food. Don' trample back there too much. We wan' it t'look nat'ral like they 'asna' been 'nyone 'round f'r some time. We surely don' wan' t'leave 'ny 'spicious signs or evidence 'round, jest in case trouble comes a courtin'. A stray traveler may stop here 'casionally, so it be a'right if'n there be a few footprints and the weeds be trampled a bit. But it needs to look like they jest found the place 'apenstance. We don' wan' it to look fresh. Sarah, ye go 'long with Tad and Lucky, and Grandmam, ye jest help Jeb here get rid o' our tracks. Ye don' need t'brush up real good, may be makin' it look like some furry creatures got inside. We need be a'gettin' down t'Tom and Millie's a'fore dark. The sooner we get out o' here, the better. Jeb, I be a helpin' ye there in jest a moment. Grandmam, rough up tha' back room if'n ye can."

Sarah, Tad and I hurried out of the building and carefully made our way back to where we had hidden the horses. I heard Grandmam telling Jeb to "gi' her tha' flimsy twig he were usin' and she'd get her share o' swooshin' done." Grumbling to himself, Jeb followed us out the door to fetch more branches for himself and Pap.

My inner thoughts and feelings did not reflect the beauty and the quiet serenity that the evening offered. In the horizon, the remaining rays of the sunlight created streaked orange and golden clouds. The shadows of early dusk were everywhere around us. We could see our breath in the cool evening air. Sarah pulled her cloak tighter around her and rubbed her arms. I wasn't sure it was the effect of the cold or the uncertainty of what might happen next. The tense anxiety of the past few days was still a nagging thorn that could not easily be extracted. All of us were wired with nerves riding on tight waves of tension.

It seemed Pap had made provisions for another harbor of safety, but I wondered if I would be able to rest once we were settled in for the night. It would also appear I was still not going to get answers to my questions here either. I hoped later in the evening there might be a quiet moment for me and Tad to talk. Just thinking about him and the way he had gotten us here through strange and only slightly familiar territory brought a warm feeling to my body and a smile to my lips. Later, I thought and I whispered a simple, silent prayer. "God, let there be time for Tad and me."

It didn't take the three of us long to make havoc of the stable area. It was a fairly simple task. There was so much dust and debris that it was easy to just mix the straw with the dirt, leaves and chunks of decayed wood lying about in the structure. I almost found myself laughing at the situation of trouncing around in the hay and dirt had it not been for the seriousness of the situation. The dry, hard ground did not leave any evidence of the hoof prints. I remembered the hard rains we had had at home before my accident. It was amazing how much I could remember since the blow to my head at the caves. The thoughts and memories came flooding back like a tidal wave – almost as if those weeks of not remembering had never existed.

We made quick work of our duties, leaving what we hoped would be little evidence of our recent habitation. I agreed with Jeb about whether soldiers might be tricked into thinking the havoc of the mill was not created – if indeed any soldiers came. Within fifteen minutes we were ready to leave for the Millers. Looking more like a caravan on holiday than fugitives from the sold'rs, we followed Pap back down the road leading away from the mill and Crawfords Point. I was more certain than before only rats and other furry critters were the entire village population. At the fork of the stream, we turned along the right channel which seemed to disappear in the distance. Near the dwindling stream was a faint trace of an ancient, well-trodden path, which we followed for maybe a half-hour. We lost sight of the village and mill.

The sunset had now completely disappeared and evening dusk was heavy upon us as we wound our way across the dry stream bed, up over a small hillock and down into a grove of trees still holding onto a few green leaves. I was beginning to wonder if we would be at our destination soon, and in a matter of minutes Pap led us on through the thick grove. There, before us stood a clearing with buildings, all of them standing and solid on their foundation. The beckoning smoke from the chimneys of a quaint, thatch-roofed cottage nestled amid several buildings on the country farmstead invited this weary party toward the luxury of shelter and protection. It would be most odd to describe these buildings as a welcoming embrace of warm arms and a friendly smile, but that's exactly how I felt at that moment.

We had just gotten to the gate attached to a stone-wall fence which bordered the front part of the cottage when we were greeted by a thin, wiry farmer. He was genuinely cordial, bordering on the fringe of deep concern. The years had claimed his age – he was not old and he was not young. His hair was neither gray nor gold, but a sort of indescribable color of sand. He had deep circles around his mouth and a wrinkled brow. His brown eyes twinkled with mischievousness.

"I were gettin' a wee bit worried 'bout ye there, bu' I can see f'r myself tha' ye be a'right," the man said with the same kind of brogue I had gotten used to from the Ringolds and Jeb. They seemed to have all come from the same area in Scotland at one time or another. That was something I would have to ask Pap about sometime.

After introductions, Old Tom said to Pap, "Ye take the ladies and go on inside. Millie be 'waitin' ye's 'rival and will take care o' ye. Like me, she were gettin' kind o' worried. Now let's see, ye be Tad. Is tha' right? Would ye mind helpin' with the horses?"

"I can help too," I said. "I often help Tad with the animals."

Old Tom looked at me and then chuckled. "I like a lass wi' a bit o' spirit. Ye are sure to like my Millie. She be a woman wi' a mind o' her own and tha' keeps Ol' Tom here on his toes."

We followed Old Tom to a corralled barn not far from the cottage. The horses were then unbridled and turned loose, to be integrated with about ten other animals already inside the pen.

"It seems ye sent ov'r grain f'r naught," Tad said. "Sorry, but we ha' t'throw it away so there be no trace o' our bein' there. But we do thank ye f'r ye's help. And we thank God f'r won'erful folk like ye."

"Bett'r t'throw it and be safe than t'worry 'bout wha' might'n happen if'n the wrong folk were t'find it. A'sides may be some o' Mother Nat're's critt'rs will find it an' make they's dinner on it," Old Tom said.

Tad laughed. "Tha' be jest wha' Pap said."

After making sure the horses had proper care, we joined the others inside the cottage. The smells, as we entered, were definitely reminiscent of those that had lingered within the walls of the Ringold's forest home. I easily liked Old Tom and his wife Millie. I wondered why he was called Old Tom. I suppose somewhere along the way there must have been or perhaps still was a young Tom. Old Tom was a likeable sort, although he seemed to be a bit more conservative than his wife. Perhaps that stemmed from being a farmer in an isolated area where life is dependent upon nature and hard work for survival. But like Old Tom, Millie had a twinkle in her brown eyes and a gaiety about her, making the gathering seem more like a festive occasion rather than the serious situation it was.

From what I gathered in Pap's telling about Old Tom and Millie, they were both people of the earth. Their weathered skin and rough hands gave evidence to the many years working the land. Pap told me later they had been in the sheep business in much wealthier circumstances during earlier years. It eased my mind considerably to find the Frosts were also here and not, as I had feared, housed in some dark forlorn cabin in the middle of nowhere. Because Pap had left the Frosts at the farm before going to the mill, they had time to rest and freshen up. It would seem the little interlude had done them a world of good. They both looked as if a giant weight had been taken from their shoulders. But, every so often they gave each other furtive glances as they looked about and listened to the news. They had not forgotten why they were here nor what the end of the trail held for them.

The hot, delicious food served to us and the congeniality of our host and hostess helped us temporarily forget our troubles and the evening hours quickly slipped by. For a short time, we all were eagerly consumed with the task of eating and enjoying the delicious food. Soon the conversation turned to a comfortable interchange of gossip about previous, old mutual friends and acquaintances of both the Ringolds and the Millers. I gathered from the tidbits of conversation Old Tom and Millie were not the strangers I had earlier thought they were. The past had caught up with the two families and provided them an opportunity for a pleasant reunion. The Millers had been Scottish refugees from the cruelty of the king before coming to northern England, just like Grandmam and Pap. They had settled here, in this quiet, pastoral countryside as farmers and were seeking to keep their identity hidden. They had easily adjusted to the country life and were settled in. That they were content in this simple life was apparent enough as I watched them carrying out their tasks. For now, they were secure in their country hiding place where they were able to offer comfort to others and help the cause by hiding fugitives of the crown.

Before we had barely finished the simple, but fulfilling meal of stewed meats, vegetables and bread pudding, the evening was well gone. Millie, Grandmam, Sarah, Mrs. Frost and I helped clear up while Old Tom and Tad brought out bedding for all of us. Pap and Jeb had gone outside, evidently for a breath of air and to contemplate our situation. I thought I might have an opportunity to ask a few questions, so I slipped out to join them. When Jeb saw me, he told Pap they could visit later and he went back inside the cottage.

"Well, Lucky, thin's ha' certainly changed f'r ye the pas' weeks, 'as' they na'? Unf'rtunately, na' f'r the best." Pap chuckled a little sardonically as he said this.

"Yes sir, they certainly have. I never would have dreamed my life would change so drastically in such a short time," I said. "On the day I left home all I wanted was a little adventure. And, I guess you could certainly say I have achieved that goal. I'm confused about my feelings and am questioning many of the beliefs I grew up with. Does it seem wrong I should question what my family taught me?"

"Na' Lucky, it don'," said Pap. "Tha' be part o' growin' up and learnin' 'bout where ye fits in t'the world. I be quite sure ye's own father would wan' ya' t'question beliefs and ideals, only so ye can know tha' many o' the thin's ye 'as been taught be true f'r ya's own way o' life. Ye 'as t'realize wha' be true for one fam'ly becomes a mute point o' dispute f'r t'others. Bu', keep this in mind. No matter wha' each fam'ly believes, justice and rights f'r all men 'as t'be upheld. An' I guess tha' be wha' the Ringolds be 'bout – providin' every person they's own right t'believe wha' be importan' f'r them."

"I understand and appreciate you talking to me about what you believe," I said. "I can easily understand those beliefs, and in some ways, it is a concept of importance to me, too. I never would have been able to have those thoughts around my own father."

I thought this was as good a time as any to jump right in and get answers to my question. "I am still a might puzzled about a good many things that I have encountered here of late."

"Sarah told me ye ha' some questions and concerns," Pap said. "May be I can help sort them out f'r ye."

"I know my deed has not made your life any easier, probably more difficult," I said. "Do you really think the soldiers knew about your helping others? And why didn't the deputy of your village know about the cave? That seems really odd to me."

Lucky, ye ha' a right t'know 'bout our helpin' others," Pap said. "I ha' been thin'in' f'r sometime tha' we be gettin' too close t'bein' discovered. Tad reported sold'rs in the area even a'fore ye came and we didna' pay much 'tention. 'As f'r the cave, those hills are so full o' nooks, crannies and 'oles that ye would ha' t'spend 'alf a lifetime mappin' 'em t'find 'em all. So I na' be s'prised the dep'ty doesna' know. Per'aps I can help ease y'r mind and gi' ye some answers f'r all our events and actions, na' only o' the last few days, but o' a lifetime."

Then Pap began his story.

CHAPTER TEN

Pap's Story

The hearing of Pap's story, along with the deeds of the last few days became the culmination of my conviction to follow through to the end with the Ringolds. Of course there was Tad and my attraction to him may have blinded me at first to see the wisdom of my actions and decisions. But Pap was a convincing story teller and from that point forward no doubt ever crossed my mind I had not done the right thing. Although the Ringolds were of different faiths, I had already justified my deeds and actions to myself. After hearing Pap's story, my heart succumbed to the rationale of what the family was doing for the grace and glory of God. My destiny was sealed, as it had been right from the very first of this incredible adventure and the fateful day I rode out of the stable yard of my father's home.

The twinkling brightness of the stars, a fading full moon and myself were the only audience for Pap's tale that night so many years ago. We had settled ourselves outside the main door of Tom and Millie's cottage on a hand-carved wooden bench, weathered from years of sun and rain. Tired as we both were, we each knew our future relationship depended upon this conversation. Loyalty and trust were dependent upon this moment in time.

I waited, almost impatiently, watching the man beside me in the shadowy moonlight. Again I was touched, as I had been when I first met Pap, by the sincerity, warm-heartedness and kindness of this man. Despite the tough exterior he presented and the fact he knew how to protect himself in times of danger, Pap was one of the gentlest men I had ever met. In the short time I had known him, I had never seen Pap raise his hand or his voice in anger. He spoke kindly of everyone, even if he did not approve of a person or notion. He often acknowledged and stated his disapproval but never, never did he belittle them.

Pap paused for a moment in our conversation and stared off into the distance. It was almost as if he was waiting to be transported into another time, or even another world temporarily, as he tried to piece together the memories and events for the story he was about to tell. A troubled sadness flashed across his whole face briefly, but only for an instant. I could only wonder what portentous event in his life had caused him so much pain and sadness. Then Pap smiled and started his tale.

* * *

"I suppose ye wonders wha' our business be 'bout and why we feel sech a strong desire t'help folk we don' know, like the Frosts – and even the kindness we ha' taken the trouble t'show ye. I guess I ha' a genuine love f'r people and ha' tried t'pass tha' down to my chil'ren. Per'aps my love f'r our fellowman causes my strong desire t'help those who be less fortunate than me. I guess tha' stems from my chil'hood. As a very young lad, na' more than seven or eight, I saw my own dad horr'bly mutilated and my gran'pap murdered. Mind ye, this 'appened right a'fore the very eyes of the young, innocent and naive lad tha' I was. Granny and mum also were forced to watch. As ye may ha' gath'red, these events left a mark on my heart – a mark t'follow me the rest o' my life. I never allow myself t'forget.

"I were very young, and wheth'r the sold'rs be justified in their treatment and actions o' my family ha' no bearin' in my mind. Even t'day, af'r all the fac's be known, I still feel the same hatred f'r their actions I felt then. Bu' hatred can only bring 'bout more evil. I ha' known many a good man who 'as succumbed t'misfortune 'cause he let hatred rule his heart and lead him 'stray. I hope, af'r all be said and done, tha' I can be judged a bett'r man. In the case o' my family, I thin' this inner hatred 'as done much good. Bu' there 'gain, tha' prob'ly depends on which side o' the issue ye be concern'd 'bout. We ha' fought long and 'ard t'defend the right to choose our religion and follow our beliefs. I thin' ev'ry man and woman 'as the right to choose how they be a worshipin' their God, or not worshipin' a God a t'all, if'n tha' be their choice. Na' ev'n the king should be so liberal wi' the privileges o' the soul.

"My mem'ries go back t'the early 1600s when I were a young lad o' 'bout seven or eight years. In our village of Evanstown, life were very harsh and many were strict followers o' the new religious beliefs pop'lar then. My gran'par'nts and par'nts chose t'follow one o' the new religions tha' ha' broken away, na' only from the Roman Church but the Anglican Church. Granny used t'complain 'bout how both sects ha' taken a toll on the poor people – 'taxed and tithed them 'til they didna' even own their souls,' she would say. 'Those churches be only f'r the well-to-do; not us common folk.

"I were brought up in the faith o' a strict Puritan house'old. I never ha' a choice t'follow other religious beliefs, and af'r Gran'pap died I didna' wan' t'change. It were as if'n I needed t'dedicate my life t'tha' faith I were brought up in. I ha' t'carry on f'r him, and this I tearfully promised t'do as I watched his life blood flow from his body.

"As I grew into adult'ood, I were serious 'bout studyin' theology and becomin' a man o' the cloth. But the older I became, the more I were angered by the treatment o' the many religious groups, even though there were a short time when Puritans were favored by the Crown. Many people ha' been victimized in the name o' religious persecution. Time af'r time, I witness'd crushin' blows again' neighbors and kin and decided tha' I couldna' devote my life t'the genteel occupation o' a church prior. Havin' come from a long line o' warriors, my Scottish blood ha' a lot t'do wi' my need t'physically defeat the 'arsh and unjust treatmen' o' my fellow man.

"I can still hear the lect'rs, or should I say s'rmons, as both Grandpap and Da' voiced they's dislike 'bout the stric'ness o' the Roman Church and its rit'als, as well as the Church o' England. My fam'ly followed a simpl'r way o' praisin' God and thankin' him f'r da'ly 'xistence, as did many other people. I suppose ye may ha' learned from either ya's catechism or hist'ry lessons 'bout the vicious and unequal methods o' treatin' people in earlier ages o' Christianity and not allowin' them the right t'worship. Now it be some differ'n', but the struggle still 'xists f'r religious freedom. I ha' learned through the years tha' ev'ry man should be 'ntitled t'believe as he wishes. Af'r all, most o' us worship the same God.

"Da' and Gran'pap were victims. Both ha' been very active and outspoken in their contempt o' not only the Roman Church, but also the policies o' the reignin' king. They were avid s'pport'rs o' the Puritan movemen'. Only a few short years later, vict'ry would ha' been theirs. Tha' is, there were somewha' of a conditional 'ceptance by the Crown to a'low f'r more religious tolerances. By then, both Da' and Gran'pap would be dead, victims o' angry battles tha' be fought in the name o' religious freedom.

"I 'member the day Gran'pap died, as vividly as if it be yest'rday. It were a warm spring day in April, one o' those days when no clouds filled the sky and the sun's rays penetrate the earth wi' a warmth tha' only edifies God's graces. We hadna' celebrated Easter yet; Granny said it were unusually late tha' year. In our little village an edict were posted by the king tha' everyone would pledge their beliefs to the Church o' England. The Crown ha' been swayin' from one position t'nother f'r a good many years. First it ha' been the Catholics then the Anglican Church, and extremes o' right or left political and religious doctrines. It were a 'ard time f'r all – from the Papis't'a the English Church, and all variations a'tween. It were a time when religious persecution ran rampan', a'though na' like in the early Roman times when large numbers o' people were crucified f'r believin' in a Christian God.

"Grandpap and Da' chose na' t'follow this edict an' carried on they's worship in private, secre't meetin' places, as did many others. I knew 'bout some o' their activities, but at my young age I were not 'ware o' all the secr'tive meetin's and gatherin's in which both became actively engaged. I were much ol'r by the time my knowledge o' these practices 'ncreased an' were understood. I guess I still don' see how they did 'nyone 'arm, but tha' were na' the way the Crown saw it. We later learned tha' a spy ha' been planted in our midst who took part in the meetin's an' collected the damagin' evidence again' Gran'pap and Da'. The spy, who ha' worked very 'ard t'become a fam'ly friend, turned in written evidence t'a the Crown again' leaders o' the secr't congregation.

"Like I say, it be a day tha' I can nev'r f'rget. The whole village were gather'd in the square, a'most like a giant celebration 'xcept tha' there be sold'rs standin' guard all 'round. The so-called o'fenders were confronted while the town pe'ple watched. The bill o' judgment were read and charges made. Best I can 'member, the men were 'cused o' leadin' a private religious sect. They were further 'cused o' falsely advisin' town folk t'follow the precepts o' the ol' tes'ament, advocatin' predestination and 'ceptin' the word o' the Bible as law. They claimed leaders o' the secr't church were against confessin' and repentin'. Treason were added t'a the list o' wrong doin's. The chanc'l'r spoke long 'bout the evils o' encouragin' pe'ple t'defy the rules o' the Crown.

"Long wi' Gran'pap and Da', several other men were 'rested and presented wi' sim'lar charges. We, the fam'lies, ha' been gather'd up, too, an' were lined up in fron' o' the crowd so other villag'rs could see wha' kind o' pe'ple they called frien's an' neighb'rs. The punishment, read by the chief chanc'l'r, pronounced the men were t'be publicly whipped, plac'd in prison f'r a time and releas'd only af'r a large fine ha' been paid.

"Ten sold'rs stepped for'ard, removin' their gloves and unwindin' long leather whips. I wan'ed t'cry out t'a the men na' t'hurt Da' and Gran'pap. I turned an' looked at my mum. Then I turned away quickly. She were a strong woman and I ha' never seen her cry. Bu' the tears were slidin' down her cheeks as she stood silently starin' 'head. I knew she would be hor'bly 'mbarrassed if'n I saw her. I jumped as I heard the firs' crack o' the whip. The crowd, which ha' been talkin' 'mongst themselves an' jeerin' at the men, instan'ly fell silent. The only

170

sound I 'member hearin' were the whirrin' and crack o' the whips. Pride filled my heart when I looked at Da', Grandpap and they's friends. They were standin' strong f'r wha' they believed in an' na' one o' them cried out when they felt the sharp blows o' the whip.

"There were six 'cused in all. The sold'rs jest aimed their whips out into the air, lettin' the blows fall where they might. They were laughin' loudly, roarin' and whoopin', as the pris'ners jumped 'round in their 'tempt t'avoid the piercin' sting o' the leather tip. It were in the middle o' this public chastisement tha' the melee broke out. A group o' 'bout ten men, none 'nyone o' us could ev'r 'member seein' a'fore, burst through the crowd an' into the group o' prison'rs and sold'rs. We were quite sure their 'nterruption ha' been planned, a'though Da' said he never knew a word 'bout it. He were never sure, he said later, 'xactly who the 'ntruders be or wha' were their 'ntent. Some said it were the king's pe'ple and it were jest a way o' gettin' rid o' more town folk than they ha' time to try, or per'aps they could na' muster up 'nough evidence f'r charges again'. Others said they be renegades who didna' like Puritans. 'Nyways, the men fired and shot in ev'ry d'rection – into the crowd o' town pe'ple and pris'ners 'like.

"Mum and I watched in hor'r; then we sought shelt'r. As a result o' the ruckus, Gran'pap and Da' both were shot down, a'though na' at the same time. Da' was still standin' when I saw Gran'pap crumple t'a the ground. He died a'most instan'ly. He were standin' brave an' tall one momen' and the nex' he were on the ground wi' his life blood pumpin' from his wounded heart. How angry I was. Mum wouldna' even let me run t'him, an'old 'im in my arms. She just held onto me tightly, whisperin' 'ye canna' help him now. He be wi' the

God he loves, ya know.' An' poor Granny. She were so brave, nev'r utterin' a sound or cryin' a tear. She jest stood quietly 'side us, tall and proud. She tol' us later she was jest silently prayin' f'r the poor souls o' the sold'rs. I tried na' t'cry, but I werena' tha' brave!

"Da' didna' die, at least in tha' incident. He ha' taken the brunt o' the beatin's and ha' caught several fragments o' the gun powd'r and pellets the sold'rs fired, leavin' him badly injured. He ev'ntually recover'd from his wounds, though ev'r af'r limped from his injuries.

"Three remainin' prisoners were still standin' in the very spot where they ha' stopped dodgin' the whips. The sold'rs shoved and pushed them t'ward the village gaol, leavin' the three downed men un'tended where they ha' fallen. In the crowd, there were a couple o' people who ha' not faired well, either. Like Gran'pap, they ha' given they's lives. Several other town folk were 'njured and na' one o' the sold'rs off'r'd them a 'pology or comfort. Frien's helped fetch up the injured, includin' Gran'pap, Da' and E'ward, an uncle an' 'nother church leader. A nearby cart was brought t'carry our three t'a small cottage on the outskirts of Evanstown, a place 'idden back in the woods. We hoped the sold'rs wouldna' come af'r us, and we ha' 'ntrusted sev'ral pe'ple t'pass the word 'round the village tha' all three ha' perished. Tha' werena' such a big lie since Gran'pap ha' died and the other two were pretty near death. E'ward lived a day and then died. So Da' were the only survivor in our family. We 'oped rumors would keep the sold'rs away, and I guess it must ha' worked 'cause none 'peared at the cottage's doorsteps.

"Granny tenderly 'ministered to Da's needs, usin' her won'erful knowledge o' lifesavin' herbs and poultices. From her, my own mum (she is Gran'mam to Tad and Sarah) learned these val'able skills – the same kind o' skills she used t'nurse ye back t'health. I a'ways admired Granny. It must ha' taken a lot o' stam'na and courage t'take care o' Da', helpin' 'im gain 'is strength and get well, while all the time her heart must ha' been breakin' wi' grief ov'r the loss o' her 'usband. Per'aps givin' the gift o' love an' life were her way o' dealin' wi' the brutality o' her 'usband's death. The two were na' like some pe'ple who jest be a married co'ple. They were frien's long a'fore they truly fell in love.

"Once Da' recovered, he found tha' many o' his frien's, 'long wi' himself and his fam'ly, were in jeopardy due to they's beliefs an' the king's new laws. The laws ha'na' changed and he werena' able to show himself publicly. A'though the sold'rs hadna' come t'a the cottage t'rest him, the word were out tha' if'n his previous activities resumed he wouldna' be f'rgotten, nor would he be dealt wi' lightly. New edicts were posted, offerin' rewards for 'nyone who reported on those 'nvolved in treason again' the king. This greatly 'stressed Da' and he vowed t'prevent the sufferin' an' 'nhuman persecutions tha' his family and many frien's ha' confronted.

"Tha' were the beginnin' o' the network f'r religious an' political refugees. Da' vowed he would help these families 'scape to saf'r locations. I nev'r understood why he didna' jest take all o' us and leave England, but I guess tha' werena' wha' he felt God wan'ed o' him. I werena' so sure I could o' made tha' decision. May be now tha' might'n be differ'nt; then I couldna' ha' done. Da' were a truly ded'cated man, and o' course, by then the whole fam'ly were a'hind him in his 'ndeavor. Granny said we'd all stay t'gether and Da' felt there were a greater need f'r him t'remain here in England, doin' wha' he could. He would say, 'af'er all, we left our home in

Scotland for the same reasons. I'll na' let it move me 'nother time. I be up for the fight.'

"And wha'ever Da's reasons, he became totally ded'cated to the cause, as did Mum, and in later years, myself. At tha' time I were too young t'be o' much help or ev'n understand wha' be goin' on. Tha' would all come later. We found a place deep in the woods and Da' became very successful at aidin' pe'ple wantin' to leave the country or findin' new lives far away from the bigger cities. He w'rked t'make up a network o' pe'ple who could help, all the way from London town up t'a the north country. At first he were very careful and names were nev'r used.

"Ventually, his fame an' skill o' aidin' others became a topic o' discussion. His notoriety 'ncreased and he became 'specially problem-some t'those o' author'ty. By the time I were eighteen, there were a price on his head, and he were livin' on borrowed time. Still, he continued wi' his traffickin' o' religious pilgrims."

Pap stopped his discourse momentarily. He got up from the bench we were sharing, stretched and started pacing. I thought he had reached the end of his tale. But then he continued.

"By this time we didna' live in Evanstown. Pap ha' listened t'the reasonin' by both Mum and Granny We moved further north af'r Pap became more deeply involved and the risk o' discov'ry 'ncreased. Finally, we ended up in this part o' the country, a'though we changed residences quite of'n a'fore we ended up where ye found us. At first it were fairly easy t'help whole families get t'new areas where their religious beliefs were more liberally 'cepted. An' o' course the whims o' the kings, 'long wi' the rules tha' Parliamen' 'nacted, made some o' these moves easier or more difficult.

"Throughout the years, I ha' seen a lot o' frien's and their fam'lies reach shelt'r and saf'ty in various ports o' the world. It were easy t'help those wi' 'stantial wealth t'travel in comparative ease an' comf'rt. F'r the poor and dedicated, 'rangements were much more difficult, but ev'n most o' those brave and 'venturous pe'ple ha' found safe sanctuary. The capt'ns o' many ships ha' been very congen'al and willin' t'provide reduced fares or gi' folk an opp'rtun'ty to w'rk f'r travel costs.

"As ye can see, we ha'na' gotten rich off'n these many ventures. We nev'r took money f'r our ef'rts, nev'r made a profit on any o' this. If'n it were money we were lookin' f'r, there were much easier methods. For most o' us, it 'as all been f'r the gl'ry o' God, an' freedom f'r our fellowman. In my case, I ha' kept my childhood pledge made to Gran'pap those long years ago. Tha' pledge keeps me goin'. I don' mean t'say we ha'na' been compensated f'r our ef'rts. Our family 'as been well fed and clothed and on 'casion, there ha' been a few 'xtra coins f'r us. E'en some o' tha' were used to help those less f'rt'nate.

"My Da' finally met wi' his demise in rather unf'rt'nate circumstances. Like my gran'fath'r, he too, were a vict'm of clandestine spyin' on the part o' the king's sold'rs. I 'member it well. It ha' been a p'rtic'larly bad weather day and an ev'n stormier night. The winds rolled in off'n the ocean stead'ly tha' whole day. Our coats whipped 'bout us, 'ats flew from our 'eads and it were really an eff'rt to walk into the wind's direction as we went 'bout our bus'ness tha' day. We were livin' 'long the coast in a small hamlet tha' I am sure ha' since been swep' away by the sea. Tha' area o' the coast ha' a'ways been notorious f'r its adv'rse weather. The wild and ferocious winds were a constan' part o' daily life. Tha' particular day

Da' an' I ha' been w'rkin' on our boats. We owned several small craf' tha' we used f'r carryin' our pass'gers t'ships at the rendezvous points.

"Travel 'rangements ha' been made f'r our pass'gers t'go out later tha' night. There were three o' them and one were a member o' the clerical staff from a large church near London whose s'rmons from the pulpit in defense o' religious freedom ang'red the Crown. The other two pass'gers we didna' know, a man and his wife from a little village none o' us knew or 'as' ev'r he'rd of. Said they were seeking political asylum.

'I am wanted for my writings,' the man tol' Da. 'I defended freedom of worship for a small congregation of people in our community.'

We believed them. I suppose ye might'n say we be a bit too trustin,' but our mission were t'help those who wan'ed our help. We nev'r gave the couple 'nother thought.

"My only worry tha' ev'nin' as Da' set sail were the bad weather and the 'proaching storm. I 'member 'monishin' Da' tha' we oughtna' take the risk tha' night wi' the wind whippin' 'cross the wat'r, whirlin' it into giant whitecaps tha' rose in foamy peaks and splayed back into the sea wi' a thud. Those angry waves rolled into the shore wi' a feroci'y tha' should ha' det'r'd any sane man. But Da' were nev'r a sane man and he ha' a cause he felt justified all his actions in life. So det'rmin'd as ev'r an' wi' a ship waitin' jest outside the rocky harb'r, he felt the trip ha' to be made. The cap'n ha' warned tha' the ship would set out a'fore dawn. It were his las' chance t'catch high tide.

"I were all set t'go 'long wi' Pap and tha' I am still 'live be pure luck. I owe my life t'Tad. Tha' very ev'nin' he decided t'nter the world. 'Liz'beth, my wife, ha' been down in bed since early mornin' tryin' to brin' the babe into the world. I

176

felt I couldna' leave wi' the birthin' takin' place. Granny also gi' orders I werena' t'be too f'r away. And I didna' wan' to. Af'er all, he were my firs' b'rn and I were feelin' the pride o' many a new fath'r. Thus it were all up t'Da' t'get his pass'gers and rendezvous wi' the ship. Mum pleaded wi' Da' to wait 'til the wee 'ours in 'opes the wind would subside an' the waves wouldna' be as treach'rous. But he couldna' nor wouldna'. He went down to the waterfron', wi' me followin' 'long t'help get them launched. I ha' strict orders tha' I couldna' stay more than a minute or two.

"It were a'ready misty and foggy an' I 'gain cautioned takin' off on the mission. I didna' introduce myself t'a the pe'ple Da' was deliverin' tha' night, but one o' the men seekin' 'sylum let me know who he be – a Mister Brandt. It be a name I won' nev'r f'rget 'til death takes me. He tol' me it were 'mperative he and his wife get on the ship and out into the deep blue a'fore mornin'. O' course Da,' nev'r thin'in' 'nythin' were amiss, complied. Grudgin'ly I helped Da' make final prep'rations. The pass'gers, jest the three o' them, and Da', settled in the boat and I pushed them out t'sea. I stood and watched them f'r a sh'rt time as the waves and wind took hold o' them, carryin' them through the dark night t'ward the larger vessel. It were the las' time I saw Da' 'live.

"Granny, Mum and I sat through tha' long evenin', waitin' and listenin' t'a the howlin' wind and waitin' f'r the babe. Later, stories were tol' by some o' the local sail'rs and the ship's crew members of how Da' and his pass'gers reached the ship wi'out problems. The trouble 'rose when the pass'gers were preparin' t'board. King's men were on the ship and threatened them all with a'rest.

"The cap'n o' the ship said one o' the men, most likely a comman'r roared out orders: 'Come 'board and s'render in the name o' the Crown, or join t'other black souls at the bottom o' the eternal deep.' The ship's cap'n said them were the very words he heard spoken.

"Cordin' to the ol' sea cap'n, standin' right next o' the comann'er were Davie Long.

He were a friend o' Da's and f'r several years Da' ha' counted on him t'make many o' the sea 'scape contacts. He most obviously were the spy and made his presence evident by claimin' he ha' 'brung prop'r trait'rs t'a the Crown.' I cert'nly hope he were well paid and his conscience didna' trouble him later. Mum said, in defense o' the man's char'cter, tha' he may ha' been granted his life f'r 'nformation. We don' know and prob'ly nev'r will. We nev'r saw him 'gain. It didna' take any urgin' for the man and wife to climb 'board and we later found out why they ha' been so eager. They were part o' the plot and the king's spies tha' were focusin' on Da'. Tha' explained why Mr. Brandt were so keen on leavin'.

"Da' and the clergyman were not as easily persuaded t'climb 'board the vessel. They tried t'get away 'mid a volley o' fire from the sold'rs firin' their muskets. I understand Da' tried turnin' the boat 'bout in the strong winds, but wi' the dang'rous waves it were a'most 'mpossible. They finally did get turned 'bout and both men frantically heaved the oars t'get some speed and distance a'tween themselves and the ship.

"The sea capt'n said it must ha' been tha' the clergyman were wounded which caused Da's distraction. In the brief instan' when Da' must ha' turned t'give his 'tention to the other man, the wind took the 'vantage. It seemed to turn instan'ly stronger and vent its 'ntire furry on the strugglin' wooden craf' and its occupants. Da' tried to gain the upper'and, but it were 'parent, ev'n from the decks o' the larger boat, tha' it were too much f'r one man to 'andle. Da' was definitely losin' the battle. An' the sold'rs continued to fire at them.

"We were tol' a large thunderin' wave, followed by a second and third tha' took Da'. It 'ngulfed the two men and the a'ready tipsy boat. Both boat and men were bounced and tossed 'round the blue-green foam as if'n they were light as feathers. When the waves reached their peak o' energy an' then died down, all tha' could be seen were riv'lets o' foam bound f'r the near'st shore. No evidence were ev'r discovered. Neither o' the bodies nor the boat were seen 'gain, a'though days later small bits o' wood fragments were found down shore. One o' the crew thought Da' might ha' been shot, but 'nother crew member said the sea jest jumped right up and claimed the two men and boat as the prize f'r the night. From what the sea crew later tol' Granny and myself, at 'bout the time the big wave came and took Da's life, his gran'son chose to enter the world. Tad were born on tha' stormy night twenty years 'go."

* * *

Pap sat back down beside me, spent from reliving a part o' his life that he had put behind him.

All I could think to say was "I'm sorry."

"Don' be sorry," Pap said. "It be wha' God wrote f'r us and how we 'as chosen t'live our life. I hope ye understands now why we be so 'ntent on helpin' others and makin' life easier f'r them t'ha' their beliefs. I don' thin' we are in as much danger these days, a'though I know there ha' been a price on my head f'r some time. We were destined t'leave our home sooner or later. And mayhap when we get t'the coast we might'n jest put all this a'hind us. I'd really like f'r my children t'ha' an easier life than mine 'as been. But f'r now, we both need to get 'nside and get some rest. We still ha' a gruelin' few days a'fore we get t'our destination."

"Thank you Pap for sharing your story. It is sad and beautiful all at the same time and it gives me a better understanding of what you all are about," I said. "I think you and your family are very brave."

"It isna' 'bout bravery," Pap said. "It be 'bout lovin' the Lord and his pe'ple."

He got up, walked over and opened the door, waiting for me to go inside. All but Millie had turned in for the evening. She had been waiting to show us our place to rest. I wasn't sure I would be able to close my eyes. Pap had given me a lot to digest. As I turned to follow Millie, Pap took hold of my arm.

"I know ye be wan'in' t'thin' 'bout all I've tol' ye t'night," he said. "But ye need t'put it 'side and store it f'r a time when you can thin' rationally 'bout wha' ye ha' he'rd and how ye might fit into our fam'ly. I can see ye's heart an' know ye care f'r Tad, ev'n though he mayna' be 'ware o' it yet. Jest close y'r eyes and get a good night's sleep."

"That's a good idea. I hope I can do that," I answered as I yawned.

"Pleasant dreams," Pap said as we both followed Millie through the cottage, down a long passageway and into a room filled with bedding pallets.

"Ye both need to close y'r eyes and jest rest," she whispered as she handed me the lit candle and turned to go to her own sleeping quarters.

I heard Pap twisting and turning across the room, trying to get settled down. I sat for a moment on my pallet, my mind in a whirlwind from the new knowledge. Just let it rest, I told myself as I wrapped a coverlet around me, blew out the candle and laid my tired head on the cushions. Only for a moment did I let my mind wander to the journey and where we were going. Was this truly my destiny, to be in the arms of the Ringolds? Time would tell. I closed my eyes and must have instantly fallen asleep.

CHAPTER ELEVEN

Reflections

The morning greeted us much too soon. Pap wanted to get an early start. He awakened us just as the morning sun was peaking over the rim of the hill which separated our hosts from the rest of the world. I had slept better than I thought I might, but exhaustion still hung over me like a cloud. Even though we had been able to have a comfortable place for a good night's sleep, I don't think any of us rested well. We were all too tired from the last few days and the strain of worry and riding long hours. Now we were up and ready to face another grueling day. Sarah, Grandmam, Mistress Frost and I straightened up the sleeping quarters we had been assigned. I poured water into the basin and washed my face. The water was cold, but refreshing. I brushed my hair and found the rest of my traveling companions in Miller's kitchen.

Jeb and Pap were in the midst of a heated discussion as we came into the room. Right away Grandmam was asking Millie what she could do to help and Millie was motioning for us all to sit down at her large table.

"Wha' be ye a thin'in' man?" Pap was saying to Jeb. " Ye canna' go back t'our home place now. Don' ya thin' the sold'rs know ye is gone. Ye said so y'rself tha' ya' thin' they

183

know 'bout the mill. I canna' be so sure o' tha' 'cause we ha' nev'r used it a'fore. Bu' f'r now, it be in our bes' interes' for ye to get on 'head o' us and make sure trav'l 'rangements be safe. Ye canna' go back, and we all may ha' to make other livin' 'rangements a'fore this be ov'r. If'n ye do go back, ye could end up like some o' our frien's – hangin' from the gallows."

"S'pose ye be right," Jeb conceded. "I jest don' like the idea o' startin' ov'r at my age. I ha' been used t' w'rkin' wi' ye and don' thin' I can change my ways. Ye knows I be best at jest bein' a listenin' post. Tha' be easy f'r me when we are 'mong frien's. I don' know how I could do tha' in a new place."

"Wha' do ye ha' t'go back to?" Pap asked. "A tiny room o'er the tav'rn? Ye 'as been mos' helpful t'our cause, but wha' good would it serve t'go back there now? I thin' many o' our faithful folk will ha' a'ready gone on t'other places, 'specially wi' the trouble at the cave. There be no one for ye t'help, ev'n if'n the sold'rs move out."

"At the presen' time Jeb I really need ye t'ride on 'head," Pap continued. "I know ye thin' all the 'rangements 'as been made, bu' ye know how they don' a'ways work out. In this case, I need ye out t'the coast to make sure ev'rythin' is as it should be. Wi' all o' us travelin' t'gether, we won' be able t'get there fas' as ye can goin' 'lone, an' we may na' ha' time to do more'n get our frien's here out t'the ship. We still be far 'nough away from the coast tha' we could definitely run into trouble. Ye knows the route and would be jest 'nough 'head tha' if'n there be trouble a brewin' ye could get word t'us. I would send Tad wi' ye, but I thin' he needs t'be here t'help me in case we run into 'ny problems. If'n there be trouble 'long the way, we might'n need a couple o' men tha' can handle weapons."

"I'll be most willing to help where I can," Albert said. He seemed quite tired and you could see the strain on him and his wife. I wondered if they felt all this was worth the effort. I'm sure it was, considering the danger they faced with their involvement in the Puritan faith.

"I know tha' be true and I thank ye," Pap said. "Mostly I be countin' on God t'be on our side. Tad 'as some 'xperience wi' our travelin' and he knows wha' t'be a lookin' f'r in the way o' trouble. But if'n we need ya', it be nice to know we can count on ye."

Albert nodded his head and said, "I hope we don't need my help." He got up from his seat and offered it to Grandmam. "Sit here, please."

"Thank ye," Grandmam said. "I could jest as well ha' stood, but it be nice t'be pamp'r'd a bit."

Jeb put his mug on the table and said, "Well, Pap, I guess I can be o' help t'ye best by stayin' in ye's service f'r now. I be ridin' 'head then and makin' sure all o' the trav'l 'rangements be made f'r the Frosts. Once they's 'board the ship, I will ha' t'thin' 'bout wha' I wan' t'do f'r myself."

"Fair 'nough and thanks, frien'. The Lord go wi' ye," Pap said.

Millie interrupted them with "come and sit ev'ryone and ha' a bite t'eat a'fore ye begins y'r journey. Jeb, ye will take a bite?"

"Deed I will," he answered. "Don' thin' I would be passin' up a meal, 'specially one tha' looks good as this one."

After filling our stomachs with Millie's enticing morning meal, she replenished our pouches with a fresh store of nourishing and ready-to-eat foods. Old Tom and Tad had gone off to the horse pen and had set each of us up with a horse, although he didn't have enough saddles to go around. Tad offered to ride his without and so did Albert. I would miss the closeness of Tad and sitting behind him as I had done the first part of our journey. But it would be nice to have control of my own animal. We gave the Millers tearful hugs of goodbye and words of thanks. Then we were on our way – closer to what I hoped would be a successful, safe and happily ever-after chapter for Catherine Grafton. I think we were all ready for a day without much adventure or surprises. Little did we know that thought would be challenged before nightfall.

Old Tom had picked animals that were rider-friendly. I patted my mount to get acquainted as I gave her a bite of oats from my hand. "Does she have a name?" I asked.

"Seesaw," he said. "Not sure why she be called tha' name. We get horses from various places and keep 'em to use f'r sech 'casions. Per'aps, if'n ye come back this way, ye can bring her back. Elsewise, I 'spect Seesaw and the rest might'n 'ventually get back one way or t'other."

Seesaw and I seemed to hit it off, and as I checked her gear I thought of Maudie. Oh, how I wish she were here for this adventure. She would have loved it. We climbed onto our chosen animals while Pap and Tad distributed the travel pouches and coverlets among us. Then it was a matter of settling in and getting as comfortable as one can when heading out for a long ride. When we were ready to leave, Jeb told Pap he would "get on 'head" and "let him know 'bout any trouble."

"God go with ye and our cause," Pap said to Jeb. "Ye knows the way we are goin' so be there 'ny problems, get back t'us soon as ye can. Otherwise, we be 'sumin' all is well and we'll see ye at the rendezvous point at t'coast in most likely three days – dependin' on how thin's go for us."

We watched Jeb start off on a trot then spring into a full gallop before he reached the hill. It wasn't long before he was out of sight. We rode after him at a slower pace following the path we had brought across to Millie and Old Tom's farm last evening. I worried about our entourage of Pap, the Frosts, Sarah, Grandmam, Tad and me.

"How safe are we with all of us riding together?" I asked Tad

"I thin' we be a'right," he answered. "Sometimes the larger group provides a bit more safety from 'ighwaymen tha' might'n be travelin' 'long our route. I 'ope Jeb can keep us 'nformed if'n there be trouble 'head. Pap and Jeb ha' done this route f'r a long time and they 'asna' seen any problems in the past. And I ha' done part o' this route, a'though right now we be in an area new to me. I guess all we kin do is pray. Ye can be sure Grandmam 'as a'ready said her mornin' prayers, askin' God t'provide us a safe journey."

I, too, prayed we would get on to our destination without any incidence. The crisp morning air was our companion as we continued our journey toward the coast. Pap led our parade of quiet, tired pilgrims ever closer to the sea. Grandmam and the Frosts were just behind him, Sarah and myself trailed closely behind, while Tad kept a close eye on the rear flank.

We settled into the routine of riding quietly and not making much conversation – partly because we were all tired or lost in thoughts of our own and partly because even a little chatter would be unwise in our present situation. It had been a pleasant visit with Millie and Old Tom, but it must have shaken the Frosts to find out the soldiers were closer to knowing the truth about the Ringolds. Pap said we were still a good three days from our destination, depending on how fast we rode and whether there would be any inconveniences along the way. I only hoped and prayed there would be none of the latter.

Our ride took us down slightly used trails along small streams, timbers and meadows. The vegetation was pale or even dead from the cool days of fall. Winter would be settling in soon and I only hoped by then we would be in a safe place and not running from soldiers, the king or the courts. Pap seemed to be avoiding villages and any designated roads. As we followed him I had time to think on our situation and speculate on what was to come. My life was changing day by day. The strength of my new friends gave me power to accept what God had chosen for me and to understand my life's destiny. This latest adventure was steering me into a path totally different than I would have chosen, or Father would have demanded, only a short time ago. In later years, when I had time to reflect on where this journey had guided me, I would see there were no other choices. Adventure and the unknown have always been a big part of my character. I have often thought if we knew the outcome of our future, how many of us would still plunge headlong into the events of our lives. This was a journey I would not have missed because I have always favored adventure over security. For now, I was committed to continue on with the Ringolds, taking whatever the future offered. The time for philosophical wanderings and pondering on what might have been would have to wait for the future. These thoughts, however, reminded me of a conversation Nathan and I had one day when we were off on one of our adventures.

* * *

It was the day we had ridden out to "Standing Stone" just a couple of years ago. We made plans for the outing, one of the few times that we did. Mostly our trips were spontaneous. Right from the beginning, we knew if Father heard of our plans to see the "Stone" we would be in serious trouble. It wasn't the kind of adventure he would ever have given his approval. At the time we considered ourselves very brave to try this trip. Not only was our destination quite a distance from the manor house, but at that particular time there were reports of highwaymen and thieves taking advantage of people along the back roadways. Still, both Nathan and I were game for our planned venture.

Our ride was uneventful, much to our disappointment. It took us about half a day to find the spot where the Stone stood as a sentinel and a symbol of what we thought of as our adventurous natures. We had dismounted and turned the horses loose to feed off the grasses and drink from the small nearby stream. We had given Molly our food pouches to fill, told her our plans and swore her to secrecy. Having Molly's picnic lunches was always a pleasure because you never knew what kind of treat she would pack. I had taken a coverlet along and laid it out on a grassy knoll where we could see the "Stone" and take advantage of shade from a nearby tree. Nathan began taking food out of the pouch: homemade bread, a few chunks of dried meat, some carrots from our gardens and Molly's famous fruit tarts. She had even slipped in a flask filled with a fruity tasting tea. After we finished eating, Nathan lay back on the coverlet and was so quiet I thought he had fallen asleep. But it turned out he was contemplating what he thought our "Stone" meant to the area inhabitants in the past.

"Do you think witches and such really gathered here and danced around it?" he said. "Wouldn't that be a sight to see? I would have loved to come creeping up the hill and seen a big bonfire and a witches' coven dancing the night away. You know, that kind of activity was part of their religion. Those folks believed in witches and ghouls and the physical consummation of young women and men to please the Gods on Midsummer Night's Eve. It would have been an exciting experience."

"Be careful Father doesn't hear those kinds of words from you," I said. "He would be livid and give us a lecture on purity and morality. Besides, I don't think a witch's coven really happened here. I often wondered if our "Stone" was really a burial marker for someone a long time ago. If you are going to dream and make up stories about why it is here, I want mine to be romantic. I think it is the burial spot of a beloved one. Maybe there is a ghost who haunts the place, wandering back and forth, looking and calling for his love."

"What a silly thought," Nathan said. "But I suppose it could happen. You know life is like a story we read once – a never-ending metamorphosis. Don't you think we are constantly changing? I mean we start out as a little tyke, cute and clever, and then grow and grow until we become stern and rigid like Father or beautiful and compassionate like Mother. It's like a caterpillar becoming a moth or butterfly. Life is also an accumulation of beginning and ending chapters; much like a book. The never-ending saga continues onward until death eventually greets us to write the final chapter."

"I had never thought about it before, but yes, I guess you are right," I said. "It's pretty heavy philosophy for a day we are supposed to be out having a fun-filled adventure." Jumping up, I picked a bouquet of flowers and began singing as I danced around the large rock. I tossed the flowers at Nathan as I sang and felt the pull of the lore that was part of "Standing Stone."

"Come join me Nathan," I said. "We can pretend we are your witches and have gathered here to greet the spring solstice. You can be a warlock and I'll be a woodland nymph. You can chase after me if you want. Do you think we dare build a fire?"

He just smiled and said I was way too wicked for his tastes.

* * *

The memory faded as I came back to reality. I thought about how life keeps changing even though you don't want it to happen. The severity and the consequences of my criminal deed had only vaguely registered in my mind. There was so much to think about and it had all happened so fast. The reality was there were two dead men. Jeb had confirmed the fact in telling his story at Crawfords Point. Death had knocked at my doorstep and subconsciously my mind was trying to ignore the accusations. Without bodies on hand to confront and confirm the terrifying actuality of what had happened at the cave, my subconscious mind seemed begging for compassion and perhaps even forgiveness. I consoled myself in acknowledging the dead men were only part of the reason Seesaw was carrying me from timber to timber and across the hills and meadows of northern England. The eminent excitement of a new adventure had certainly camouflaged the totality of my involvement.

My mind seemed to be a jumble of thoughts as we rode. As I recalled Pap's tale, I thought about his remarkable story.

I am not sure the ramifications of it all had soaked in yet. But I certainly felt the sadness and strength of the man as a result of the horrifying events he had experienced as a young child. His turning to faith only increased my admiration for him and his whole family. They had taken tragedy and turned it into what I saw as something wonderful. Death for his grandpap during those years of religious upheaval had only created a path for him and his family to aid political and religious fugitives from the Crown. I wanted to ask him how many people he had helped, but I was sure he would just shrug his shoulders and give me some evasive answer. I could just hear him say, "I only helped those who wan'ed to love and w'rship God in they's own way." I couldn't even begin to realize the intensity of their help, although this journey was beginning to make me understand how important it was to have personal freedom for worship.

Sewsaw sneezed which brought me back to reality again. I closed my eyes for a moment, feeling her steady gait as she followed Sarah's horse. Seesaw seemed to sense she was in charge and I let her take the lead. The easy, consistent pace Pap had established gave me further time to think about the Ringolds and their mission.

I recalled the history lessons which had filled many long hours in our school room at Grafton Manor. History in general had always been a subject I enjoyed and Father had been adamant his children should know about world events. We were always well-versed in some of the major happenings, especially church history and how it impacted our Catholicity. Much as I hated to admit it, I found people, places and their deeds in time fascinating. Perhaps my interest came about because I was a daydreamer, or maybe it was just my adventurous nature. Father would be proud to think I had gleaned a bit of knowledge after all in the world of church history. I am thankful he had been so persistent.

I was kind of awed I could remember historical facts because of my accident and the amnesia. It seemed odd I hadn't been able to remember the lessons about church and religious beliefs during that time. Instead, I had eagerly accepted my Puritan friends and their faith and had not thought it wrong. Now my memory was back and I thought about those lessons and the strict religious discipline Father had expected of us all. I think even then I was open to learning about and even accepting other forms of worship. For now, it would seem the Puritan way of worshipping fit my needs. I could only think it was one more way my father would be greatly displeased with me. But was it so wrong? What made one faith better than another?

* * *

I can still picture Armond, the current tutor before I left home. He would be standing in front of his desk, a stern and knowledgeable replica of Father. He was waving his long stick, often used for pointing, prodding and attention-getting. This time he was pointing at one of Father's maps. Father always insisted we know locations of the places and events we studied. Armond was urging us to reflect on the rules and regulations of religious beliefs set by English kings and queens for their subjects. He especially liked to pick on Henry VIII.

"It was Henry who really started it all. The church reformation began with his many wives and his refusing to adhere to the Catholic Church and papal authority," Armond had said. "In order to get his way, he established the Church of England to fit his lifestyle. That church became the mode of worship and people had to avow their loyalty to the church and the king. This created problems and conflicts for many Catholics as well as other forms of beliefs. Included in this new church were Puritans."

"The Puritans were a varied group of religious reformers, often called Calvinists and Presbyterians who broke away from the authority of the Church of England," Armond went on to explain. "The original name 'Puritan' was a term of contempt assigned to the movement by its enemies. One reason groups broke away from the Protestant Church of England was the rituals and formality it retained from the Roman Church. Worship was to be directed toward personal religious experiences, sincere moral conduct and simple worship services. The Puritans were absolutists and felt all Catholic influences should be eliminated."

Armond had given us an assignment to look up the word absolutism. We were to write about how it related to church, state and the kings or queens. I can vividly recall Armond expounding on the subject day after day for several months. At the time, I remember thinking I will never need to know any more about this subject and would sometimes let my mind wander into more adventurous daydreams. But Armond had a way of telling a story and some days he made the historic time frame come to life. He went on to explain absolutism was a popular idea which gave "absolute" power to one or more rulers. He said rulers used this idea to determine the laws, rules and beliefs of their kingdoms. As I listened to his comments and wrote my report, I considered the idea Father could be considered an absolutist – at least by me anyway. Armond went on to say the absolutist concept had severe repercussions in the mid sixteenth century. Because of their belief in absolutism, various renegade and political groups created widespread destruction of sculpture, stained glass, rood screens and other religious images.

In thinking about bits of history drilled into us by Armond I could easily see how Pap and his family might have gotten caught up in the conflict. In his Scotland, Queen Mary of Scots practiced her Catholic faith amid a growing Protestant community. Armond told his students –David, Nathan and me – the dissension between Catholics and Protestants tore at the very heart of society. This was one of the many crises Queen Elizabeth I faced as she came into power. Known to her subjects as Good Queen Bess, her country was in the midst of religious clashes during her 45-year reign. I was always daydreaming about Good Queen Bess – just her name made her sound like a very nice person. However, it would appear from Armond's stories she was not so friendly and understanding of all faiths. She ruled with a strong arm. In the early years of her reign, Puritans were accepted, but fate stepped in and they suffered a series of reverses lasting through the reigns of Bess and her successors.

Armond talked about the many people who lost their livelihood and were dislocated because of their political and religious convictions. He made us think about the events which stirred the pot of religion, the political and religious turmoil and the conflicts which encompassed Europe for centuries. I could easily visualize violence erupting in various parts of Scotland and England in the name of faith. There again, I could see where Pap and his family fit into this society and the kind of trouble they would have run into because of their beliefs. I wondered how Grandmam and Pap had fared when they were living in Scotland. It seemed so much of Pap's story was about the trials and troubles they faced after moving south into England. I recalled Armond's stories of James I. He was not only an English King but also a King of Scotland. Armond actually acted out a scenario to help us understand about the upheaval caused by religious uprisings in Scotland. In England, King James I replaced his court with Scottish people, providing much fodder for criticism. It was most likely during this time period that Pap and his family were facing strong opposition to their beliefs and perhaps came into dissension with the Crown. I suspected this dissention was what culminated in the Ringolds becoming involved with their livelihood of sheltering down-trodden political and religious victims.

"The Puritans grew discouraged with reforms," Armond told us. "After James I became king of England in 1603, Puritan leaders asked him to grant several reforms. He rejected most of their proposals, which included abolition of bishops. Even though Puritanism gained popular support early in the seventeenth century, a repressive government and church leaders caused many Puritans to emigrate."

I at least knew Charles I was the current king. Father used to expound on the antics of Charles and felt he was doing everything he could to bring an impasse between Catholics and Protestants. In a discussion about Puritans with Sarah and Grandmam, they had talked about how King Charles tried to get the Puritans out of the Church of England. And once out, Grandman had said many looked for their own ways to practice their beliefs, including immigrating to America. Those Puritans who remained in England continued the struggle for reform. Little did we all know the conflicts would continue, eventually leading up to war in which the Stuart kingdoms of Scotland, England and even Ireland would be ripped apart by the religious and political unrest.

One topic Armond introduced to our young minds was the witch hunts occurring as a result of religious beliefs and upheavals. These hunts had resulted in trials and death, sometimes for innocent people. I was interested in this aspect and vaguely recalled there had been talk of an actual witch burning in our village, long before I was born. I asked Father about it once, but he told me I was too young to know about such violence. I asked Molly about it too, and she told me the accused family lived on the outskirts of our village. Whenever Nathan and I would go past their small cottage, we would try to get information out of our escort for the day. Armond was the only one who would talk to us about the incident.

As I got older and traveled into the village alone, I would wonder what had happened and who had done the accusing. By then I had read enough to know witch hunts didn't always seek the truth. I could imagine how the accused might have been a bit different in their beliefs or maybe even too shy to stand up for themselves. Once a finger was pointed, the accusations would escalate. From my readings, I know some of the accused were enmeshed in herbs and healing, providing treatments for people much like Grandmam had done for me. This, along with other strange or unusual incidents, was enough for local people to question the conduct and beliefs of those accused. A few village people might have become vindictive and made up stories. That would have been the final straw and those accused were brought to trial.

* * *

A whistle from Pap brought me back to the present. He stopped and we all gathered around him. He said the morning was almost gone and we might want to stop for a bite to eat,

197

rest our horses and our bones. We had been riding through a timber and a small stream was close at hand. He thought this would be a good place to take some time out. As on previous occasions, we all slowly lowered our tried bodies to the ground, waiting for the lower limbs to accept the weight and give us some momentum for motion.

"We can gi' our 'orses a rest, too. Jest let them graze on the grass there a bit," Pap said. Tad, Albert and Pap grabbed the reins of all the animals and led them to the stream so they could refresh themselves.

As tired as Grandmam had to be she made sure the Frosts found a proper spot to sit and rest. She made sure they had a flask of water and some of the food Millie and Old Tom had placed in our pouches. Sarah and I made sure the rest of us had something to eat. It was good to sit on a solid surface even it if was the ground. I guess we relaxed some – Tad even fell asleep. It wasn't a long rest. I felt we had just gotten off the horses when Pap said it was time to get back into the business of continuing our journey to the sea.

Once more we climbed on our animals and continued our single-file trek into unknown territory. We began our steady pace again and my mind continued its wandering. I wondered how many miles we had covered during the long morning hours and how many more we had to go to complete our journey. Was it just this morning we had left Millie and Old Tom with their secret hide-away? I hoped it could remain a safe haven and retreat for others like us. If the soldiers knew about the Miller's place, wouldn't they have been there before we left? Or, were they holding out for bigger game. They might just be planning to meet us at the ship and implicate even more people. But I felt deep in my bones Old Tom's place was safe enough, at least for now. As tired as I was already, I hoped Pap would find a comfortable shelter for the evening like the spot at Millie and Old Tom's farm. And above all, I wondered what fate had yet in store for all of us.

CHAPTER TWELVE
The Journey Continues

The afternoon was as uneventful as the morning. We were thankful for the sunshine which warmed us through and through. Without the sun's warmth our traveling day would not have been so pleasant. The winter solstice was approaching with shorter days and cooler temperatures. A warm fire was always welcome. Tired though I was, I began to make mental notes about our surroundings. I had been too worried and concerned about our journey up until now, but observing nature had always been an enjoyable part of my riding. We were still hugging the large forest area which had been our constant companion since we left the Ringold cottage. Riding off the roadway as we were, there seemed to be little sign of life. I thought it odd we didn't see a cottage or two in the landscape along our route, but when I inquired, Tad told me very few people lived in or near this part of the forest. He said what few did live in this heavily wooded area were in small hamlets north of where we were riding.

About mid afternoon, in the near distance we sighted the remnants of an old castle. Its gray stones seemed to beckon us as a welcoming shelter even though it appeared to be abandoned. Even from our vantage point, we could see the decay and rot, emphasizing it was in sad need of repair. The wind-whipped banners that must have once furled out a welcome to visitors were now short rags of cloth. When I asked Tad if he knew what it was called, he said he wasn't quite sure who had called it home.

"There be lots o' 'bandoned castles in this area," he said. "Guess there were a lot o' diff'rent tribes o' folk who settled this land. Wars and battles were pretty prev'lent up this way and it be 'ard t'keep up wi' who were the landl'rd or f'r tha' matter how long."

The still standing unique spires gave my romantic spirit a chance to speculate on who might have lived there at one time.

* * *

In my younger days I would have invented a story about the abandoned castle. In my daydreams there would, of course, have been an elegant princess and her strict father, King or Lord Somebody, searching for a handsome prince to bring new blood and money to his stronghold. I could almost see the noble Earl of Somewhere riding in with his fellow companions, flashing a standard and whooping it up as they rode up to the thick walls of the drawbridge. As with every romantic tale, and adding conflict to the story, there would have been the peasant boy who had fallen in love with the princess. It was the age-old fairy tale of kings, queens and other royalty and told throughout the days of time. I shook my head when words my father spoke in the past came to mind. He would chide me for spending my afternoons reading romantic stories.

"Catherine, you spend way too much time in idle daydreaming or reading nonsense stories." It was a comment was to hear time after time. "What latest book of bad writings is filling your head with fluff this afternoon? If you must spend your afternoon reading about kings and queens, why don't you read about real kings and queens and what they have done to our country with their political and religious views? Maybe you can learn more about why we worship the way we do. That would be much more beneficial to you and give you a better understanding of our Catholic world."

I would try to ignore him, and he would stump away. But by then, my afternoon would be ruined. I would give up my thoughts and books to reality and usually try to find Nathan or go to the kitchen and check out what Molly was preparing for the next meal. She always loved to chat and could make me feel welcome anytime.

* * *

My mind returned to the present just in time t'see Pap raise his hand for us to stop. I was just beginning to wonder what he wanted to tell us when we all saw riders in the far distance coming in our direction on the nearby roadway. Pap motioned us to gather close. He told us to quietly and slowly move closer to the trees and "jest wait to see what the two be 'bout."

"What do you think is going on?" I whispered to Tad.

"Riders o' some sort," he answered. "They be a'most like sold'rs. I don' thin' they are and f'r sure they canna' be king's men 'cause they don' ha' red coats. But 'pears they be wearin' the same kind o' clothes. I don' like the look o' this."

"Obviously if we can see them, they can see us." I whispered to Tad. "What are we going to do? Do we have a story to tell them that will justify us being here together and riding along the woods instead on the trail?"

"Don' worry none," Tad said softly. "I be sure Pap 'as been in this kind o' situation a'fore. 'Sides we be 'arder f'r them t'see than they be t'us. Pap knows wha' t'say and ye can be sure he 'as a story tha' they be believin'. I canna' thin' word o' our deeds might'n ha' reached here yet. But they might'n jest be lookin' for Puritans in gen'ral tha' be headin' ov'r t'the coast and out o' the country. We ain' the only folks who gi' help to fellow Puritans. Pap and me is jest one o' many who bring fellow believers t'the coast for a safe trip away from England. Aye, this could be serious. But ye jest ha' faith in Pap and the Lord t'get us safely on our way 'gain."

As the riders came closer, I heard Grandmam whispering one of her usual prayers: "Lord pr'tect us from evil tha' others do. Keep us safe and guide us on our journey. We 'as ha' 'nough trouble these las' few days and could ye jest be kind 'nough t'lead us safely on our way? Thanks and Amen."

We could see their uniforms now. They were dressed in blue tunics with gray trousers and wore no hats or helmets. The two didn't seem very threatening and as far as we could tell, they appeared to not have any weapons on them. They carried no flags or standards to acknowledge who they might be. As they got closer we heard them laughing and joking. And then wonder of wonders, they just rode on by, not even acknowledging they saw us. Slowly we turned our horses around and continued to watch them. We had all been holding our breath and let out a sigh of relief as we watched them ride out of sight. Up the small hill they went. Their bodies disappeared over the rim, and then their heads. We stayed in that spot without moving for what seemed an eternity. Finally Pap told us to gather close.

"We be getting" close t'the end o' our day," he said. "I be 'fraid our 'commodations t'end this day's journey be not as plush as the last few nights. Jest a short distance back in the woods, be an ol' woodcutter's hut. Won' be 'igh comf'rt, but there be wide benches f'r restin'. And we ha' our supply o' food. There be a stream close by. I be sorry 'bout this, but where we usually stay, the couple came down wi' the flu and they both died, wi'in a day or two o' each other. 'Member Jeb told us tha' bit o' news?"

"So who do you think those fellows were that rode past us?" I asked Pap. "Did they really not see us or did they just think we weren't worth stopping for? If that's so, I don't care. But, I wonder if they will think later they saw us and then come back for us."

"Well Lucky, those be good questions," Pap said. "I 'as seen fellows dressed like tha' a'fore. They don' be king's men and they don' be any thin' to worry 'bout. I ha' seen similar garmen's on men workin' wi' some o' the big travelin' ships.. I thin' those fellows be part o' a ship's crew tha' provide the 'igh class payin' customers wi' s'rvices. Arrivin' t'port, they 'as a few days o' 'oliday an' sometimes the men borrow 'orses f'r a ride out t'see the countryside. I though' it mightn' be them when I saw the riders, bu' didna' know f'r sure so felt it be safer f'r us back here near the trees. We be dressed in dark 'nough clothes tha' we blend in good wi' the shadows. Nev'r know whether t'trust those fellows, so I a'ways try to 'void them."

Turning his horse around, he motioned us to follow him, again leading us single file along the forest's edge. We rode another half-hour and watched the sun edge slowly down toward the western horizon. I had just begun to wonder how much further it would be when he turned onto a slightly used path into deep shadows of hemlock and pine trees. A few minutes off the path, we saw the small, rustic lodge. To say it was a spectacle of comfort would be an understatement. But when you are bone-tired weary, sometimes any port in the storm at the end of the day will do. Pap motioned us to wait in the shadows of the trees while he rode closer to the building and then on around it. He seemed satisfied, but dismounted and silently walked to the door. He cautiously and slowly pushed on the door, then kicked it wide open. After a moment, with weapon in hand, he slowly eased himself inside. He was out of sight only a few minutes. He came out and waved to us to come on in. As we got to the cabin, he came out and helped Grandmam down. The rest of us slowly climbed off the animals and stood for just a few minutes to get our legs under us again.

"Do you think we are going to be safe here tonight?" I asked Pap. I wanted him to reassure my fears. I was not usually afraid of dark shadows, but this setting seemed eerily silent and somewhat foreboding.

"Far as I can tell, I thin' we be safe 'nough t'night," he said. "Looks like Mr. Rondell, a nearby residen', 'as provided f'r us, makin' sure we na' be in any danger. There be food and drink on the table and plenty o coverlets. Most likely ye'll find water out back f'r the animals. I as'na' called on him for help much, but Rondell be a good man – one ye can count on t'do the job required o' him. I know it is goin' t'be a cold night, but we canna' ha' a fire. The smoke comin' out o' the woods might 'tract unwan'ed 'tention. So we ha' to jest wrap up in the coverlets. Besides, ye won' be here tha' long. I wan' t'get an early start in the mornin'."

Pap told Sarah to help Grandmam inside and set up the food and sleeping quarters. He, Tad and I grabbed the reins of the horses and led them behind the building to a small grove of trees. Pap said the horses would have to spend the night in their gear in case we would need to leave in a hurry. Tad pulled a bag of oats from his knapsack for the animals, but soon discovered he didn't need it. The mysterious Rondell had taken care of the animal necessities. One wooden trough was filled with water. A bag of oats was hanging from the tree near the other trough. Tad poured out about half of it and put the rest into the bags on his horse. Once the animals were secured, fed and bedded down as best they could be with their gear still on them, we found our way back around to the front of the lodge and inside. I couldn't wait to see our accommodations.

The lodge consisted of a very large room with a huge fireplace at one end. Under normal circumstances there would been a great roaring fire which easily could have warmed the entire room and our cold bodies. Now the cavern stood black and empty. In the center of the room was the table. It was surrounded by benches and could easily seat a dozen or more people. Along three walls were low, wide benches to seat a crowd or offer sleeping arrangements for more than a dozen people. The wooden floors echoed as we walked across them, which made us turn to make sure we weren't being followed. The building reminded me of hunting lodges my father and his friends had used on a number of occasions.

It was good to sit in a spot that wasn't moving. We all gathered around the table to share the simple meal Rondell had left. Grandmam and Sarah had added some dried fruit from our own supplies. Before we sat down to the meager, but satisfying food Grandmam led us in prayer. She gave praise to God for keeping us safe throughout the day, thanked Him for the food and good friends who were helping us on our way to the sea and asked Him t'keep us safe through the evening and guide us safely on our journey the next morning. We all answered "Amen" and as tired as we were, began to devour the food before us.

Darkness soon filled the lodge and Pap allowed us to have one small candle on the table. It did not do much to ease the shadows filling every corner. Since we were all very tired and there was nothing else to do, we cleaned up the table and made up our beds. I think sleep came easily to each of us. Morning came – again too soon. Pap awakened us all and told us to make ready to travel as soon as we could. I did feel somewhat rested. Sarah said she, too, had gotten a good night's sleep despite the hard benches. Grandmam laid out a bite to eat while Sarah and I straightened up the lodge, eliminating traces of our visit. After the quick morning repast, Pap and Tad brought the horses around to the front of the lodge. This would be the routine for the next few days. A short distance off the trail of what I called the "forever forest" would be a lodge or a shanty concealed by a thicket of tangled weeds, shrubs and trees and filled with years of dirt and grime. I doubt soldiers would consider these hidden bowers as hiding places, or for that matter, even know about them. A supply of water, dried food for us and grain for the horses was always awaiting us in each of these stopovers. I was just beginning to understand the network Pap had established along his route to the sea.

Despite the tenseness and strain of the journey, we relaxed a bit and talked quietly among our small groups. Of course there was always the danger of soldiers finding us, but we hadn't seen any sign of trouble. Sarah had a way of helping all of us forget the seriousness of the situation. Oh, how she could tease. She especially liked to pick on Tad. Even the Frosts smiled and chuckled at her antics and meaningless, light-hearted prattle. At this time in all our lives, her chatter about inconsequential happenings, events and even places was just the antidote we all needed. From what I had observed of her in the few months I had been with the family, she was not one of those empty-headed girls who chatter to hear their own voice. She was a very practical girl and I admired how she bravely made us all feel more secure and comfortable during our journey. Both she and Tad seemed to be very knowledgeable in the ways of the world and nature. I began to understand that they were much wiser than one would have expected of what my father would have called "cottage people." Although, he had prided himself on the knowledge and learning that had been provided for his own "cottage people."

I found myself joining in her banter and the two of us teased and cajoled Tad at every opportunity. In looking back at memorable times during that trip, I remember one conversation, as if it were only yesterday...

We had been traveling along a stretch of what could have been grazing land hidden within a small protected valley. It reminded me of a perfect place for goats and sheep to graze, although we did not see any, nor even a cottage or other kind of dwelling. Instead it was filled with the gray rocks we had been encountering more and more as we rode ever closer to the sea. Here and there, amid the rock there had been a sprinkling of yellowish grasses and as we continued on, they had become taller and more frequent.

"This looks like it mightn't be a good place t'rest a bit," Pap said as he motioned us all to stop and get down from our horses. "Thin' we could all use it. Mayhap, we'll jest have some lunch and I may even catch a short nap."

Pap was a great one for just sneaking a few winks of sleep whenever he could. It seemed he could fall asleep in the blink of an eye, wake up fifteen or twenty minutes later, refreshed and ready for whatever activity he was doing.

The small lea where we stopped was still boasting a few daisies from the summer. The cooler weather had not dampened their spirits, and when I commented about them, Tad said they liked the cooler weather of fall. It felt good to walk about and stretch tired muscles in the mid-day sunlight. The Frosts and Pap were walking about and talking about the countryside. Earlier in the morning, the ground had been heavy with dew, but now the sun had warmed the grasses, providing an inviting, thick cushion to sink into and relax. I found a good grassy spot and sat down, using the surrounding smooth rocky outcroppings as a back rest. It was good to sit and rest and bask in the warmth of the sun's rays that were filtering through the cloudy sky. Tad came over and sat down beside me – it was a nice gesture which made my heart flutter a bit and gave me a warm feeling from head to toe.

Sarah started to sit down but spied a small patch of daisies. As full of spunk as ever, she leaned down and picked one of the daisies. Plucking off the petals one by one, Sarah began dancing around Tad and chanting:

"Behold the daisy, the beautiful daisy o' love,
A true symbol o' the maiden and her turtle dove.
The daisy whispers a tale of love so bold –
One that be greater than all the coffers o' gold.
Who be your true love my princely young man?
Be your heart taken by Helene or little Laurianne?
Or do ye love the naughty Liza or fair Aileen?
Upon which maiden be y'r heart most keen?
Does she love me or does she not?"

By this time, Tad was turning several shades of red as he blushed; then he became quite gruff as he said, "Leave me 'lone. My soc'al life be none o' ye's concern. Ye need t'sit down and rest whilst ya' can 'stead o' carryin' on wi' ye's nonsense."

He reached out to grab at her skirts but she swished and turned as she continued to dance merrily around Tad and me. Laughingly, she continued her poetic country song. Then she started in on me, dancing and teasing as she whirled around the two of us.

"Let me find a flower for Lucky," Sarah said as she reached down and plucked yet another daisy. She again began to recite her made-up verses:

> "I' will tell you a tale, a tale I will tell –
> of the name bespoken at yon wishin' well.
> By a young maiden beyond wood and river –
> a name to make a young male heart quiver.
> 'Tis a lad called Tad wi' wonderful charm!
> The maiden would mourn e're he came t'harm."

Sarah continued her chant as she plucked the petals.

> "She loves him, she loves him not,
> "He loves her, he loves her not…

I glanced at Tad to see how he was reacting to this whole scene. He smiled at me and just for a moment I could feel his eyes probing deeply into mine for answers. Then he held up his hands and shrugged his shoulders. Joining in Sarah's gaiety and looking at me, he echoed her chant: "She loves me, she loves me not. Would that be true Lucky?"

I blushed and cast down my eyes. If he loved me, I would consider that my good fortune. Where was this conversation going?

"What be the matter Lucky," he teased. "Cat got ye's tongue? Oh my, do I detect a bit o' shyness? Is tha' an answer o' yes, then? I nev'r thought ye would be shy 'round 'nyone, 'specially ye's new family. Nev'er thought ye'd ev'r be at a loss f'r words, but certainly ye be at this moment. Now wha' do ye thin' o' tha' Sarah?"

Pap came over to where we standing, breaking up our conversation and letting us know it was time to travel again. I wondered how much he had heard. He already knew how I felt about Tad, but I wondered if he knew how his son felt. The moment had slipped away and there would be time later to rekindle the happy spirit of the afternoon. Later, as we rode toward our destiny I puzzled over the whole event. I had seen the look in Tad's eyes and hoped I was not mistaken in seeing a look which said he cared for me. I felt elated and exhilarated the rest of the afternoon, lost in my own world of enchantment. I was floating absently above the danger that was awaiting all of us in the not-to-distant future.

We arrived at our usual lodging arrangements and prepared for our evening's stay. After we had a bite to eat, I asked Pap if it would all right to go outside for a bit of fresh air. I just couldn't begin to settle down for the evening and thought a little outdoor scenery and air might help me unwind. I didn't think about what danger might lie in wait for us; I was still living on the exhilarating thoughts of my afternoon of day dreaming – to think Tad might really care for me. Or, at least I hoped that is what I had seen in his eyes early in the afternoon.

"I don' thin' it be a good idea t'go 'lone," Pap said in answer to my request. "Per'aps Tad and Sarah could join ye, then the three o' ye might jest walk a bit if'n ye stay close t'a the cabin here. I don' thin' there be any danger; at least I 'asna' seen anythin.'

"I could use a little walkin' t'stretch my legs," Sarah said. "'Ow 'bout ye, Tad. Would ye care to join us?"

"Sure, I wouldna' mind doin' some walkin'," Tad said as he winked his eye at his father. "Anyone else f'r a bit o' air?"

Grandmam and the Frosts declined, saying they were going to bed.

"Mind ye, don' go far – stay right close t'the lodge," Pap said as he followed the three of us out the door. "I know how ye youngin's 'as an extra bit more energy than we ol'r folk. I'll jest kind o' look 'round a bit f'r any signs o' other travelers who might'n ha' taken 'vantage o' the cabin in the pas' few days or weeks. An' I be checkin' on our 'orses, makin' sure they is restin.' When we rode in, I didna' see 'nythin', but we canna' be too cautious."

Once outside, Sarah, Tad and I walked just a short distance down a narrow path into a small grove of trees just adjacent to the cabin in which Pap had hidden us. None of us spoke and I think we were just enjoying the night air. The lodge had been a bit stuffy, despite the cold. I looked up through an opening in the pine boughs and saw a cloudless sky with a multitude of stars just beginning to start their night's work of twinkling. It made me think of long ago nights at Grafton Manor when we would do our sky watching.

"Look at this sky – it is a glorious picture," I said. "It does make me a bit homesick because I had views like this at my home before I left. I have to admit Father was a good one with stories about the evening skies. My brother Nathan and I were

213

the ones who would plead for his stories and he would give in. When I think about it, I find it against Father's nature to believe in the myths of the sky. But perhaps he felt it was just another way of educating us."

"It is a won'erful sight," Sarah said. She shivered a little and pulled her shawl closer about her. "I be cold and am goin' back into the lodge. 'Sides, I thin' ye two could use a little time for y'rselves."

"Ye don' need to run off," Tad told Sarah. Then teasingly he said, "Do ye wan' to be 'lone with me, Lucky?"

"I.. I.. I.. well, if you want to talk, that would be fine," I stammered.

Tad laughed heartily. "Lucky, I be 'stounded. I canna' believe ye be at a loss f'r words – and twice in the same day. How can tha' be?"

"Get on with you, you silly boy," I said as I tried to cuff him on the ears. But he was too quick and ducked away.

"I'll just get on back, but don' stay out very long," Sarah said. "I can let Pap know I be goin' inside. I bet ev'r'one inside will be talkin' and won'erin' wha' the two o' ye be up to, that is ifn' they 'asna' fallen 'sleep a'ready. Then 'gain, I thin' they all know how the two o' ya feel t'wards each other, even if ye don' know yet."

I felt somewhat awkward as I turned back to Tad. My mind was a whirl with the tumultuous feelings beginning to stir within me when I was around him. I wondered if he felt the same way.

"Sarah's leavin' us 'lone was really all right wi' you?" I asked, prattling on like I sometimes do. I had never been so nervous, not even when standing up to Father. I felt like a young miss at her first cotillion. I wanted to go slow because I realized this fragile relationship meant a lot to me and I was

214

not about to throw caution to the wind. I wouldn't want to lose Tad by being too eager before our relationship had really had a chance to begin.

"I hope you won't be angry with me for being so premature," I said. "I realize we hardly know each other and have not had the best circumstances for meeting. And I also realize we still need time to get to know more about each other. But I can't help the way I feel – I hope you don't think I'm too forward. My father always told me I was much too persistent and wanted everything to happen all at once. I hope I haven't overstepped the boundaries of friendship. I.. I.. ah.. just wanted.."

Tad stepped closer and put a finger on my lips.

"Either ye talk too much or get all tongue-tied," he said. "Lucky, ye jest might be a lucky girl 'cause I ha' come t'care a great deal f'r ye. Like ya said, we 'asna' ha' a lot o' time, bu' I know people who ha' made life commitments goin' on less time than we 'as t'gether. Ye don' ha' to be 'mbarrassed for speakin' ye's mind. And ye may thin' I don' pay 'tention to wha' be happenin' but I could see tha' ye ha' been a carin' f'r me. I guess I knowed right from the very firs' time I set eyes on ya tha' ye could be a special p'rson in my life. We 'as a'ready been through a lot t'gether, so we kind o' 'as a special bond. An' once we are past all this mess, we may ha' lots o' time t'get to know each other. Like ye, I 'ope tha' might'n be years and years o' t'getherness."

"Will it be that easy," I asked. "I only wish it would. Remember, there is a dead man to account for and we are still not safely out of the woods, so to speak."

"I know, and tha' be a big worry f'r us all right now," Tad said. "But ye must ha' 'ope and faith in the future. Look at Pap. Life 'asna' a'ways de'lt fairly wi' him, an' he ha' more faith and confidence than 'nyone I know."

215

"It is so good to know you care for me, even if it is just a bit," I said. "I do have faith and believe there will be a time for us when this is all over."

Tad then stepped closer and took my hands. "Right now, I canna really promise 'nythin' more than I will take care o' ye as long as I can," he said. "Bu' jest so ye know, when I am 'round ye, I be very, very 'appy – ev'n though ye may thin' I don' show it. Mayhap tha' be wha' real love be all 'bout. I don' ha' much 'xperience wi' this kind o' thin'. Would ye mind if'n I held ye close for a moment?"

I was never certain later if he took me into his arms or if I took him into mine. But at last we held each other close, clinging together like it was our last embrace. For now, the promise of a future with Tad was good enough to make me happy. I could feel the warmth of his body, the beating of his heart and the sweet smell of musk from his hair. I wanted him to hold me close like this for eternity. I thought for a moment he might kiss me but we were interrupted by the crunch of a foot stepping on dry twigs. We jumped apart as Pap came into sight.

"Did ye find 'ny evidence tha' others 'as been usin' the lodge," Tad asked quickly covering up our intimacy.

"No sign o' 'anythin' but two young lov'rs so tha' 'as t'be a good omen," Pap said laughing. We both turned red with embarrassment. "We best be gettin' back inside a'fore the others worry 'bout us. I don' know 'bout the two o' ya', but I sure could do wi' a bit o' rest."

He turned and walked up the path quietly, the two of us close behind. It was good to settle in for the evening and I think I slept better than I had for some time, cherishing the promise of a future with Tad. We still didn't know a lot about each other's past, but it didn't really matter. I hoped we would have plenty of time to share with each other our past lives and enjoy the pleasure of each other's company in the future.

Although there was little time the remainder of the trip for Tad and me to have a more than just a few moments alone, general conversation seemed to be much easier now that our feelings had been openly revealed. Tad had said there would be time later, and that was enough for now. I let my thoughts dwell on that rather than on any misgivings I had about whether the life I had awaiting me at the end of this adventure would include Tad and his family. With all my heart and soul I prayed that nothing would interfere with my dream.

Like many nights, it felt too short. Pap had us up and ready to leave just as dawn was breaking. He informed us we were on the last leg of our journey and "God willing we would reach the coast sometime t'day." We all seemed to feel the weight of the world leaving us. What a relief to be close to our "ship of freedom" – the one to carry the Frosts, and perhaps even us, into a new life.

We had spent the last few days looking over our shoulders. There had been no sighting of any other people other than the two sailors we had seen a couple of days earlier. Our destination was close at hand. If soldiers were on our trail, we had seen none. Perhaps Pap had been right in predicting the soldiers would be awaiting us at the ocean rendezvous. I felt my stomach begin to knot up again with fear from the thought. My mind had been preoccupied and I had not had time to dwell on the dangers which might lie ahead. Instead, my thoughts were about Tad and how good it had felt to be in his arms. I wanted to revel in his promise of a future once life settled down. For a few briefs moments I had even allowed myself to forget the real reason for our exhausting journey. I had appeased myself with a false sense of security, thinking perhaps Jeb and Pap might have been too pessimistic and there would be no soldiers looking for any of us. After all, we had seen no sight of Jeb. Wasn't that a good sign? What a silly and mistaken idea!

The last morning on our trek to the coast started off cold. There was a misty rain, making our ride most unpleasant. It was close to midday when we stopped for a rest. Grandmam dug deep in her food pouches and brought out biscuits and dried meat for all of us. As she handed out the rations, a deluge of questions were being poured out to Pap. We were getting close to our destination and we were all beginning to wonder how safe we were and what we could expect at the coast.

"I know at this point it is hard for you to be sure, but I guess the missus and I need some assurance this long trip will get us safely away," Albert said. "Ye can understand we are nervous and anxious to be away."

"I know it 'as been 'long and 'ard on ye, na' bein' 'customed t'the rough kind o' travelin' we ha' been forced t'use," Pap said sympathetically. "Best I can tell ye is tha' Jeb should ha' all the 'rangements made when we 'rive at the coast. We 'asna' he'rd from him, so I am cert'n a small boat be 'waitin' t'take ye out t'a the sailin' ship an' on y'r way t'a new life."

"I don' spect any trouble," Pap continued. "I ha' been takin' care o' good folk like y'rselves f'r a long time and I 'asna' lost nary a client. So rest assured. I be gettin' ye t' the ship ev'n if'n I ha' t'leave me fam'ly a'hind f'r a while. We be a'most there and soon ye be bo'rdin' the ship and restin' comf'rt'bly in a private cab'n. Course, I canna promise ye a smooth and trouble-free voyage, but at least on the ship there should be little danger 'cept from the wrath o' God an' nature. And I pray tha' God will be kind t'the captain, crew and ye."

As I listened to the conversation, I could only hope Pap's optimism would hold true for the couple.

"Well Pap, we do mightily appreciate all ye have done for us, the missus and I," said Albert. "And the rest of you too, we thank ye for all your help. Surely God will protect us all a bit longer, but if that not be his judgment, we want ye to know how grateful we are for all ye have done. If there be a problem, let your conscious be at rest; ye have given more than we expected. Our future safety now rests in God's hand and we are at his mercy. I don't understand what drives the soldiers of the king. I daresay, some of those soldiers surely must worship a different kind of God than we do to cause so much misery and hardship throughout the countryside."

"Don' worry, we be gettin' ye on t'safety best we can in no time," Pap said. "I thin' the 'orses 'as sufficient rest, so I thin' we be gettin' on our way. I hate t'urge ye on, but we do ha' a ship t'meet up wi' t'day."

We all laughed and got back on the horses. I think we all were feeling a little giddy just knowing our journey was coming to an end. It was about mid afternoon when we drew close to our destination. We had stopped only once more for a mid-day break and bite to eat and drink for both ourselves and the horses. The rain and mist had stopped but the day had not warmed up much and I think the cool, damp weather was beginning to have an affect on the two older ladies of our party. From what I was hearing from Pap and Tad, it sounded like we would soon be safe and secure in some kind of shelter.

Thank goodness, I thought. I wasn't sure how much more of this kind of traveling Mistress Frost could take. She was not a frail woman, but she had been under a strain for more than a week, what with traveling to the cave and finally the continuous riding through woods, hills, moors and lush leas. And Grandmam, no matter how much she boasted she was "fit as a fiddle and ready f'r action," she was not as young and hardy as she claimed. Though she never complained, I know the dampness and the long ride had been a hardship for her. I had even felt the tiredness in my young bones, along with the effects of my previous injuries from which everyone claimed I was still somewhat recovering. And, we were all tired – not one of us had rested properly for some time now.

"Can ye smell it?" Tad asked as he sniffed loudly. "Just smell the saltwater, the seaweed an' dead fish. We be definitely gettin' close. I can a'ready feel the spray o' water as the waves hit shore and rocks."

Personally, I couldn't detect anything different in the air, but then I have been a landlubber all my life. Never having ventured this close to the ocean would make a difference.

"I can a'ways tell when we be gettin' close," Tad said. "I jest feel it in my bones and my nose perks right up. There be somethin' 'bout the air – it jest be differen' than bein' inland. Mayhaps it be 'cause I were born near here and my body feels like it 'as come 'ome. We should soon 'ear and see the gulls swoopin' and cryin' f'r they's dinner. Wait 'til ye see them swoopin' and grabbin' a poor 'nocent fish. They be a picture o' gracefulness."

"I am looking forward to my first adventure with the sea," I said politely. My thoughts had turned to evaluating the fear of the unknown and what awaited us here rather than observing the picturesque beauty of water and beach Tad seemed to be looking forward to. It was hard to feel like we had just arrived at a scenic vista when my mind clung to the potential of a harmful fate and future. My thoughts were putting a damper on enjoying the beauty of the area. Had I known at that moment our seaside visit would prove to be more eventful than even I could have imagined, my enthusiasm would have been further deterred.

"Sarah, do you smell the ocean as Tad does, and is it one of your favorite spots?" I asked.

"Deed so," she answered. "Course, I am na' as 'nchanted as Tad be, but the sea do get into ye's bones, Lucky. We grew up 'ere and no matt'r 'ow far away ye goes and na matt'r wha' other pretty scenery ye might'n find 'nland, us sea folk a'ways yearn f'r the briny green. Sometimes when I thin' 'bout livin' 'ere I close my eyes and jest sit back – 'njoyin' my mem'ries. I were little, but in my 'magination, I can a'most feel the vibrations o' the waves beatin' the shore. An' I be a feelin' the feathery foam on my skin as it washes 'shore and then silently sifts back into the sea. We 'asna' lived here f'r a very long time, but the sea still be a part o' who Tad and I be. Guess once ye 'as 'xperienc'd sea life, ye become one wi' it and it wi' ye. It becomes an 'ntegral part o' who ye be. I didna' realize 'ow much I missed the sea."

"Nor I," replied Tad sadly. "I 'as greatly missed it. In my mem'ries there be the days we used t'walk the beach, feeling the san' a'tween the toes and the salty mist splashin on ye's body. I were but a lad then, but it still feels like my real home. Some day, when life be differen' and more 'commodatin', may be I can make my 'ome 'mongst the gulls, the whal'rs, the break'rs and the roarin' tides?"

Turning to me, he asked, "Lucky, wha' would ye thin' 'bout tha' kind o' life f'r the likes o' ye?"

"W.. W.. Would that be some kind of proposal?" I stuttered, feeling my heart flutter and flip-flop with the wonderful thought. "It wouldn't matter where I lived. I.. I.. I would be happy anywhere my love would take me."

I looked at him and then lowered my eyes. I could feel myself blushing. Sarah laughed at me and reached out to touch my arm, offering her encouragement and friendship.

Tad laughed. "I loves it when ye get all tongue-tied. F'r now, our lives are jest gettin' out o' the mess we be in and seein' the Frosts on t'a safe life a'fore we can thin' 'bout wha' be 'waitin' any o' us in the future. I pray God will see us all safe as we wend our way into new and differen' lives than we 'as ha' in the past."

We continued to ride and I tried to take in the sights and sounds as the sea came into view. My first glimpse at the expanding blue-green vastness loomed before us. Pap said we were not too far from a coastal village but he thought this nearby cove would be better for the rendezvous point than at the wharf in the village. We slowly followed Pap as he turned off the trail and picked his way down a well-worn path. He began winding his way downward to the ocean across a beach filled with sandy soil and sparse vegetation. Rocky outcroppings and jagged pilasters of gray stone were enmeshed in sand while sudsy foam-filled waves rushed ashore. As far as the eye could see there was water and sky – intermingled and indistinct at the horizon's edge. What a wonder to behold. I felt mute, and unable to express how I felt about the infinite greatness of the scenery before me. I could easily understand how this great expanse of water and sky could compel men to become fishermen and sailors. The landscape reminded me in many ways of pictures I had seen in my school books. One picture came to mind – it was of mountains somewhere near India. Whenever I saw those pictures I was reminded of the beauty and wonder God has presented to man in the form of nature. This view of the mighty ocean made me feel the same way.

I was startled from my reverie. The peaceful air now became filled with the piercing shrieks of seagulls. The roaring of thunderous waves could be heard as they belted the shore and spread debris far inland and across the sandy flats. Farther down shoreline, smaller rocks were intermingled with white sand and the ocean seemed calmer as it came ashore.

"It's beautiful," I uttered, not even aware I had spoken my thoughts aloud.

"Aye, that it be," said Pap, riding up beside me and talking loudly above the noise. He had let the others pass and was waiting for Tad to catch up to him. "The sea be a whole w'rld unto its self. I a'ways f'rget 'ow much I love bein' near the water 'til I come 'ere. May be tha' is part o' why I help others. Guess it be God's way of givin' me a piece o' my soul while I be doin' His work."

"Are we going to be much longer?" I shouted to Pap. "Do ye think we will get the Frosts out safely? What about us? Guess I'm full of questions."

"Same as the rest o' us," Pap answered. "I can only 'ope our trip will go as well as those in the pas'. We 'asna' ha' any trouble f'r a very long time and I 'xpect this time t'be jest the same. 'Bout 'nother half-hour a'fore we get down t'the cove where the boat be 'waitin t'take the Frosts out t'the ship. We be stoppin' jest 'round tha' large bend and soon as the Frosts be on the boat, we be headin' over t'yonder village f'r the ev'nin.' At least tha' be the plan f'r now. Ye can see down there is the cove, jest a short distance cross the sand. Pray t'God tha' he guides us there safely."

"Looks like our venture be 'bout at the end," Pap told Tad. "I don' s'pect no trouble, but I need ye t'be on the lookout f'r any poss'ble danger. Ye knows the plan and our sole purpose be t'get the Frosts on they's way. If'n there be any trouble, ye get Grandmam, Sarah, Lucky and y'rself out o' danger best ye can. Be lookin' 'round t'see where ye might'n go if'n there be a need for hidin'. Else, jest ride like the wind. I be the one worryin' 'bout the Frosts and gettin' them 'board the ship. Jeb should be 'round somewhere, 'though I did 'spect him a'fore this."

As we continued to ride closer to the destination point, I wondered if this would be the beginning of the end. Will we put the Frosts on the boat, all shake hands and say how pleasant it all has been and each of us then go on our own merry way? I was sure that wouldn't happen. Tad had promised a future and I was going to hold him to it.

The last leg of our journey was eminently near and in the distance I could see the outline of a ship. It stood like a silent sentinel against the horizon – a ghostly apparition as it swayed with the current in the late afternoon sun. So far, there did not seem to be any danger; I was relieved to see no sign of the anticipated and dreadful soldiers. The beach seemed safe and peaceful, at least on the surface. Except for the noises and beauty of nature, we were lulled into a false security. I don't think any of us were prepared for the surprise awaiting us. But as fate would have it, our adventure would soon take on a new twist, completely sealing my destiny forever. I shall always associate the sea and the tragedy which was to follow conjunctively with fear and death.

CHAPTER THIRTEEN

At the Coast

We continued our journey across desolate rocks and sand as we moved ever nearer to the ocean. By this time, it was getting close to late afternoon. We were a weary crew, letting the horses and Pap lead us to what we hoped would be a safe place to rest and see the Frosts, and perhaps ourselves, bound for a new life. I think we were so relieved to be at our destination we were unmindful of the danger whispering around our shoulders and nipping at our heels.

At the top of the sandy hill leading down to the beach, Pap stopped for a minute, looking and listening. The beach was almost an isolated island among the high rocky cliffs which seemed to consume much of the coast in this area. No sign of life could be seen. It was a solitary scene of water, rocks and sand. The only activity on the beach was ocean waves and birds — a good omen. There was very little vegetation, only a sparse spattering of shrubs or willow bushes. I thought Pap had chosen a good rendezvous point.

"It would 'pear the Sea Witch be 'waitin' on us – well I thin' tha' be her. She don' look quite right, but it ha' been a while since we 'as been over this way," Pap said when he saw the ship. "She be a pleasin' sight. But I don' see anythin' f'r gettin' us out t'her. I be 'opin' a small craft be showin' up soon. I won'er where Jeb 'be and why he ain' down there wavin' t'us. Mayhap he be hidin' and a watchin' f'r trouble."

The ship was anchored quite a distance out into the water because of the rocky barrier extending from the shore. It was waiting patiently like a tired mother at the end of a long day. The giant wooden hull boasted a conglomerate of tall masts and sturdy rope rigging, black spiral silhouettes piercing the sky in the fading daylight. From this distance, there seemed to be no movement aboard the sea-going vessel. It was as if everything on and around the ship itself was in suspended animation, awaiting the culmination of this dangerous liaison. For a moment, as brief as the blink of an eye, I felt throughout my whole body a warning and dreadful premonition of pending disaster. Calm down I told myself. "Don' be borrowin' trouble" as Grandmam would have said. I smiled. I was becoming more and more like her and Sarah and less of the spoiled girl I had once been.

I closed my eyes and instead of danger I saw a picture of hope. Although I had never sailed, in my daydream I envisioned white billowing sails, bulging with the wind – the giant vessel cutting through foamy waves which lashed at its wooden sides. I pictured myself, the Ringolds and the Frosts all standing in the prow, feeling the cold wind on our faces as the ship sped lightly through the water. I could feel the taste of freedom as the miles fell behind, bringing us closer to safety and a new beginning. But these thoughts were only an overactive imagination and a wistful hope this adventure would have a happy ending.

"I thin' we be safe 'nough' f'r now. Be ye ready f'r a short rest?" Pap asked, bringin' me back from my daydream. "We be goin' ov'r t'tha' small cove. It be a good place to wait, 'ide the 'orses and take a bit o' rest while we wait for Jeb an' the boat to come f'r us. Canna' figure why he isna' here."

We followed Pap down across the sand and rocks. Near the shoreline seagulls gracefully floated just above the water, diving every so often for tidbits or calling out to their mates in a screeching, piercing cry. They seemed to be gloating over their good fortune in finding palatable morsels for their existence. I viewed the great expanse of water within my vision and felt awe and wonder. The wide-open space with nothing but miles and miles of water made me feel very small and unimportant. I felt the omnipotence of God. I smiled at this thought. Only a few months ago, before meeting the Ringolds, such serious thoughts would never have crossed my mind. I always enjoyed nature, but I would have rarely given the glory to God. These thoughts would never have been put into words by me unless prompted to do so in the classroom or when questioned by Father. No doubt he would be pleased with at least part of me. I shook my head and returned to present reality.

A faint outcropping of what appeared to be buildings could be seen further up the coast line. We were far enough away they were only faint shapes and forms, shimmering in the distance. When I asked Tad if he knew about it, he said it was a fishing village and the closest port to this beach.

"I thin' it be called Ravenston. It isna' a busy port and very few ships stop 'long there," he said. "Mostly, the bigger ships and trad'rs dock further down the coast where the larger wharves be more numerous. Bu' all up and down the coast there be a vast shippin' business. It be the mainstay and livelihood f'r most coastal towns and villages – tha' and fishin'."

"The ocean kind of smells – maybe I don't like the ocean," I said.

"Salt water and dead fish," Tad said as he laughed. "It be somethin' ye get used t'when ye live 'long the water. I ha' forgotten tha' many o' the shores don' ha' such a pleasan' odor."

I nodded and watched the strange birds along the water's edge. They were small with long bills, short bodies and long legs. I watched as they pecked at the discarded offerings of the sea. They weren't making any noise, just running frantically along the shore, digging and eating.

"Funny-looking birds too," I commented. "Do you know what they are?"

"They be a type o' ocean snipe tha' live 'long these rocky shores," Tad said. "I s'spect they be a lot o' creatures here differn' than ones ya be used t'seein'. Ye can call it an outdoor classroom. Did ya ha' those at y'r Grafton Manor?"

"You would be surprised at how many outdoor lessons we had," I answered. "Father was always taken with nature and felt his children could be no less fond of the ponds, lakes and woods surrounding us."

Tad smiled and turned to look at the ocean. I followed his lead, devouring the breath-taking view of the water and rocky cliffs as we rode. On a high promontory point at the edge of the cove where we were headed was a lone tree. Rock surrounded the tree and I wondered how its once fragile roots could have ever taken hold. But they did and now they were agglutinated within the rocky structure – almost as if they were one. The leaves had earlier left the branches bare and the gnarled trunk and twisted limbs protruded out into the sea as if a tall giant had leaned against the tree trunk for a very long time. This only gave evidence to the strong and vicious wind currents which most likely swept down across the cove and beach regularly. Today's winds were just enough to send a chill through the body, but they had certainly blown strongly in the past to leave the tree as misshapen and gnarled as it was. Despite all the odds, it had survived in this solitary and stark place. In the fading afternoon light, it stood like a lone sentinel – and left a picture in my memory of beauty, endurance and even a hint of despair. The tree became for me, then and throughout the remainder of my years, a symbol of what determination can do.

Pap led us past the rocky promontory where my lone tree of courage stood and into the small cove surrounded by high rocks on three sides and the ocean on the other. A tiny stream, which must have had its beginning in the tall rocks, flowed into the ocean. It was a small but cozy spot for a retreat, leaving us concealed and isolated from the rest of the world. The cove sheltered us as though we had taken refuge in the midst of a deep green forest. I had to give credit to Pap or whoever made the arrangements. It seemed a perfect location from which the Frosts could safely depart, or so we thought. After the long ride, the sea-green water of the ocean was inviting, in spite of the smell. The only noise was the clapping, slapping thud of waves skimming across rocks and sand, leaving behind a trail of suds and debris. I told Tad I wanted "to rush down to the water's edge, feel the waves and splash my face and hands to wash away my tiredness from the journey."

He laughed, then said, "I bet ye mightn' be a bit dis'point'd. Tha' wat'r won' leave ye feelin' very refreshed. Ye may be f'rgettin' it be salty. And ye can be sure it be cold."

"Even so, water has a way of making a person feel refreshed," I said. "It is sure to renew my energy."

I wanted to throw caution to the wind and run into the water like a small child who has just found a new toy or diversion. Pap put up his hand and signaled us to stop before we got close enough to the water for me to act rashly or foolishly. "This be the end o' our journey, at least f'r some o' ye," he said, chuckling at his own joke. He winked his eye, which did a great deal towards making us all feel a little more at ease and a bit safer.

Once we dismounted, I looked around for the promised boat, but saw nothing. I was worried. Perhaps it was hidden near some of the larger rocks along the coastline. Tall gray stones were blocking our sight of the water in some places, creating a safe niche for a small boat. Pap, too, seemed to be searching the nearby shore for signs of the boat and Jeb.

For a few moments we all just stood where we had set foot on solid ground. It was good to just stand. Not one of us spoke as we continued to search with our eyes for a boat to carry our party out to the sailing ship. I still believed it was hidden in one of the little recesses of rock and water. By now, we were all in tune with each other and there seemed little need for conversation. Either the boat was here and all would be well, or there was a problem we needed to learn about before the situation was out of control. I knew about how things can be "out of control" and was still feeling extremely grievous about my bout with the king's soldiers. "Please God, don't let it happen again," I whispered as I prayed quietly to myself.

Slowly, fear began in each of us – pumping through our veins with every beat of our heart, radiating outwards and spreading like a contagious disease. Each of us glanced back over our shoulders and all around, looking from one to the other. As we made contact, eyes seemed to spell out the word "fear." I was holding my breath I realized and could almost hear the others holding theirs as well. Of course I was no judge of sounds, but there didn't seem to be anything except the splash of waves hitting the water and the birds fighting for their dinner. Even the constant wind following us most of the day was now just a cold breeze. Perhaps it was the lack of wind which made the scene startling and frightening; or perhaps it was just the quiet itself. It felt eerie and ominous and caused our uneasiness. When I look back, I wish that could have been the case.

By this time, Pap had motioned Mrs. Frost and Grandmam over towards a grassy area in the sandy cove. "Tad, why don' ye, Albert and Lucky take our 'orses and 'ide them a'hind tha' large rocky area near the back o' the cove," he said. "Jest leave they's saddles on in case we ha' t'leave in a hurry. If'n I ha' my directions right from the local, they be a small pool o' water hidin' near the rocks and ye can gi' the animals some o' the grain we been totin' 'round f'r the past few days. We need to keep our furry friends here in a good disposition, 'ealthy and 'appy."

We three easily completed the assigned task. Behind the rocks, along the high cliffs was the pool of water Pap had talked about. It was fed by a small spring at the base of the rocky formation – more specifically, it was just clumps of moisture gathering on the rock then dripping into a shallow pool below. But it was enough to quench the animals' thirst, as well as our own. I filled a small flask full of water to share with the others. We gave our horses a quick brushing down as best we could while still leaving them saddled and ready to run if we had to.

Returning to the cove opening, we still saw no sign of a boat. Pap suggested it would be a good time to rest while we were waiting. It didn't take much encouragement. Exhausted as we were, we just sank into various spots in the cove – all within view of the opening to see what was happening down on the beach. Some chose the grassy plot, while others sat on nearby rocks.

Although I'm not sure how any of us could rest until our small boat arrived, it felt good to sit in a spot which wasn't moving. The fear we had earlier felt seemed to vanish as we relaxed. Pap did not appear to be too worried there wasn't a boat yet, and we all accepted a false sense of safety and a security we would live to regret. For the moment, while we caught our breath and felt the solid firmness of ground under us, all thoughts of our mission were given over to exhaustion. We were all tired from the long ride and the day had not gotten much warmer. Our clothes were still damp from the morning mist.

It really amazed me at how well the Frosts, Grandmam and even Pap had adjusted to the daily grind of travel. I didn't know how old any of them were but they did have age on their side. I know my own grandmother would never have withstood the strain of such a trip. Even myself, Tad and Sarah were tired, and we had the advantage of youth. I had momentarily forgotten the Ringolds were used to this type of life. All of them, from Sarah and Tad to Pap and Grandmam, were used to the hardships of arranging secretive meetings, scheduling long arduous trips and foregoing all but the essentials in life to provide for those in need of their help. Even the Frosts had handled the strenuous trip well. Was it inner strength or just plain fear? I recalled an earlier conversation with Sarah about the Frosts.

"They be used to travelin' 'round from one village t'the next, promotin' Puritan ideals," Sarah had said. "Don' ye worry 'bout them none – they be used to it, and probably wouldna' been so eager to get away if'n it ha'na' been for their son and family. Ya' see, they were killed by sold'rs f'r settin' up a meetin.' They though' the location were secure, bu' turns out, like 'appens many times, tha' someone wan'in' revenge tol' the local constable abou' the meetin'. Albert and Mistress Frost got t'the meetin' a bit late tha' af'rnoon 'cause o' their w'rk in gettin' some folk safely away t'nother part o' the country. When theys did 'rive, all they found were dead folk and sold'rs. They didna' stay 'round. Once burial 'rangements were made, it were pretty mandatory they move on. They also were instrumental in writin' sev'ral pap'rs tha' ha' been distrib'ted throughou' the 'und'rgr'nd system.' The two really ha' an urgent need to leave the country."

I shivered at the thought of what they must have been through. It was similar to Pap's story. Until my woodland excursion, I had certainly lived a very sheltered and pampered life. I had a lot to learn about the world outside Grafton Manor.

We hadn't been in the cove very long when Pap got up and headed for the shoreline.

"Wan' I should come wi' ye?" Tad asked.

Pap held up his hand. "I jest be stretchin' the legs." He disappeared from sight as he followed the rocky cliff down to the beach. I couldn't stand not knowing what was going on and I don't think Tad could either. We both followed him to the edge of the cove where we had a good look at the water and the beach. I think we were all getting a bit anxious as we saw the afternoon slipping away. I hoped the smaller boat would show up soon or we would be going out to the ship in the dark. We watched Pap pacing back and forth. I suspect he thought a problem had arisen and he was a little worried. I know he didn't want to upset the rest of us, but I couldn't help the panic I was feeling and the knot growing in my stomach. Where was the boat which should have been anchored on the shore?

Then, not more than a few feet from where he stood was movement. It was a man and a boat. It was almost a mirage, as if he had appeared out of nowhere. One minute there was nothing. The next, the man was climbing out and docking the boat. I thought for a moment it might be Jeb. From our distance I couldn't see his face. But I didn't recognize the clothing. Add a long white beard – it was the face of a stranger.

"Who is that person?" I asked Tad.

"Don' know," he said, as we watched the tottery, ragged and white- bearded man emerge from the run-down fishing skiff. He seemed a bit disoriented – almost as if he didn't know what he was supposed to do or why he was there. Maybe he was checking out the rocks and finding a place to anchor the water craft – if one could call it such. His boat was so decrepit I doubted it could stay afloat long enough to get away from the rock-encrusted shoreline and out to the waiting ship. There were patches of color mixed in with the gray and the small boat must have once been beautifully painted or oiled. Now the boards were so gray with rot they appeared to be almost porous.

"Do they call that a seaworthy boat," I asked Tad. "Disastrous and unsafe is how I see it. I hope they have a bucket for dipping water out as it skims out into the sea."

"I didna' thin' ye knew much 'bout boats and oceans. And t'tell ye the truth, ye'd be s'prised at how strong and water tight tha' old boat might'n still be," Tad said. "It don' look like much, but I ha' seen worse. Much worse."

I felt sorry and worried about any of us climbing into what I considered a stack of wood ready for the wreckage pile. Even I, who was young and sporting for an adventure, although not so eagerly as before, would not be too keen on taking a watery ride. I think Pap had thought we might join the Frosts and board the big ship, but I could see we all could not possibly fit into the small skiff. It would probably sink before we got past the rocks.

Thinking about climbing aboard the dilapidated boat and the dead soldier brought back memories of other times my adventurous nature had placed me in unsafe situations. While we waited for Pap, I recalled those long ago days at Grafton Manor and told Tad a story about my wild childhood.

* * *

"You should have seen some of the adventures Nathan and I had. I was kind of a rowdy in those days and Nathan and I often found our selves in danger. Sometimes a few of the older children on our estate would take part in our escapades, and on occasion, our elder brother David might join us. But most of the time he was too much of a prude to take part in what we younger children did."

"What fun we had in those days," I said with just a twist of wistful reminiscing. "Nathan and I would often ride our horses out into the fields at a fast pace – dashing through the thickets and not giving a second thought to the dangers lurking from low-hanging branches or protruding tree roots."

"There were the times we hid from the elders secretly in the heavily-scented, suffocating stacks of straw and hay in the fields on our estate. The huge mounds of dried grass drew us into their fold – an excellent place to hide from each other, tutors or even Mother or Father. There was an especially large pile near the stables we likes to pounce in or slide down the side. Mother had cautioned us many a time not to hide in the hay stacks. But we would just laugh and keep right on hiding from each other in the moldy stacks. Once I fell asleep in the straw pile and was discovered by David. I could hardly breathe by the time he found me. Thank goodness Nathan told on me. It was late afternoon one day when Nathan I had been hiding from each other. I had kept waiting and waiting for Nathan to find me, but I guess he must have gotten tired of playing. I found out later, he had gone off to play with a boy who lived on the estate. When I hadn't shown up for afternoon tea and treats, mother became worried."

"When David found me, he reiterated her words." 'Those stacks are extremely dangerous,' he had scolded. 'You might easily have smothered in there had I not found you. And, you never know when one of the farm workers will come along with the hay prongs, stabbing into the stacks and gathering straw for the animals.'"

"Not being able to catch my breath and catching a bad case of the sniffles sort of deterred me from the hay stacks after that," I said. "It gave me goose bumps to think of being pronged by a fork. But I guess the incident didn't do much to keep me from trying other dangerous things. Nathan and I liked to pretend we were a brave knight and courageous maiden as we walked on fallen trees and limbs across rain-swollen creeks and rivers. Between Nathan and me, we had quite an imagination, often stirred by the books we read and the lessons in our classroom."

* * *

"I guess I didn't slow down much on my adventures considering it was just a few months ago I rode into the autumn sunshine. You might say the ride proved to be a bit unsafe for me," I said. "Or perhaps it was a good omen. Just look where I ended up. But for my adventurous nature I would not have met you and your family."

"I was sure all 'long ye were a 'venturous vixen," Tad said. "Y'r stories only confirm wha' I be suspectin' 'bout ye."

"After hearing my story, have you changed your mind about me?" I asked.

"I thin' not. I a'ways wan'ed a 'venturous lass f'r me girl," he said.

I gave Tad a big smile, grabbed his hand and squeezed it. "I thank ye for that," I said.

I returned to the reality of watching Pap and the boatman. Pap did not seem to be the least bit perturbed about the boat's appearance or its occupant. From our short distance, Tad and I both smiled as we saw the frown disappear from Pap's face and he broke out into a hearty hello and laughter.

"Ahoy there," we heard Pap yell above the noise of the waves as he approached the boat and the stranger. "Wha' be keepin' ye? Where be Jeb? Isna' he joinin' us? We ha' been here quite a while. And normally tha' wouldna' matter, but I thin' we are not so safe as we ha' been in the past."

Pap waved to us, hollered for us "to stay put" as he climbed over the rocks, to what some might call a floating wooden cockleshell and greeted its captain. He and the man hailed each other heartily. I surmised from their greeting they were old friends, although later I learned this was a misconception on my part. In fact, it was their first encounter. All the arrangements for the man to show up at the beach had been made through Jeb who had contacted a local resident. The conversation seemed, at least from where we sat, congenial enough at first.

Tad and I sat on a rock near the inner cove, content to let time pass without conversation. As the two men carried out the preliminaries of their greeting, I glanced at them with only slight interest. My mind wandered aimlessly again, as it was wont to do these days. I was beginning to wonder about my distractions the last few days and decided it was partly because my body was drained of ambition and the power of concentration.

* * *

I dreamily watched the clouds in the fading daylight. The sun was fading slowly, beginning its retreat into the horizon for the day. Its yellowish golden glow radiated sparks of white-light which filled the late afternoon sky. The sun alternately slipped in and out from behind white cottony, mushroom-shaped puffs of clouds, playing hide and seek with the rocky, violet-colored asymmetrical shapes of the rocks and cliffs in the distance. It was another one of those moments in time when I felt the glorious wonder of God's presence. How at peace I felt for those few minutes. I, who had never really taken the time on my own to acknowledge the glory of God, was amazed at my own thoughts. That I could think so profoundly – and twice, within the same afternoon.

My tutors from my old school days would surely have been astounded at this since I was never one for deep serious thoughts back in the classroom. I, like Nathan, was a dreamer and had not given religious beliefs and God much time in my short numbered years, at least by my own choice. That is, until now. Had my way of thinking about God and religion changed so much in just the short time I had known the Ringolds? Could I have so easily become influenced by these people and their way of thinking? Or was I just at the right place and time to experience the way God works. It would seem perhaps this was so.

I was surprised at how much I had absorbed because the Ringolds never spent a lot of time discussing their religion or even political views. Those concepts were intricately woven into their life. I had gathered more than just a smithering of information and knowledge in the past few months through osmosis – it was as though their scattered, short and fragmented thoughts, sentences and actions had become part of me. Pap and Grandmam were always saying such things as "No king should ha' power over man." I had heard this time and again from them, as well as Sarah and Tad. "Only God should 'xact sech a toll on man and set the rules," Pap had said on several occasions, and with animosity. "It be every man's choice to'respect and follow these rules."

I was surprised I felt in total agreement. I know my father had extolled the virtues and rules of the kings most of the time. But those beliefs were part of his training as a barrister. I had grown up under the guidance of following papal beliefs and the king's laws, which at various times were not always on the same plane of thought. That was the climate in what I once called home. My father would have never understood disobeying rules of the church and making the king's rules fit into those beliefs. In future years I would look back with wonder on those long ago days with my family and my adventures with the Ringolds. I will sit and ponder on the rising and setting of the sun, the beauty of a starlit evening, the power and glory of God and to relive these delicious moments of peace I was feeling now. I think the impetuous youth I had been was getting a brief glimpse of new philosophical convictions that might follow me all my days. It was a new and exciting experience for me. Some might call it my moment of awakening. I wanted to share those feelings about God and his breathtaking, mystical beauty of golden clouds.

"Look at the sky, Tad. It is as if God is telling us to be safe," I said.

It was as if we were one. He caught my thoughts and feelings about the ethereal beauty before us. He reached for my hand and gave me one of his sweet smiles. He seemed about to say something when our dreamy thoughts were interrupted and we were jolted back to the present by a ruckus on the shore.

* * *

From the dock, the two voices of Pap and the old man began to increase in volume. The tones reaching our ears were short, angry staccato-like sounds, rising and swelling to a musical crescendo. It was like the ocean itself when the tides roll in and out, bellowing and roaring as the waves hit the sand and rock. Our attention suddenly became attuned to the two as we strained to hear the angry words being exchanged and the impact of what seemed to be an argument.

Soon Pap's head was nodding sporadically and he threw his hands into the air. Once he even turned and looked toward us, nodding his head and jerking his thumb, then pounding his fists in his palms. We couldn't really tell what the problem was but the two appeared to be haggling like fishwives about something. They were both talking loudly now, but the roar of the waves hitting and bouncing on the shore made it impossible to catch the whole conversation. They also had their backs to us and we could only hear brief words such as late, money, midnight, ship, safety and payments. We even heard Jeb's name shouted a couple of times. We guessed from the bits of conversation that Pap was agitated and angry with the arrangements.

Grandmam came over to where Tad and I were sitting. Like us, she had been watching the goings on at the beach. "Tad, do ya' thin' ye better get on down their and see wha' be the matter?" she asked. Her brow wrinkled and her voice cracked with concern. "Can ye hear wha' they be sayin'? I cain' tell, but it sure don' sound like Pap be 'appy wi' the gen'leman there."

"Don' worry Grandman," Tad said, trying to sound unconcerned. But I could detect the tenseness in his voice. "Pap ha' been doin' quite nicely wi'out help from me or ye wi' his 'rangements in the past. I thin' ev'ry thin' will be a'right. They jest ha' t'w'rk out a few misunderstandin's far as I can tell."

Despite Tad's indifference, I perceived all was not well and hoped it was not too serious. The only thing I could piece together from the few words were heard was the old man must have thought he was not properly being paid for such a risky job. We sat, rather impatiently, watching the scene at the dock. As I looked at the two men, it struck me rather humorously and I had to stop myself from laughing right out loud. They seemed almost like the street mimers I had seen once at a fair in Skipton. They were waiving and flinging their arms in the air as though they were chasing clouds of insects from their faces or practicing some kind of signaling code. But the fact of the matter was Pap seemed very upset.

Again Grandman turned to Tad. "Do ya thin' me boy tha' ye might'n be getting' down there and findin' out wha' be happenin'?" I noticed panic in her voice as she gave Tad a slight nudge.

This time Tad took her advice. "I thin' ye be 'bout right and was beginn' t'thin' the same."

He got up and started down to the beach. I got up to follow, but Grandmam motioned for me to stay and wait. By this time the rest of our party had seen our concern. We all had gathered close together as renewed fear placed its stranglehold on us. Sarah reached for my hand and gave it a squeeze as we both tried to comfort each other.

"Don' worry; it canna' be anythin' too distressin'," Grandmam said. She tried her best to comfort us with boastful words and more confidence than I'm sure she felt by saying "those men can take care o' the sit'ation." None of us were fooled for a minute.

"Tad jest went down to see 'bout the delay. 'Member, God takes care o' his shepherds," she said. "I thin' it might'n only be some little financial dis'greement between Pap and tha' man wi' the boat. Some o' these ol' sea capt'ns thin' the sea is theirs and they can be mighty cantankerous."

Grandmam winked and burst forth with a nervous laugh as she tried to ease the seriousness of the situation. I did notice the Frosts moved closer together. I speculated whether it was fear of the pending new danger we all felt, or only a need to offer comfort and encouragement to each other as Tad and I had. We watched for a few minutes more, then Tad and Pap came back up the beach toward us while the good captain, if indeed that's what he was, began making apparent preparations. What did it all mean? Pap did not look nearly as angry as before, but he wasn't smiling either. Was the deal still on for the Frosts or was the boatman taking off without them? We started down the beach toward the two men, anxiously awaiting news of the plans.

"It be all set, finally," Pap said. "Seems either our friend Jeb didna' take care o' all the 'rangements or the ol' man be misinformed from the local. 'Nyways, he panicked when he saw all o' ye on the beach. He ha' only been 'xpectin' one person t'take out t'the ship. Wait 'til I get a hol' o' tha' Jeb."

"Where be the ol' man?" Grandmam asked. "Why 'asna' he shown his whiskery ol' face? Been sippin' too much ale to take care o' his bus'ness?

"Now Grandmam, don' be so mean," Pap said. "I don' know 'bout Jeb and the capt'n down their didna' seem t'know much 'bout 'im either. I cert'nly do won'er where he be. Na' like him – he a'ways 'as all the details in place. He prob'ly be at the local tavern sippin' ale an' thin'in' ev'ry thin is goin' 'cordin' t'plan. Tha' poor man down there, his name be Tinker, ha' no idea why it were so 'mperative t'get these pe'ple boarded and didna' know they be a deadline. Tha' be why he were so late, and I guess tha' be fine by me. The fewer pe'ple know wha' we be doin', the safer we be."

"Tinker also werena' tol' t'be secretive so he mentioned his sailin' contract t'a few o' his frien's there in the village," Pap said. "It 'pears the ol' boy seems t'enjoy his ale as much as our frien' Jeb and boasted las' night in the tav'rn tha' come t'night he'd be treatin' f'r drinks 'cause he be doin' a little boatin' job. I asked Tinker if'n very many pe'ple coulda' he'rd his boast. He swore on the good book it were only a couple o' his frien's he tol' 'bout his good fortune. We may be in more trouble than we bargained f'r but I guess tha' canna be helped now."

"But he can take us to the ship?" asked Albert.

"Yes, but there be a bit o' problem," Pap said. "Seems the contact fellow tol' the good cap'n we would pay him af'r delivery ou' t'the ship. I asked him if'n he ha' a'ready got part o' his cash. He didna' and was confused 'bout the

243

whole bus'ness. Still canna' thin' wha' Jeb be doin' and why he wouldna' ha' paid him half in 'vance like we a'ways do and the rest af'r he returned t'the village. Jeb knows we ha' a'ways done our trips tha' way. I didna' ha the cash to gi' the cap'n, but asked him if'n he would be a'right gettin' his fee t'morrow. He 'greed rather reluctantly and said he be at the tavern in the mornin' He threatened tha' if'n I didna' show up, he would waste no time findin' sold'rs or the local dep'ty."

Pap laughed and said, "As if tha' 'asna' a'ready 'appened this trip. 'Nyway, soon as I and the cap'n get the Frosts out t'sea and put them 'bo'rd the ship, we be comin' back. The rest o' us will be goin' t'the village to see if'n we can find Jeb. I do ha' a bit o' money and 'ope it be 'nough. I don' wan' no 'ditional price on my head. So the good cap'n be waitin' for ye Albert and Mistess Frost."

"I don't have much money with me," Albert said. "But I'd be glad to help out with whatever I can. I feel bad we have caused people so much inconvenience. Ye know I am beholding to ye. I don't know if I'll ever be able to repay all those who have pledged to help us make this trip."

"Don' ye worry none," Pap said. "We be takin' care o' ever'thin'. Ye ha' a'ready paid wha' ye can t'get on t'a safe haven. There be many in the arms o' God right here in England willin' t'help pay f'r those who ha'na' means t'pay. I know it be 'ard on ye, 'specially when ye be used t'thin's a bit nicer. Jest 'member, God takes care o' those he loves. And it 'pears tha' we all canna' be gettin' on tha' ship like we ha' talked 'bout. Firs', it don' look like we need t'hurry 'nywhere's so we can jest run down to Grandman's fam'ly f'r a while 'til we figure ou' wha' t'do. Second, there isna' 'nough room in tha' boat down there t'carry us all t'the ship and we still ha' the 'orses t'thin' 'bout. Tha' were one o' Jeb's tasks. If'n we were leavin', he were t'take the 'orses and sell them. For the life o' me, I canna' figure ou' where the man be. F'r now, best get Albert and Mistress Frost t'safety. Tad, run and fetch the Frost's thin's from the 'orses so we can get goin' t'the sailin' ship."

Tad turned and traipsed across the distance into the cove where the animals were hidden, leaving his departing footsteps in the sand. I thought how the pattern of those foot prints gave me a feeling of loneliness as they stretched in the space from me and the others across the austere gray rocks. I shook my head to get rid of such sad feelings.

"I noticed that boat does not look very seaworthy from here." Albert said. "Are the missus and I going to be alright?"

"It mightna' be the most 'commodatin' skiff I ever seen in my day and it do look a bit o' dilapidated. But ye won' ha' t'worry 'bout gettin' out t'the big ship," Pap said. "God speed ye on y'r journey, and keep up the good work ye ha' been doin'. Wi'out men like ye, our destiny wi' God might'n not ha' been so successful."

Tad returned with the Frosts' baggage. We hurriedly said good-bye to the couple so they could get on with their journey. Grandmam gave Mistress Frost a hug, saying "Good luck my dear. The Lord 'bove gi' ye 'is blessin's and a good strong wind t'blow ye safely 'cross the sea. The rest of us gave hugs and shook hands, expressing our best wishes for a safe ocean voyage. Albert shook my hand.

"As for ye young miss, I think this journey has been more of an education than ye have bargained for. Again I thank you for all the risks you have taken for a cause that wasn't remotely yours, especially in regards to your own future. I suspect your ideas of life have greatly changed and I hope God is smiling down on ye and protecting ye. I've also noticed the look ye have for Tad. I used to have that same yearning for Mistress Frost. I hope ye's future will include that young man and you will have years of happiness as we have had, despite our current problems. God bless ye."

As Pap turned to walk down to the boat, he handed Tad a money pouch. "Ye knows the plan if'n 'nythin' 'appens t'me. Don' waste time if'n ye see 'ny trouble. Jest get the 'orses an' y'rselves ou' o' here best ye can."

"Are ye goin' ou' wi' them then?" asked Tad.

"Aye, I wan' t'make sure they get bo'rded safely. Tinker said he would bring me back t'shore and meet me t'morrow f'r his money."

"It doesna' seem like there by 'ny trouble," Tad said.

Pap only held up his hand and said, "Ye never know. Do as I tell ye lad. At the firs' sign o' 'ny trouble, whether I be back or na', get up t'the village and make ye self as 'nconspicuous as pos'ble. I be takin' care o' myself best I can and I don' wan' t'worry 'bout 'ny o' ya'. I know ye ha' some money t'cov'r our costs and here be a bit more. Once we get down to Grandmam's brother we kin settle up. And if'n 'nythin' 'appens t'me, get y'rself t'the tavern t'morrow an' take care o' payin' Tinker. Once tha' be done, ye can get on down t'Grandmam's fam'ly. I can find ye there if'n we get separated."

We watched Pap and the Frosts walk down the beach toward the skiff taking them on out to the sailing ship. I think we all breathed a sign of relief our long journey was coming to an end. It seemed all was well even though I still didn't know how this adventure would end for me and the Ringolds. I felt some closure was taking place and I could begin to think about a future with Tad and his family. But, as with the rest of this journey, fate was again at our doorstep and awaiting another opportunity to alter our lives.

CHAPTER FOURTEEN

Dangerous Mission

Pap and the Frosts hurried down the sandy, rocky beach
to the awaiting boat. We watched Pap introduce Albert and
his missus to the captain. They shook hands and talked a
few minutes. Then the captain motioned for them to climb
aboard the sea craft. Once they were seated, he climbed in
and motioned Pap to push them out to sea. We could see Pap
was taking his time, looking around carefully at the scenery
and checking to make sure they were safe. I guess he felt
there was no sign of danger or any kind of trouble because
he turned and waved to us. He began pushing the weathered
boat off the rocks and out into the foamy waters. The four
were on their way to the Sea Witch – what I had labeled as the
"freedom ship."

Once Pap was aboard, he sat at the back of the boat,
manning the rudder. In the middle of the boat, the captain was
doing the rowing, trying to keep the oars under control and
not bending in towards the boat as the waves smashed into
them. The Frosts huddled together in front of the boat. We
watched the weathered boat tossing, bouncing and enduring
the waves lapping at its sides and finally rushing and smashing
ashore on the beach. I hoped the Frost would be on board

ship before dark. The sun was beginning its downward slide into the horizon. And the western sky was a soft orange with whispers of clouds. Before long, the evening sky would be upon us with a new challenge of riding up along the rocks to get back to the trail. Maybe we would have a star-filled night, although it had been cloudy all day and I suspected many would be hiding.

My gaze turned towards ship. There still seemed to be no movement. "Will they not put the sails up until the Frosts are aboard," I asked Tad.

"Don' know," he aswered. "I would'a though' they might'n ha' them up a'ready since they wan'ed t'get out into the seas jest soon as the pass'gers bo'rded. They 'as t'get out while the tide is runnin' high. Seems odd they don' ha' the sails up a'ready, but then I don' be knowin' how those sailin' folk thin' or run their ship."

We had no more than finished our conversation when in the distance I could see the sails beginning to go up the rigging. I pointed at them and Tad nodded.

"Looks like they do mean t'sail soon as the Frosts are 'bo'rd," Tad said.

"How long do you think it will be until Pap comes back?" I asked. "Is there anything we can do or are we to just sit and wait?"

"We could ha' a bite to eat," said Grandmam. "It ha' been a long time since we ha' some sustenance."

"Sure, tha' would be good," Tad said to Grandmam. And to me, he said, "Pap were not sure how long t'would be a'fore he got back. He said for us t'keep back into tha' smaller cove and jest rest. He didna' foresee 'ny trouble an' though' it might'n be a good time f'r us t'catch up on some much needed rest a'fore we head into the village."

"That's a good idea, since we don't know where we will stay for the night or what kind of greeting awaits us," I said. "How far is it down to your brother Artie's home? Is this his village – the one we are going to for the night?"

"My, ain' ye jest full o' questions," Grandmam answered instead of Tad. "Me brother lives in a little coastal town jest south o' here and we wouldna' be but 'nother day gettin' there."

"And as f'r where we be stayin' t'night, I don' know," Tad said. "Pap be takin' care o' those 'rangements when he gets back since it 'pears our frien' Jeb didna'. He were 'sposed t'take care o' ev'rythin' we needed."

"Jeb was supposed to be here wasn't he?" I asked. "Where do ye think he might be?"

"Don' get me started on tha' no good louse," interjected Grandmam. "He most likely be at the local tav'rn swizzlin' down his share o' ale. Prob'ly thins' he 'as ev'rythin' 'ranged and we don' need him. He sometimes don' see tha' he be part o' our worries."

"Now Grandmam, be kind," Sarah said. "He be a fam'ly frien' even if'n ye don' thin' so kindly 'bout him. 'Member, God said we must forgive our enemies and ya' don' know – may be he 'as ha' some trouble."

"Don' lecture me none, young'un," Grandmam said to Sarah.

"I guessed Jeb be 'round," Tad said. "I don' know wha' he and Pap 'ranged. I thin' Pap were so disturbed by tha' small boat he kind o' f'rgot t'find out where Jeb mightn't be. I guess we will jest ha' to wait 'til Pap returns. It canna' take too long t'get out' t'the big ship. Bu' the distance on wat'r sometimes be a might d'ceivin'. Wha' seems kind o' funny t'me is there didna' seem t'be movement on tha' big ship 'til jest a bit ago

249

when the sails wen' up. I woulda' thought ev'n from here we would be seein' some o' the crew workin' and gettin' ready t'take off when they's pass'gers 'rive. I thin' it seems kind o' odd."

"May be we should be movin' back into tha' cove where we 'as a bit more protection," Tad added, sounding a little anxious. The four of us moved further into the cove, but curiosity soon got the better of us. Before long we were standing back at the entrance. I suppose that is when we began putting our hands up to our eyes, like we had spy glasses, and tried to see what was happening on the water. My stomach seemed to be doing flip-flops and I had a bad feeling all of a sudden about this whole ship business. Still, nothing seemed unusual. The small craft was fighting the waves as it made its way closer and closer to its destination. Suddenly, the small skiff seemed to be turning around. It was sort of spinning, almost as if it were in a whirlpool. For a moment it looked like they were heading back to the beach. It was hard to tell with the wind tossing them about. It was then we could see some activity on the ship. The stick figures were running back and forth. In the distance, we could hear an unusual rumble.

"What do ye make o' it?" Grandmam asked Tad. "What da ye' thin' be the matter? I don' like the looks o' it."

"I don' either," he said. "I thin' we need t'be ready t'leave at a moment's notice. We need t'get our 'orses here by our side so we can leave if'n we need."

Before we could even turn to get the horses and bring them closer, there was a loud hiss and a thundering crack. Then we saw flames and pieces of Tinker's boat flying into the air. The small craft seemed to be exploding.

"What's happenin'?" Sarah said. "Can ye make out wha' be goin' on?"

The small craft continued spinning around as smoke and orange flames reached for the sky. We couldn't even see the big ship because smoke filled the space where it was anchored. We stood there in stunned silence for a few seconds until Sarah screamed. Tad turned around to shush her, and then took her in his arms. They stood entwined together. Then Tad reached for me and pulled me close to them.

"Oh my God, my God," I uttered as the tears began to stream down my cheeks. "What is happening? What caused the flames? Do you think they could have gotten out? The poor Frosts – they were so close to freedom."

Tad's face was pure white and his eyes were filled with tears. "The pe'ple on the ship jest blew them out o' the water," he said in astonishment.

"Why would they do that?" I asked. "I thought we were safe here."

The smoke began to clear as we stood there watching and trying to see any sign of the small boat. But there was nothing. The sails were up and blowing in the wind as the big ship began slowly moving out to sea, leaving only a huge wake and small pieces of burning wood.

I turned to Grandmam to console her. But she brushed me away. Then she spoke so calmly it scared me, "Tad, pull y'rself t'gether. We 'as no time t'waste. We need t'get out o' here fast as we can. Run boy, and get them 'orses. Ye knows wha' Pap would 'xpec' out o' ye. We canna' stay 'round to see if'n anyone got away a'fore the 'xplosion. We ha' to do our grievin' later."

I was surprised at her stamina and how she was taking charge when we were all utterly shattered. Tad was running across the sand toward the animals. I should have helped him but I was just too stunned. I was rooted to my spot still trying to sort out what had gone wrong. I had expected there might be some trouble, but I never dreamed it would lead to this. And in the back of my mind was the nagging thought I was partly to blame for this horrific and tragic event. I turned to look skyward and said to the God I had newly found: "What were you thinking God? They were such good people. Did you need both Pap and the Frosts up there to help you? Couldn't we have had Pap to help us?"

"Get y'rself on a 'orse, Lucky," Tad said gruffly, handing me the reins of Seesaw. I gave her a hug and told her we had to hurry out of this place.

We followed Tad back the way we had come down across the beach. We were a quiet group. The sadness had left us doing what had to be done routinely. The urgency of finding a safe haven kept us going. As we rode up the beach, we could still see fire bouncing on the waves. One would think it would have gone out with all that water around it.

In the early twilight, the sailing ship was almost out of sight now. And just as it had seemed eerie and ghostly when we rode onto the beach, so now it had the same effect. Who was the enemy? We could only guess it was soldiers. There had been no flag on the ship, although it appeared Pap had seemed to recognize it. Hadn't he called it by name? But when I thought about it, I remember he wasn't quite so sure it was the same ship he had used on several other occasions. There were a lot of questions and it was obvious none of us knew where to look for the answers. As tired as we were of being on our horses, it seemed only logical we would further depend on them for our future.

By the time we had retrieved the horses and mounted up, darkness had flooded the sky. Adjusting to the dim light, we carefully wound our way across the sand and back up the path through the rocks and weed patches to the main trail. I had lost track of time, but my stomach told me it was well past the dinner hour. We hadn't gotten around to Grandmam's "bite to eat" with all the concern about the small boat and its passengers. By the time we rode across the beach and found the road into the neighboring village, it was getting well into the evening.

Every little sound echoed in our ears and when Tad heard something he wasn't sure what it was, he would hold up his hand and motion us to stop. Then we would hear nothing except the splashing waves hitting the shore. Except for that it was dead calm. Dead – what about the Frosts and Pap? Were they all dead? It seemed impossible anyone of them could have escaped. How awful it must have been on their little boat. Did they see the movement on the sailing ship and think there was something wrong? I still wondered if they had been trying to turn back or if it was just the water and wind spinning them around. What about the old man? Would there be anyone looking for him? Was he a victim of circumstances or was he the one who led Pap and the Frosts into danger?

I caught up with Tad, reaching out to touch his shoulder in sympathy.

"I am so sorry." I spoke softly so my voice wouldn't carry into the night. "I know how ye loved your Pap. I have come to love him too, perhaps even more than my own father."

He nodded and said, "Pap thought a lot o' ye. I thank ye for carin'."

"How far is it to the village?" I asked. "We didn't go very near it when we rode in."

"Na' far, at least I don' thin. I 'asna' been to this p'rticul'r point or village a'fore," Tad said softly. "This whole trip 'as been a new 'xperience f'r us 'cause Pap were so worried 'bout sold'rs knowin' his reg'lar pattern o' helpin' and gettin' pe'ple out t'the big ships. Several times in the pas' he brought fo'k to tha' town 'cause it be a small place where they would jest catch a ship in p'rt. When he he'rd 'bout this cove, he thought it a good idea. On various trips ou' this way he talked to the locals who tol' him 'bout this place. It be jest really odd tha' Jeb didna' show up. How be ev'ryone doin'?"

"I think we won't know until we get to safety," I said. "I feel it is partly my fault. And maybe, just maybe, Pap got away. Is he a good swimmer?"

"Don' count on 'nyone gettin' back to shore," Tad said sadly. "Tha' boat was blown apart. I don' thin' there be 'ny survivors."

I could see my talking to Tad was choking him up and he was having a hard time trying to be strong, brave and in charge. I backed off and let Sarah and Grandmam pass by. I don't know why I thought I should be last. I didn't know what to do if anyone took aim at me or anyone else in the party. I didn't have a gun. And having a gun had once got me in a heap of trouble. Wasn't I part of the reason we were riding away from the sea with a coat of sadness so thick it would take a very warm sun to melt it. So far, there didn't seem to be anyone else about. By this time it was getting quite dark and finding our way among the rocks and small trees was becoming very difficult. I don't know which was worse, having the darkness and not knowing what was going on around us or not having it dark enough that we couldn't hide easily if we needed to.

Just as I was beginning to question whether we would find our way to the village, I saw the twinkling of lamp lights coming from a few windows in the near distance. Soon we found the road leading into the heart of the ocean-side settlement. I was surprised Tad turned onto the road instead of staying just off to the side as we had done throughout our journey. But with the dark, he probably felt it would be safer. And too, I guess he was just as anxious as the rest of us to get this night over with. I wondered if he had any ideas about what we were going to do once we were in the village. All Pap had told him was to get to the village as fast as he could if there was trouble. And trouble there certainly had been. I was still reeling from the explosion and I was sure the rest of our party was just as stunned. I wanted to just to stop and cry, but grieving would have to wait. We had to think about our selves and what was in store for us now without Pap to guide us. Where would fate lead us now? All we could do was put our trust in God that he would get us through this difficult time.

Again I rode up next to Tad and asked if there was a plan. "What do you think we should do?" I asked. "Do you know the contact person or do you have a name?"

"I don' even know where t'start," he answered. "I don' ha' a name. All's I know was Jeb were s'posed t'be at the boat t'help. I don' understand wha' 'as 'appened and why he werena' there. I guess the only thin' we can do is 'ope they be a comf'r'ble inn and see if'n they be 'ny rooms 'vailable. I don' know if'n our money be 'nough. Pap did gi' me a bit in case there be a 'mergency. An', I guess we won' ha' t'pay the boatman in the mornin'. I don' thin' he be sharin' ale wi' 'is frien's 'ny time soon. I thin' af'r we fin' a room an' ye three be settled, I mightn' jest step down t'the tav'rn and see if'n Jeb be there and get a lay o' the land. I know ye all be wantin' t'help, but I thin' this plan will ha' to do f'r the night. It wouldna' be seemly for ye ladies t'go inside sech an establishment, 'specially at night."

Tad seemed to be thinking out loud as he said, "Come firs' light, I thin' we should get back down the road t'Uncle Artie's place. He mightn' ha' some ideas and he surely needs t'know 'bout Pap. I can check out t'see if'n there be any sold'rs 'round here or if'n they were all on the ship. We canna' count out tha' the ship might'n a been full o' pirates. I he'rd tell o' tha' 'appenin' of'n, though it nev'r 'as 'appened to Pap. I thin' he would ha' spurned the idea. More'n likely, tha' ship were full o' sold'rs and once they got the boat they were t'leave. I don' thin' we ha' t'worry so much 'cause I don' thin' they could see us. We were far 'nough from the water. But we be needin' t'be on guard f'r a while."

"I think you have a good plan," I said, trying to console Tad on the huge responsibility which had fallen into his lap. "Grandmam may have some ideas. And just maybe Pap or Jeb might have mentioned to her the name of the contact person."

We rode on into the village in silence. There didn't seem to be anyone about. Many of the cottages we rode by were dark, and as late as it was, I assumed at least a few villagers might have turned in for the night. How I wished I could be asleep in a nice warm bed. We continued on down the main street of the small berg. The shops were closed and shuttered, except for the inn and tavern. It appeared the two were joined together. How convenient I thought. Once Tad found a room, he could just slip down and see what was going on in the tavern. As we rode by, it didn't seem overly noisy like some taverns I had seen when Father and I had gone to villages near our home.

Grandmam rode up beside Tad "I thin' us ladies should stay in the shadows while ye go into the inn," she said. "Why don' me and the girls jest wait for ye up 'round tha' corner. Be sure t'find out 'bout stables and wha' be the cost. I don' know if'n ye be 'ware, but I ha' some money tha' I ha' saved through the years. It be my life savin's and some moneys I got from y'r grandfather's fam'ly when he died. Guess I ha' been good at savin' but we can use it if'n need be. An' Pap ha' taken good care o' us."

Tad stopped in front of the inn and tavern and motioned for us to go on up the street and wait for him there. He watched to make sure we were safe before turning into the inn. The town seemed eerie to me. I think we were all feeling the effects of the explosion and thinking danger was lurking for us at every corner.

"How are you doing Sarah?" I asked.

She shivered. "Awful," she answered. Although I couldn't see the tears, I could feel her grief and knew the tears must be running down her cheeks.

"Wha' do ye thin' wen' wrong?" she asked. "I know Pap and I ha' talked a'fore 'bout this kind o' thin' 'appenin' sometime. But ye never thin' it be y'r turn to feel the brunt o' the religious battles. Pap jest went 'bout his bus'ness and nev'r ga' danger much thought.

"Grandmam, are you alright?" I asked as I reached out and tried to put my arm around her shoulder while still keeping my horse under control.

"I don' thin' I be feelin' anythin'," she said. "I feel dead like Pap. We ha' been lucky all these years o' Pap helpin' others. I thin' we a'ways knew there would be a day. It be so hard 'cause it ain' nothin' ye can pr'pare for. But Pap be in a better place now. He and the Frosts be lyin' in the arms o' the Lord. Well, the cap'n, too. We don' know much 'bout him, bu' he surely do need t'know God 'as been watchin' ov'r him. I know Pap be lookin' down and helpin' Tad thin' through wha' t'do.

It be a big 'sponsibility f'r the lad. An' I don' like to say bad thin's 'bout other folk, but I blame Jeb. He ha' been slippin' on his duties lately. I thin' he be helpin' the king's men and I ain' so sure tha' Pap didna' thin' the same. I jest would like to see tha' dowdy man and gi' him a piece o' my mind."

"Now calm down Grandmam," Sarah said. "We canna' bring Pap back and it don' do no good t'blame other folks when we don' know the whole story."

Sarah always seemed to find the good in people and situations, no matter how bad it appeared. I admired her for that. I was not feeling forgiving at the moment and wanted desperately to have some answers. I was angry at Jeb, the soldiers and anyone else who fought against the right to practice whatever faith and political concepts they wanted.

I shivered, not only from the sadness we all felt, but from the evening's chill. How good a warm fire would feel. I hoped our room at the inn would have a fireplace so we could warm ourselves. I was wishing Tad would hurry. Waiting on the street corner didn't seem the safest spot and with our extra horses, I thought we looked rather conspicuous.

"Wha' do ye thin' is takin' Tad so long?" asked Sarah. "I am freezin' here and my 'orse is even shiverin'. I so 'ope he can find somethin' f'r us. I am jest so tired."

"Take it easy there lass," Grandmam said to Sarah. "It ha' been a very sad day, but I know ye can be strong. I need ye t'do tha' for me 'til we can get down to Artie's place."

It was another five or ten minutes before Tad came around the corner and saw us. "I got us a room," he said as he rode up. "It were not so costly, but I be 'fraid it isna' very big. Ye girls will ha' t'share the bed and I can sleep on the floor. But ye will be happy t'know, there be a warm fire in the fireplace t'take the chill of'n ye. It will do f'r the night and in the mornin' we

258

be headin' down the road. I wanna' be out early. It seems tha' many o' the rooms are bein' used by sold'rs. I don' wan' to be 'round 'ere very long wi' those fella's. I peeked into the tav'rn and it didna' seem a very rowdy group. There werena' 'ny sold'rs tha' I could see, so I be wonderin' where they be. I thin Grandmam tha' ye and Sarah should go on up t'the room right 'way while Lucky and I take care o' the 'orses. When tha' is done, we be up."

"Oh, and one bit o' news. The 'nnkeeper were 'xpectin' us. Said there be a genle'man in earlier in the week makin' 'rangements f'r him and us," Tad said. "He didna' ha' any other 'nformation 'bout the man, jest tha' he ha' some frien's comin' in. But the odd thin' was tha' he told the 'nnkeeper he would be back later t'make reservations. Then he seemed t'have dis'pear'd. I plan t'question the man more, but though' I should jest get ye settled in firs' and outa' the cold."

We escorted Grandmam and Sarah t'the fr'nt o' the hotel. Tad helped the two down and handed them their belongings.

"Jest go on in and tell the 'nkeeper who ye be, tha' I jest reserved a room f'r the Graftons – I 'ope ye don' mind Lucky tha' I used y'r fam'ly name. He can show ye up. Lock the door. When we come up we'll knock and identify ourselves. I don' thin' there be a problem, but 'cause o' our af'rnoon we canna' be too careful. Sarah, ye come t'the door and wave if'n ev'r thin' seems a'right."

We watched the two of them go into the inn. After a few minutes, Sarah came to the door and waved us on. We waited long enough to see a candle flicker in one of the upstairs windows. That, at least, gave us some sense of security. We rode on down the street leading the extra horses to the stables, located just a few doors away. No one was about and Tad said the innkeeper had told him to jest find a couple o' pens and do what we needed to take care o' our animals.

"I guess the sold'rs ha' their own corral," Tad said. "The keeper said there wouldna' be a problem wi' havin' 'nough room."

The two of us worked together to take care of the horses. It was comforting to do the mundane task of taking saddles off and combing the animals down with brushes lying about the stable. It must have taken us a good hour to complete the task. We worked well together, with neither of us really saying anything – just taking care of the business at hand. When we were finished, I think we both let out a sigh of relief about the same time.

"Are you doin' all right?" I asked.

He nodded, then put his arm around my shoulder.

"How 'bout y'rself?"

"I think I'm fine, but I just can't figure it out. Are you surprised at the turn of events or is this something you expected?" I said.

"I canna' be so surprised," he said quietly. "Ye knows we be in a bus'ness tha' offers danger at ev'ry turn. I canna' say I thought our day would end so tragically. Pap knew the dangers and was a'ways on the lookout. I don' know if'n he 'xpected anythin' or not. I kind o' got a glimpse o' how he was feelin' though when he lef' f'r the boat and tol' me 'bout gettin' away. Foolish tha' I was, I thought he were jest bein' ov'rly cautious. Lookin' back, I thin' he might 'o been jest a wee bit 'fraid – 'specially when Jeb werena' there and tha' strange cap'n were late and not knowin' wha' be goin' on."

"What are we going to do?" I asked. "Are we in danger too?"

"Not sure wha' t'be 'xpectin' next," he said. "I guess there a'ways be the possibil'ty o' us bein' in danger. Don' know wha' the pe'ple on the boat saw – whether they could see us or na'? We couldna' see them very good and I thin' by the time Pap ha' got out t'sea, we were close enough t'the cove tha' we might'n ha' only been small dots. And mayhap they won' care. They got wha' they wan'ed – Pap."

He turned to me and took my hands. Holding them tight, he said, "All I know is I be 'appy ye are 'ere and givin' me strength. I thank ye f'r tha'. Jest hold on and help me when ye can. I thin' Grandmam is strong and I can depend on her help t'make plans f'r the future. Sarah is jest plain 'fraid, but I can feel ye be ready t'fight for anythin' tha' is goin' to 'inder us. I ha' thought f'r a time we would be 'oppin' bo'rd tha' big ship and be on our way t'a new life, but there 'gain, wi' the way ev'ry thin' w'rked out, guess tha' couldna' 'appen. I know there were jest too many o' us, and the final straw I thin' was when tha' derelict boat and it's cap'n rowed into the cove. Pap jest seemed to feel the danger, I thin'. All's I can tell ye is tha' we ha' t'get out o' here firs' light in the mornin.' I don' feel safe here and I don' know wha' t'do next. I don' know if'n Uncle Artie can be much help, but it 'as to be a safe haven for a short time while we figure out where t'go."

We walked the short couple of blocks to the tavern and inn. As we went into that welcoming hostel, the noise from the attached pub seemed to have gotten a bit rowdier than when we first came into the village.

"Soon as we get settled in upstairs, I be comin' back down an' see if'n I can find out any news tha' might be o' 'mportance t'us. I 'specially need to follow up on the fact tha' Jeb were 'ere and now he isna' anywhere t'be found. Tha' be mighty curious, don ye thin'?" Tad said.

I agreed with him, telling him I had been wondering the same thing. Tad greeted the innkeeper who recognized him from his earlier stop.

"Sounds like ye ha' some mighty rowdy patrons t'night," Tad said to the man.

"Sold'rs o' some kind 'as come back into port and they be lettin' off 'n a bit o' steam from their day's w'rk," the innkeeper said. "Long as they pay and don' break thin's up, I don' care."

"Tha' be wha' earnin' a livin' as a tav'rn and 'nkeeper be 'bout," Tad said. "Well, sir, we bid ye a good night."

We headed up to the room we had taken. Tad rapped quietly on the door and it was immediately opened by Sarah. She almost leapt into his arms, crying as she spoke. "Wha' took ye so long? Grandmam and I ha' been worried sick."

"Now, now, ye knows it takes a bit o' time to prop'rly take care o' the horses. Ye should ha' lain down and rested," Tad said.

"How could we do tha' wi' all tha' 'as 'appened t'day?" she asked.

"I be here now for ye," Tad said as he took her in his arms to comfort her. He gently rubbed her back and whispered to her to "lie down and get a bit o' sleep." Then he said to all of us, "We ha' t'be on the road firs' thin' t'morrow mornin' and gettin' down t'Uncle Artie's fas' as we can. Right now, I be goin' back downstairs f'r jest a wee bit to see if'n there be any news tha' might'n help us wi' our travels."

"Ye take care, boy," Grandman said. "We be dependin' on ye now. Ye's all we got. Y'r Pap 'as taken good care o' me these las' few years and I be mighty beholden t'both him and God. And I know ye will get us safely where we need t'go. I trust ye like I do God."

"I be tryin' t'do my best Grandmam," he said. "Now why don' ye three jest lay down an' get a bit o' sleep while I go down t'the tav'rn. I canna' rest meself 'til I find out where tha' rowdy bunch o' sold'rs 'as been an' where they be a'goin'. And there be the matter o' Jeb an wha' 'as 'appened t'him. We know he were 'ere an' I be puzzled where he might'n ha' gotten to. I know ye don' like the man Grandmam, but he 'as a'ways been there f'r Pap and nev'r let him down. I 'ope I can find somethin' out 'bout 'im. I am beginin' t'thin' like Pap and be worryin' 'bout danger lurkin' at ev'ry turn. Tha's na' good, so I ha' t'get a sense o' where t'go next."

"I know ye be worried and I canna' blame ye there," Grandmam said. "I guess I 'as lived wi' danger nippin' at our toes so long tha' I thin' it jest be a nat'ral part o' life f'r us. Take care down there and don' be too 'spicuous. At the firs' sign o' any danger or concern, ye get right up here. And, if'n we 'as to leave in the middle o' the night, we can do it. We all be tired, but I thin' once we get down to Artie's we can rest a good while. I wish there ha' been some way t'let him know, but I reckon when we get there, he will greet us wi' open arms."

Tad left the room while the three of us tried to stretch out on the bed. I knew I wouldn't be able to close my eyes for worrying about Tad and what he might find below. I think that was the same for my two companions. Sarah was crying – it was more that I could feel her sorrow than actually hear her. I reached out to comfort her, but Grandmam already had Sarah in her arms. She was shushing and consoling her, telling her Pap needed her to be strong right now.

"There be time f'r grievin' later," I heard Grandmam say quietly.

I lay there reviewing my own thoughts. How had our journey to search for freedom come to have such a sad ending. Although it had only been a week, it seemed that we had thought about and done nothing else for an eternity except concentrate on getting the Frosts to safety. They and Pap had all fought for their beliefs and eluded death on numerous occasions. And just when it looked like everyone would be getting a fresh start, death had finally knocked on their doorsteps and come in.

Another chapter had closed on our adventure, only leaving us to wonder what we would find in the next leg of our journey. I found it most interesting Jeb had made some tentative plans for us. But where was the man and why hadn't he been at the point? It was all very puzzling and only added to our sadness and fears.

I shivered a little and snuggled closer to Sarah. I needed a bit of consoling myself. I thought again about fate and my future. More than ever I wanted to see this battle of beliefs to a safe end for these people I had come to love and consider my family. My destiny had blown me into their arms and hearts and it was where I wanted to stay. My fate and future were sealed. Tomorrow was a new day and I wanted to be a part of this family's adventures. Hopefully, we would end up in a safe haven that was forgiving and enduring – a place where people of all faiths and political views would be tolerated and accepted.

CHAPTER FIFTEEN

Secrets at the Tavern

It was well past midnight by the time Tad wound his way down to the tavern, wishing all the while that he could have stretched out on the floor above. Upon entering the establishment, he found a quiet corner where he could watch and hear what was going on. From his observations, this is Tad's story, told to Grandmam, Sarah and me the next morning.

* * *

"It were a large crowd o' fellows in the room ev'n at tha' time o' night. The air in the tav'rn were an overwhelmin' smell o' ale, sweatin' bodies, smoker's pipes and oil from the lamps. Ov'r a dozen men crowded 'round the bar, while 'nother dozen or so sat on chairs and benches at the tables. The men 'peared t'be celebratin' some kind o' vict'ry. They would slam their mugs on the bar and the barmaid slopp'ly filled 'em t'the brim. Then they would lift they's filled mugs in the air, shoutin' toasts, roarin' wi' laught'r and slappin' each other on the back. As with most tav'rns, the dim lightin' from candles and lant'rns made it diff'cult t'tell one rowdy patron from 'nother. As I watched, 'nother round o' ale were drunk, wi' more cheerin', yellin' and slappin' on the back. I won'ered wha' they be celebratin'.'"

"The men 'parently were part o' one group, 'though I doubted they were sold'rs o' any sort – or at least not king's men or any other sold'rs we be knowin'. Too bad Pap werena' here. He'd most likely know who they be and wha' they be 'bout. For jest a moment I felt the loss o' Pap heav'ly. Then I shook my head and the ghos' o' my father wen' away. Bu' I could hear him sayin' t'jest pay 'tention and gather facts. Tha' be the best ye can do,' he would ha' said."

"A major'ty o' the men were dressed in dark bloomer pants and whitish blouses tha' opened down the fron' wi' no collar. Some wore a dark kerchief 'round their neck, while others ha' leather necklaces wi' some kind o' medallion on them. The thought crossed my mind they jest might'n be seamen from a big ship docked f'r the ev'nin' rather than 'ny kind o' sold'rs. It may be they ha' brought in a supply o' goods, ha' a good fishin' catch or their cap'n jest ha' enough o' the sea and chose this port t'dock f'r a day or so. On the cap'n's part tha' would ha' been a good plan. A quiet little burg would ha' been jest' wha' were needed to gi' his men a chance t'be a little rowdy wi'out gettin' in t'a big fight or any other trouble tha' larger ports might'n offer. "

"I looked 'round to see who else might'n be in the tav'rn, but wi' all the hootin' and hollerin' from those men – some were ev'n dancin', it were diff'cult t'see 'ow many other people were seated 'round the room. It were af'r the third round o' ale tha' a'most by signal, the group o' men filed out o' the tav'rn an' t'the street. Ye could 'ear them still laughin' and yellin' as they headed on t'ward the wharf. I started t'follow them, but

266

thought better o' it. I got t'thin'in' I might'n ha' better luck o' findin' out wha' be goin' on by jest hangin' 'round the tav'rn a bit longer."

"Once the group I thought might'n be sailors left, there were very few patr'ns left sittin' 'round and enjoyin' their ev'nin' brew. The few who lingered af'r seemed t'be most 'preciative tha' the noisy crowd ha' left – ye could a'most hear their sigh o' relief. Several small groups o' most likely local men were huddled 'round a few tables near the back o' the room, quietly talkin' 'mongst themselves. I walked up t'the 'laborate bar, bein' careful na' t'touch the top tha' were littered with tankards, ale glasses and puddles o' ale. The barmaid looked up and smiled."

'Can I help ye now stranger?' she asked as she began cleanin' off the top o' the bar and placin' tankards in a tub for washin'.

'Do ye ha' any ale left or did tha' rowdy crew drink it all up?" I asked. 'If'n ye do, I would take a short tankard.'

'Ye be in luck there young fella. Where be ye from and wha' be ye 'bout tha' y'r out so late?' She continued to clean the area, using a small, stained cloth t'wipe up the mess.

'Comin' down from the north country,' I tol' her. 'I be passin' through f'r the evenin' on my way down the coast where I got some bus'ness t'do. I 'as a room upstairs and was feelin' the need for a sip o' ale a'fore settlin' in f'r the night. Didna' know it would be so rowdy and noisy 'ere or I might o' passed. But once I be in, I though' I mightn' jest set a spell and see wha' were goin' on? Wha' be the ruckus; those blokes in 'ere seemed t'be havin' a good time. Wha' be they celebratin'?'

'I don' thin' I found out clearly wha' they were celebratin',' she said. 'All I know is they came in 'bout a couple o' hours ago and were a'ready a bit heady 'bout somethin' they ha' done earlier t'day. I canna' help bu' thin' tha' at least a few o' them werena' from England 'cause they be talkin' pretty strangely. I thin' they came in on a ship and I were a bit s'prised they were docked here. But as to wha' they be 'bout, I couldna' tell ye.'

"She set my cup o' ale on a portion of the bar top tha' she ha' cleaned. Ev'n though the ale ha' a good smell, I werena' so sure I wan'ed t'drink out o' the mug. I looked 'round and saw the awful mess the sailors left behind and felt sorry f'r the barmaid if'n she were doin' the cleanin' up af'r them. As I picked up the mug, I saw somethin' floatin' on top in the liquid. Tha' were all it took for me t'thin' twice 'bout enjoyin' the tav'rn's brew."

'Na' much f'r drinkin' af'r all,' I said, placin' a few coins on the counter t'pay. 'Tell me 'bout ye's town. My Pap said ye don' ha' much boat traffic 'round here. Reckon most ships be goin' further down t'the bigger ports?'

'We get our share,' the woman said.

"Her blonde curls were carelessly pulled back and tied, bu' many strands ha' broken loose and were hangin' 'bout her face. She looked t'be 'bout mid-thirty, though wi' women it be sometimes 'ard t'tell age. Her face tol' the story 'bout a woman who 'as w'rked 'ard all her life. I won'ered if'n she be the innkeeper's wife. Tha' of'n be the case in these small villages. The inns and tav'rns are run by a fam'ly."

'We are na' very big and most o' our residen's w'rk wi' the boats or make they's livin' catchin' fish,' she said in answerin' the question 'bout the village. 'We ha' a good market down by the wharf where ye can ha' a choice o' the catch f'r the day. Most o' our fishermen, though, go on down to Kingsley where they ha' a bigger pop'lation and a much bigger harb'r. We don' ha' a big port here, so we can only take care o' a couple ships at a time and us'lly they be bringin' in goods. Sometimes we do get a few ships carryin' pass'gers, and o'course pe'ple of'n catch a ship out o' 'ere when they make 'rangements. Ev'ry so of'n we get a crew like the one ye saw this ev'nin'. Don' know where they come from, but they be a'ways dressed kind o' odd and they cert'nly like their ale and rum. We do ha' people north o' here who come down t'get goods rather than goin' down the coast much further.'

'Wi' all the timber 'round here, I s'pect there be a lot o' woodin' 'ere and ye get the woodsmen. Do they come into the tav'rn?' I asked.

'We get them all – from the boaters t'strang'rs much like ye passin' through. Ha' a swell fellow here t'other day. He were dressed pretty fancy and though' he might'n be royalty, though he didna' talk much like someone wi' a lot o' learnin' t'his credit. He surely were a dandy though, wha' wi' his brightly colored frock coat, ruffled blouse, and feather hat. Might'n still be 'round the village. Said he ha' some bus'ness here and would be 'round several days. But come to thin' on it, I 'asna' seen him t'day. Guess he may ha' taken care o' wha' he came for.'

"I listened as she described Jeb perfectly. It were all I could do t'keep my composure."

'Ma'am, I s'pose ye do get all differen' kind here,' I said. 'Tell me more 'bout tha' dandy. I mightn' be lookin' f'r jest such a person. So ye say he 'asna' been 'round t'day? Do ye w'rk here all day?'

'I 'asna' been here the whole day,' she said. 'My husband, Master Rodney an' also the innkeeper, were here most o' the day. We got some youngun's and I come ov'r here af'r dinner t'help out. Me mum comes in t'take care o' the chil'rens in the ev'nin's when we both be keepin' our livelihood 'live. It 'as been a good crowd in here this week, so my mister been taken care o' the inn. Ev'n ha' a few o' the queen's sold'rs f'r couple o' days.'

'We are usually sech a quiet little tav'rn,' she went on t'say. 'Very rarely do we get such a rowdy crew as come in t'night. But, it be good f'r the purse. Those boys were flingin' coins ev'rywhere. 'Bout ye's friend, ask Master Rodney – he might'n know more.'

'I didna' say he were a frien', I told her, instantly panicking tha' she would thin' I were attached to tha' person. If'n it were Jeb, I didna' wan' 'nyone t'a know 'bout tha' bus'ness 'til I found out wha' he were up to."

'Sounds kind o' like a fellow I ran into while travelin',' I said. 'He were comin' t'this part o' the country. I had a little bus'ness up north and said I might'n see him when I got o'vr this way. I jest won'ered wha' he was doin' here or if'n he got this f'r. I didna' thin' this were the port he were plannin' t'stop at. But it sounds like it were. Too bad I missed him.'

'Too bad ya' ev'n got mixed up wi' the likes o' tha' one,' she said. 'He seemed kind o' on the shady side. Nice young man like y'rself surely wouldna' wan' t'spend much time in his comp'ny.'

'S'pose na', bu' when ye be travelin' a familiar face be a nice way t'spend the ev'nin' as ye chat and sip ale,' I said.

"It was when I turned to leave tha' one o' the patr'ns motioned me t'come over t'his table. He and his frien' seemed to be havin' an ev'nin' out. One o' the men were portly in size and seemed t'be o' the gen'lman class. He were well-kemp' and 'tired in a brown woven suit and a green satin vest. A carved cane was standin' 'gain the table an' his watch fob snug in his vest pocket."

270

'Good evening to ye there young man,' he said. 'So ye be a visiting our fair village. What brings ye into our midst?'

Cautiously I turned to meet the man face to face. 'I jest be passin' through on my way down the coast. Jest needed a place t'stop f'r the night and a cold mug o' ale a'fore I turn in. It 'as been a long day's trav'l and I jest needed t'get unwound a'fore I headed up t'my room. 'Ow 'bout y'rself? Be ye a member o' this community?'

'Aye, me and my friend Ernst over there have been here ever since we were young lads. Let me introduce myself. I am Archie Graves and live down at the end of the lane at the edge of town. Why don't ye come and join us for another mug. We heard ye talking about the strange fellow. He came in here a couple of nights ago and we wondered about him ourselves.'

"I were beginnin' to feel a bit nervous and won'er'd where this conversation were goin'. I were turnin' ov'r in my mind whether t'take off on a dead run, wake ye all up and head out o' town or join the two and see wha' they had to say."

'Archie, canna' ye see the young man be ready t'call it a night?' the barmaid hollered 'cross the room. 'Ye be a'ways a botherin' pe'ple.'

'Oh, ye are always a getting into our business there Mistress Sinclair and then telling Master Rodney what we be up to,' said the man who called himself Archie.

'Sure, I kin set with ye and take a bit o' ale,' I said. 'I ha' t'be up and on the road pretty early in the mornin' though. An', I need t'catch a few 'ours sleep, but I ha' a few minutes t'be cordial t'the two o' ye.'

"As the barmaid and Archie bantered back and forth, she filled a new mug and set it on the table afore me. She laughed and said the two were pretty safe company ev'n though they liked to stir thin's up a bit."

271

'They be such busybodies bu' pretty 'armless,' she added.

'Pay them na mind,' she tol' me. 'Ernst and Archie are reg'lars here and know more 'bout wha' goes on in this place than ev'n the dep'ty. The two o' them could keep ye 'ntertained all night 'bout the antics they ha' been in and the pe'ple they have seen come through our doors ov'r there. They 'as been here as long as my mister and I ha' been in this village. Guess we don' ha' many secrets from each other. They prob'ly can tell ye mor 'bout wha' 'appened to y'r 'quaintance than 'nyone I know. All I can say though, it be good if'n ye don' catch up wi' the likes o him.'

'Now that we have Mistress Sinclair's permission, perhaps we do know some gossip ye might find interesting,' Archie said. 'Quite a brogue ye have there young man. Where ya' hail from?'

'I grew up in Scotlan',' I told them, as I looked ov'r the new mug o' ale t'make sure it were drink'ble. Slowly took a couple sips and said, 'Tha' mos' likely 'counts for 'ow I talk. Bu' o' late I ha' been livin' over in centr'l England, up 'round Keighly way. Reckon tha' be the closes' big village t'our neck o' the woods. I come from a little burg north o' there and woodcutting be my trade. I came ov'r t'the coast t'check on some tools f'r woodin' and t'stop down further 'long the coast t'visit wi' some family I got down tha' way.'

'Wha' do ye gen'lemen do here in the village? Do ye ha' a bus'ness or are ye jest lan'owners?' I inquired.

'We just hold down the tavern,' said Ernst, winking his eye, laughing and holding up his glass of ale. 'Here's a toast to ye young man.'

'Don't mind him,' Archie said. 'Ernst is our village drinker. He can hold more ale than anyone we know. We have even had contests and he always wins. As for me, I guess ye might call me a landowner, although my land isn't worth much these days. We have had some mighty big rains and I cannot even get out to my home for all the flooding and mud. So I stay here and keep Ernst company.'

'Ye mentioned the man I ran into on my trav'ls,' I said. 'What can ye tell me 'bout him? Did he come into the tavern?'

'Aye, he was an interesting chap – a great one for enjoying taverns, and telling stories,' Archie said. 'He fit right into our company easily. It was a couple of days ago he first came in. There's no doubt in my mind he were a real dandy with his fancy clothes. And though he tries to be a gentleman, he is more like the old sea captains we know. He can certainly tell a few yarns to make ye's hair raise. He was most interesting.'

'Wha' kind o' stories?' I asked, feelin' the hairs on my own arms raise in 'larm. I were 'opin' Jeb wouldna' ha' gi'en away secret 'nformation 'bout our religion an' the bus'ness o' helpin' those in need.

'Oh, he said he was traveling around the countryside, helping little old ladies and keeping them company while doing chores around their homes,' Archie said. 'Not sure I believe all he was telling us. He was dressed too fancy to do any useful work. Told us he was a woodcutter in his younger days. Seems like he, too, had once lived in Scotland. He had a few tales about his younger days down in London town when he was fighting against the king's army. He told about some friends he helped who were shot down during some kind of uprising. Sounds like he's had one busy life – that is, if ye could believe half of what he said with all the ale he consumed. Me, I personally think he is a bigger drunk than my friend Ernst here and I cannot believe anything Ernst tells me.'

'Do ye know wha' might'n ha' 'appened t'the man? Did ya say he left town?' I asked.

'Not sure what happened to him. He talked about seeing us later after he took care o' some important business. But, we haven't seen him since. It may be he is still up in his room, sopping drunk. Wouldn't surprise me! He surely had more than his share of ale,' Archie said. 'Was it last night we saw him Ernst or was it night before?'

'Can't 'member,' muttered Ernst. The man was sitting on only half of his chair and seemed to be completely wiped out. About that time, he fell off and landed on the floor. We laughed, as Ernst tried to get up.

'I best be getting my friend home,' Archie said. 'After a night of drinking, it is my job to get him down to his little shanty by the river that flows into the ocean. He's married ye know and his wife just shakes her head when I drag him in and throw him on their bed. I be sorry for the lady. She has certainly had her hands full with Ernst. It can't have been an easy life for her and I don't know why she continues to stay with him. But she's as loyal as the day is long. It was nice meeting ye young man. Hope ye find y'r friend, if indeed he be a friend. But like Ernst, every man liking his ale needs a good friend to take him home at the end o' the day. Good luck to ye.'

"Archie grabbed Ernst, lifted him up and 'alf carried him as the two 'obbled out the door. As for myself, I ha'na' found out much 'nformation. And my need for sleep were ev'n greater than a'fore. I bid Mistress Sinclair a good night and headed back t'ward the inn and our room. As I reached the inn desk, Master Rodney were still there, checkin' his room lists and takin' care o' his 'counts f'r the day."

'Sorry t'bother ye there sir, but y'r wife tells me the man I be lookin' f'r came here t'the inn a couple o' days ago,' I said. 'Ye mentioned tha' he ha' 'nquired f'r us and was comin' back later. Y'r wife thought mayhap ye mightn' 'member when he checked out. He were the one dressed kind o' funny wi' the big hat and feather, ruffled blouse and colorful trousers? She thought it were a couple o' days ago tha' he might ha' been lookin' f'r a room. Do ye know anythin' more 'bout him?'

'Ah, yes, I do recall tha' gen'leman,' Master Rodney said. 'He be quite a fella. Came in an' got his self a room. Said he needed one f'r 'bout a week and paid right then. I thin' it were a couple o' days af'r he 'nquired whether I ha' a couple o' 'xtra rooms f'r three ladies and a couple o' men. Tol' him I most likely would ha' space but he didna' reserve a date then. I kind o' f'rgot 'bout him. Come to thin' on it, I don' know tha' he ev'r checked out. Tha' seems odd. Usually pe'ple stop and let me know they be leavin'. He were an odd one, spent a lot o' time talkin' t'folk at the inn and in the tav'rn. He did come in one night wi' an old'r man I thought might'n be a sea cap'n. Bu' I werena' sure. The two o' them sat an' talked in the tav'rn f'r a bit and then both left. I saw him shake hands wi' the fella and then head up the stairs. I thin' tha' might'n be the las' time I saw him.'

'Ye don' thin' he might'n still be in tha' room?' I asked, 'oping agains' all odds tha' he would say tha' were so.

'Na', I let tha' space night a'fore las' to some sold'rs. I thin' they were king's men,' he said. 'Come to thin' on it, I ha' not seen them since. Tha' 'appens quite a of'n. Pe'ple come and take a room but fin' some other kind o' 'ntertainment where they spends the night. Guess those sold'r blokes don' ha' to worry since the king pays f'r their lodgin'.'

'If'n ye be the folk he were wantin' rooms f'r, wha' 'appened t'the other man? Or did he ha' it wrong?' Master Rodney inquired.

"We jest ha' some mix up and he werena' able t'join us," I said, tryin' t'keep my voice steady. I didn'a wan' to gi' away our problem.

"I ha' done 'nough talkin' and tryin' t'find answer f'r one night. I were way too tired t'thin' on it 'ny more. All I wan'ed at this point were t'get up stairs and find a spot where I could rest a bit a'fore headin' down t'uncle's home. So I bid the innkeeper good night and headed up the stairs. I guess ye know the rest from there."

* * *

Rapping softly on the door of their room, Tad wondered if anyone would hear him or would we all be asleep.

"Lucky, open up," he whispered. I could tell he was happy to see the door open, and before he could get completely inside, I was in his arms.

"I was so worried. You were gone so long and I was sure that something had happened."

"Shhhh, don' wake Grandmam and Sarah," Tad whispered. "It jest took me longer than I thought t'find out anythin'. Then, I canna' be sure tha' I ha' found 'ny 'nformation worth while. I thin' Jeb didna' leave here and s'pect he may still be here at the inn. I canna' be sure."

"Tell me all that's going on. Maybe I can help with the puzzle," I said.

"In the mornin', Lucky," Tad said. "I ha' got t'get a bit o' rest so my head is clear and I can thin'. We canna' do much t'night 'nyway. Get y'rself into tha' bed and get t'sleep. I be tellin' ye a story come mornin'. Good night t'ye f'r now."

He turned and took clothes and packs off the only padded chair in the room. Pulling it close to the end of the bed, he sat down and propped his feet up. I threw a coverlet across him. Before I could check the door lock and get into bed Tad was sound asleep.

Sleep did not come easily for me. My mind was racing and I was wide awake, wondering what kind of news Tad had found in the tavern. It was evident he had consumed some ale which surprised me because I had seen neither him nor Pap indulge. I recalled Sarah saying once Tad often went down into their village to the tavern. Maybe there is more to Tad than I know. What a silly girl I can sometimes be. How else would he converse with the men at the inn unless he had a cup or two. I only hoped he was able to find out why Jeb had forsaken us. I finally settled down and fell asleep. It seemed just a short time before Grandmam woke us all up and said we needed to be on our way down to Artie's place. She handed out food from one of the packs and asked Tad if he had any ideas or thoughts about where Jeb might be.

"Na' sure," Tad answered, as he nibbled on the biscuit Grandmam gave him. "From all my talkin' last night I thin' we may be at a dead end. Na' one person I talked wi' either knew or seemed to care 'bout Jeb's where-'bouts. Guess he really 'ngratiated himself on this little village. I thought it curious though tha' he didna' show up at the cove. An' much as I know some o' ye don' like the man he 'as a'ways been a trustw'rthy and reli'ble fella when it comes t'the religion bus'ness. I 'as known him t'be unnecessarily worried ov'r the smallest incidents an' details. At this point, I don' know wha' it all means."

"Wha' it all means is the varmint sneaked ou' on us and ga' Pap over t'the King's men. It 'as 'appened a'fore if'n ye might'n recall," Grandmam said.

"Now wait, Grandmam," I said. "First of all, Tad said the men who were here didn't have the red uniforms of the king's men. And at the distance we were from the sailing ship, we couldn't see what kind of uniforms the men on the boat wore. They seemed dark and muted, but that's not to say they couldn't have been hired by the king's men. We have no idea to what lengths the king's men will go in enforcing the laws. Those men in the tavern may have had a job to do with a good chunk of gold at the end and did not even know the reasons why. Do you think that is possible, Tad?"

"May be. It cert'nly could be an answer t'wha' they were celebratin'," Tad said. "I jest find it rather puzzlin' tha' no one 'as seen Jeb f'r a couple o' days. Sometimes he likes t'make a big scene o' his comin's and goin's, s'pecially if'n he 'as gotten 'quainted wi' folk. Jeb be a pretty soci'ble fella an' I thin' it most likely he would ha' taken 'vantage o' tha' kind o' 'tention, despite wha' he be doin' here and wha'ev'r 'rangements he were makin.' An' the lan'lord did say they saw him talkin' t'an old'r man, so tha' part o' the 'rangements were no secret. Course he didna' say he knew wha' Jeb be talkin' 'bout, so I thin' we can 'sume he kep' his bus'ness to his self."

"Wha's this thin' 'bout his room?" Sarah asked. "Wouldna' the lan'lord or his wife know if'n Jeb ha' left a'fore they rented the room? Wouldna' they ha' cleaned it up a bit a'fore the sold'rs came and reserved it? Do ya' thin' there be more t'tha' story? Wha' if'n Jeb be still in the room?"

"I doubt tha'," Tad said. "Why would the lan'lord be keepin' tha' kind o' thin' a secret? He didna' seem t'me like he be hidin' 'nythin' when I talked wi' him las' night. I canna' thin' there be 'ny more than wha' he a'ready tol' me."

"I thin' we be wan'in' t'see tha' room, ev'n though it be taken," Grandmam said. "We gotta be checkin' ou' ev'ry situation."

"S'pose I go down t'the stable and see if'n there be any sign o' Jeb's 'orse," Tad said. "I been thin'in' 'bout tha' idea. If'n I were goin' t'hide a man, I cert'nly wouldna' leave his 'orse 'round. I do need t'settle up wi' the stable master 'nyways, so I can do tha' while ye get ready t'leave. We should be gettin' on down the road. I don' thin' we wan'a' be hangin' 'round here much longer. I be gettin' nervous wi' won'erin' wha' is really goin' on here – wha' wi' the celebration party las' night, the dis'pearance o' Jeb and the unusual circumstances 'round Pap at the cove."

"Want me to go down with you?" I said, hopin' he would say yes so we could have a minute alone.

"Na' this time," he answered. "Ye help Sarah and Grandmam get our thin's t'gether so's we can get on our way. I be lookin' 'round a bit, takin' care o' our stable fees and then comin' right back. I might'n jest ask the lan'lord if'n he could let me see Jeb's room. Once I come back, ye be ready so we can get our 'orses an' leave. Don' wan' t'rouse 'nybody by saddlin' 'em up right now. We can save tha' 'til jest a'fore we be ready t'ride."

Tad left for the stables and I tried to help get things ready to leave. I was worried and began to sum up the situation in my mind. It just seemed to me something didn't add up in the way the story went. Why were the men celebrating? If they were the ones who blew up Pap's boat, wouldn't they be aware of a stranger like Jeb? What if the landlord was telling the truth – he might not be the one who takes care of

279

the rooms and could have been given the wrong information. I was more than a bit suspicious and there seemed to be the potential of others being involved and he not aware of the plans. His wife just might know more than her husband about Jeb and his comings and goings. It was kind of presumptuous on my part since I hadn't met her. Still, she could easily be a spy for the king's men or even a part of their intrigue. And it could be Jeb was the traitor himself, taking off and leaving us to face the consequences. It seemed the web of destiny just kept getting tighter and tighter and drawing me ever closer to the Ringolds.

I had to laugh at myself. Just a few short months ago I would never have been so suspicious of people. Adventurous as I was, I had always thought people were honest. I do remember Father warning me time and again about not to be so trusting of ev'rythin' I saw and heard. I was always surprised about his opinion of people and thought he was rather a "stuffed shirt" when it came to trusting others. Now his words came back to haunt me and I felt a bit homesick as I thought how I might have to heed what he had told all of us. He had urged us to "always look beneath the surface and make sure what we saw and heard were the true facts."

The door opened to interrupt my thoughts. It was Tad and he seemed distressed. "Jeb's 'orse still be in the stables," he said excitedly. "The master there said he ha' been waitin' f'r the man t'come and pay his bill, but 'asna' seen 'nythin' o' him f'r several days."

"Jest one more thin' t'na' trust the man," Grandmam said. "Canna' even take care o' his own bus'ness, let 'lone ours."

"Grandmam, slow down," Tad said. "Stop and thin' 'bout it. Why wouldna' the man ha' come f'r his 'orse? Tha' don'

280

make sense. I stopped by the desk downstairs, but I didna' see 'nythin' o' the landlord. There werena' a soul t'talk with."

"Wha' do ye thin' it means?" Sarah asked. "Wha' are we goin' t'do 'bout this new predic'ment?"

"I've been thinking on this situation and I have a couple of ideas," I offered. "Do ye think both the landlord and his wife are telling the truth? I mean one could be working with the king's men and the other not know anything about what was happening. From what you have said Tad, it appears the wife may know a bit more than she was sharing."

"I s'pose tha' be possible," Tad said. "I don' know where t'turn or who t'trust at this point."

"Who is in the tavern right now?" I asked. "I assume it is already open. Maybe ye could go in and find out whether the landlord is in there. I think ye should find out the room number and see if he will open the door for us to have a look around. And was more than one room provided to the soldiers – why don't you pursue that idea? Think about how Pap would want you to solve this problem. I am most sure he would get right to the heart of the matter by asking those he thinks might be involved. You know how these little villages are; maybe those two men last night were part of the plot also. If they don't have work, might be the king's men provide them with enough gold coins to live comfortably in the world of taverns and ale."

"I thin' Lucky be right," Sarah said. "We should be talkin' wi' ev'ry one who 'as ha' contact wi' Jeb while he were here."

"I been thin'in' much as I don' like the man, Jeb may ha' gotten his self into a bit o' trouble," Grandmam finally conceded. "Like Lucky, I thin' there be some thin's tha' jest don' add up. An' the best place t'start might'n jest be down there in the tav'rn. I won' be 'shamed t'set foot inside if'n it means we can get the lan'lord or his wife t'tell us all they know."

"I don' know 'bout ye all goin' down there," Tad said cautiously. "I can find out wha' we need to know."

"And jest wha' we be doin' if'n ye dis'pear too," Grandmam said. "We be stayin' t'gether right now and I f'r one be ready t'get downstairs and find us some clues 'bout our frien' – an he do be tha' most o' the time. Na' matter wha' I thin' o' him, we got t'find out wha' 'as 'appened an' help him."

"A'right then, leave ye's thin's and we can go down t'see 'bout some answers," Tad said. "I 'ope we won' be too late."

The four of us trooped down the stairs, past the innkeeper's desk and on into the tavern. It took a few minutes for our eyes to adjust to the dimly-lit room. It was a good sized-area, much bigger than I had expected. I was surprised there were a few people sitting on the benches at the large tables even at this time of day. All eyes were on us as we swept inside. I blinked my eyes and felt a tear as the strong whiff of ale, beer and smoke from pipes took my breath away. The innkeeper glanced around at us as he filled a tankard with brew from a large vat behind the bar.

"Good mornin' to ye," he said as he sat the tankard on the bar and wiped his hands on the apron he was wearing. "Welcome. There be breakfast 'vailable ov'r t'the inn dinin' room. Jest gi' me a moment."

He picked up the tankard and carried it to a nearby table, sitting it in front of an old man who seemed more asleep than awake. The innkeeper, Master Rodney, picked up an empty container in front of his patron and carried it back to the bar.

"Now, wha' can I be doin' for ye?" he said.

"I s'pose ye 'members us from las' night," Tad said. "We ha' one o' ye's rooms upstairs. Do ya 'member?"

"Cert'nly I do. How d'do Mistress and young misses," Master Rodney said. "Did ye' find ev'rythin' to ye's likin'?

I could see Grandmam wasn't too pleased at the sight of the patrons and their "lapping" at ale so early in the day. I hoped she would just let Tad do the talking. But that was not to be.

"Lis'en here Mister," she said. "We do 'preciate the room, but as ye may know a frien' be missin' and we thin' ye got him 'idden somewhere's here in ye's fine 'stablishment. Now would tha' be so?"

"Grandmam!" Tad admonished. "Don' mind her. But we do be a bit concerned 'bout tha' friend o' ours. Ya' 'member I asked 'bout him las' night and you seemed to thin' he a'ready departed. But ye see, there be a problem wi' tha' idea. His 'orse be still bedded down in yon'er stable and it isna' like him t'leave his 'orse un'tended – well, tha' is 'less'n he be dead or 'idden somewhere. He werena' the kind o' man careless 'nough t'get hisself killed."

"We be won'erin' if'n ye can tell us more 'bout the man wi' the strange hat an' fancy clothes?" Tad continued. "Do ye thin' it poss'ble we could see his room? I know tha' be an 'mposition but we be tryin' ev'ry thin' we can t'find the man. Ye's wife said she ha' seen him in the tavern. Could she know anythin' tha' might'n help us find him? Ya see he were s'posed t'be at a 'pointment yest'rday and he didna' come. Tha' be most unlike him an' we jest thin' somethin' bad 'as 'appened to him. Can ye help us?"

"Like I tol' ye last evenin', sold'rs took the room," Master Rodney said. "Don' know 'ny more 'n tha'."

"Who cleans the rooms af'r guests leave, or don' ye take care o' tha'?" Tad asked.

"Course we clean up the rooms, usually," Master Rodney said, feeling somewhat insulted we would think so badly of his establishment.

"I didna' mean 'ny o'fence," Tad said. "But we would greatly 'preciate 'nythin' ye can do t'help us."

"On this o'casion, the sold'rs said they'd take the room as it were an' would let us know when we could come t'clean," the innkeeper said. "Like I said, I ha'na' seen the sold'rs or ev'n he'rd from them. I guess ye might'n thin' tha' be a bit 'spicious. I thought my wife ha' cleaned the room, but when I tol' her 'bout ye's concern las' night she said na' a bit o'cleanin 'as been done by us. The sold'rs tol' her they'd take care o' it. Do ye thin' ye's frien' were 'idin' from the sold'rs and they got 'im in the room?"

"More an' more this sounds like Jeb might'n be in a bit o' trouble," Tad said. "Do ye thin' we could jest look in his room an' the other one the sold'rs took? I don' mean t'stir up trouble, but I thin' it be on ye's doorstep."

"Well now young man, I don' know," Master Rodney said. "We don' like t'overstep our bound'ries when it comes t' guests and they's rooms. Wha' pe'ple do af'r they pay f'r a room doesna' be o' concern f'r us. We jest give 'em space and they pay f'r it."

Grandmam had enough of the man's excuses. "Ye listen t'me mister, I wan' ye t'get up those stairs an' op'n both o' those doors so's we can see f'r ourselves whether our frien' be up there an' in trouble. Jest get y'r keys or I be findin' the local dep'ty and askin' him f'r help."

We all looked at her in disbelief. How could she be threatening to bring in the deputy? But it seemed to work because Master Rodney gathered the big ring of keys off the bar top and turned to go up the stairs. We were right behind him. I wondered what we would find waiting for us. Perhaps nothing, but it couldn't hurt to find out if there were any clues about Jeb's departure. Master Rodney huffed and puffed as he climbed up the stairs.

"Ye know, this is 'gainst my will," he said. "But ye be so 'nsistent and I guess somethin' here doesna' seem quite right. Tha's why I be helpin' ye."

We reached the room Jeb had occupied. Master Rodney rapped loudly on the door.

"'Nybody here?" he shouted. He waited politely for an answer, but none came. He rapped again but got no answer to his query. Slowly he inserted the key, opened the door and entered, with the rest of us right behind him.

"Well, I be damned," Master Rodney said. "They ain' nobody here. I don' see any o' the sold'rs thin's and the room 'as been thoroughly cleaned. It be a'most cleaner than we ha' for new guests. Tha' be pretty strange."

Tad wandered around the room, opening the wardrobe and peeking behind the curtains, under the bed and in every corner of the room. The room was immaculately clean, ready for the next guest. To see there were no clues was a bit disappointing. Or was the clean room a clue in itself?

"How 'bout the other room? Can we see it?" Tad asked.

Master Rodney grumbled as he turned down the narrow hallway to the next room. We were right behind him and waiting impatiently while he put the key in the lock. He jiggled the key several times and pushed on the door. But it would not open. He kept trying several keys, twisting and turning them.

"This here be the key," he said as he inserted it one more time. "Don' know why it won' op'n. I thin' somethin' be blockin' the door."

He turned the handle, shoving, pushing and trying to get it open.

"Why don' ye help me Tad?" he said. They both pushed and shoved until the door moved a couple of inches. "I don' understand," said Master Rodney. "This be very odd an' now I be concerned 'bout ye's safety. Why don' ye ladies go down the hall there a bit and get back out o' the way?"

Grandmam, Sarah and I did as he bid while he and Tad continued to shove and push on the door, moving it only inches at a time. It was slow work, but they were making progress. Finally, they got the door open enough for Master Rodney to squeeze through. He held up his hand for Tad to stay where he was.

"Wha' in tarnation?" we heard Master Rodney exclaim. "Tad, Tad ye best come quickly."

We three women started down the hall to see what was going on, but Tad held up his hand. So we waited, wondering what they had found. It didn't sound good and I had a sinking feeling in my stomach. The fear returned that had constantly been in the back of my mind ever since our journey began. With Pap's death it had sort of vanished. Now it was back. I could feel the hair on my arms standing up and a cold chill made me shiver. I looked at Grandmam and Sarah. They, like me, looked scared.

Tad came back out the door and motioned us to come.

"We ha' Jeb," Tad said. "He be tied t'the bed an' isna' in very good shape. I don' thin' he be dead, but he isna' goin' t'talk for some time. I knew it ha' to be the sold'rs. I thin' they must o' followed him here or found him af'r he were askin' questions. Or, he trusted the wrong person. Once he is better, if'n he gets better, I 'ope we can find out wha' be the story."

"Jest let me at 'im. I be makin' him well jest t'find out wha' the scoundrel been doin'," Grandmam said. "Sarah, go back t'our room an' bring my 'erbal satchel. Move aside there Tad and let me through."

Tad stepped aside and Grandmam squeezed through the open door.

"Oh, ye poor, poor man. Wha' kind o' trouble ye been doin' t'get ye in this condition?" we heard her say. "Tad, can we move him? Help me get him untied. Then I thin' ye should move him t'our room."

"I can help Tad move him down the hall f'r now," Master Rodney said. "I don' know wha' ye frien', or f'r tha' matter the rest o' ye be doin' here, but ye best be long gone by the time the sold'rs come back – if'n they do."

Sarah returned with the herbal bag and handed it to Tad. He told us we should get back to our room, and as soon as he and Master Rodney could, they would bring him there. As I started to go back down the hall, I heard a groan. Something Grandmam had pulled out of her bag of concoctions had at least aroused Jeb enough for him to make noise.

"Wait Lucky, come help us move this piece o' furniture tha' has been stashed 'gainst the door," Tad said.

When I entered the room, I tried not to look at Jeb lying on the bed. I wondered how long he had been held captive there without food or water. At least two or three days since that was the last time anyone had seen him. It was a struggle to move the heavy cabinet but between Tad, me and Master Rodney, we pushed it back into place in order to open the door..

"I thin' we can safely move him to ye's room f'r a short time," Master Rodney said. "Bu' 'gain I must 'mphasize tha' ye need t'get on the road soon as possible. I be sorry I didna' take ye seriously las' night. We might'a found a healthier man. Do ye ha' a place to go?"

"We do, and plan t'get goin' soon. Lucky, ye and Sarah get back t'our room and leave the door open. Make the bed ready for Jeb so's Grandmam can take care o' him," Tad said.

It was all Tad and Master Rodney could do to get Jeb down the hall and into our room. He did groan a bit as they moved him. Once settled on the bed, Grandmam already had a bit of herbal tea to spoon-feed him. The rest of us just stood around with fear and shock written across our faces.

"I thin' I sort o' knew those soldiers were up t'no good when na' one o' them came back," Master Rodney said. "I 'spect there be more t' this story tha' you mayn't be a tellin', is tha' right?"

"Aye, ye be right there," Tad said. "But the less ye know 'bout our bus'ness, the safer ye be. Ye don' know where we might'n get a wagon t'take our friend further down the coast, do ya? We ha' 'nough money to buy it from ye. I 'gree we canna' be safe here and we don' wan' to bring any trouble on ye. The sooner we can get our frien' down the road, the better we and ye be. The sold'rs will find out soon 'nough tha' you might'a discovered a dead body in your inn and they will be back lookin' f'r 'nformation."

"Why don' ye check the stables," Master Rodney said. "Tell the master tha' ye 'as permission from me t'take the ol' cart. He be knowin' wha' I mean. It ain' worth much so ye can jest ha' it f'r all the inconvenience I caused ye. Fill it full o' straw and hitch it up wi a couple o' ye's 'orses. I can find ye a couple o' coverlets. By the time ye get tha' done, the missus there may ha' him pumped full of 'nough herbal tea so tha' he can survive the rough, bumpy journey wi'out too much pain. My missus can come up and clean the rooms af'r ye be gone. While ye be takin' care o' the wagon, I can gather up ye frien's belongin's and put them wi' the rest o' y'r thin's. Don' waste 'ny time. Soon as ye ha' the cart ready, bring it here and I can help get ye goin.'"

"We 'preciate ye's help," Tad said. "Lucky, ye come wi' me. Sarah, ye stay and help Grandmam wi' wha'ever she may need. We be back soon."

Tad and I went down the stairs, looking in every direction to make sure there were no soldiers around. We were spooked good by now and wondering if we would get away safely. I think we were both lost in our thoughts and we just followed our instincts of doing what needed to be done. We arrived at the stables and once we explained what we needed, using Master Rodney's name, the stable master helped us get ready to travel in a short time. While he and Tad worked on the cart, I saddled Jeb's horse and the other animals not needed to pull the cart. I thought we would be able to pull this off because it was plenty early and most people were either just getting up or had already gone to the fields or whatever work they did for the day. I glanced out the stable door way and saw workers already on the dock, getting things ready for the next ship to come into port. It would seem the one with the celebrating men at the tavern last night had loaded up and set sail – either late last night or very early this morning.

"Lucky, be ye ready? The cart and the 'orses are hitched," Tad said. Turning to the stable master, he said "We thank ye f'r y'r help. I don' ha' much money, but ye can ha' wha' I got f'r Jeb's an' our fees.

"Don'cha worry 'bout it young man," he said. "If Master Rodney be takin' care o' ye, then I guess I can' help ye out too."

"We do thank ye 'gain an' would greatly 'preciate if'n ye wouldna' mention seein' us. We wouldna' wan' t'find ye in trouble and ye could be if'n ye talk 'bout the likes o' us. I don' know if'n ye be a God-fearin' man, but we praise God daily and will ask him f'r blessin's on ye and y'r fam'ly. Thanks be to God."

"Get on with ye then," said the stable master. "Good luck and I 'ope ya' get to ye's destination safely."

Tad climbed on the seat of the cart, clucked to the horses and drove the team on down to the inn and tavern. I climbed on Seesaw and followed, leading the rest of the animals. As soon as we got to the tavern, Tad jumped off the cart and told me to wait while he went up to get the rest of our party. I was really nervous people would come by and see me with all the horses and cart. But as luck would have it, not a soul came in or out of the inn while I waited. It was just a short time when Tad and Master Rodney came out carrying Jeb. They gently laid him in the cart. Following him were Grandmam and Sarah. Grandmam had some coverlets and gently tucked them around Jeb, while Sarah put our few belongings in along the edges.

Tad shook Master Rodney's hand and said, "We thank ye f'r helpin' wi' our dilemma and f'r carin' 'bout us. God be good to ye and the fam'ly."

He climbed up on the seat of the cart while Grandmam and Sarah got on their horses. We were quite a parade. The Frost's horses were pulling the cart. I handed Sarah the reins of Pap's horse and I took Jeb's as we began winding our way down the road we had brought into the small village yesterday afternoon. It seemed more like a couple of days ago because so much had happened. I prayed we would get to our destination without any more trouble. As for Jeb, Grandmam said he were lucky to be alive and would most likely make it down to her brother's place.

"How long will it take us?" I asked.

"Most o' the day if'n I reckon right," Grandmam answered as she rode up along side the cart to check on Jeb. "Poor soul, I be sorry I ha'na' been so kind t'ye wi' my words. Ye take care o' this man, God, and help me make him well and back t'his on'ry self. Oh, and God, could ye let us get down t'Artie's wi'out anymore trouble. We a'ready 'as' a lot o' sadness t'deal wi' right now. Thank ye, from ye's 'umble servant."

Our entourage followed the road from the village, making our way slowly down to where Grandmam's family lived. None of us spoke as we plodded along. It was hard to concentrate on anything, much less what had happened to us in the past few days. First Pap, and now Jeb who would take a long time to heal. I couldn't quite fathom it all. I watched Tad's head and body bobbing as the cart wheels slowly took us down the road, hopefully away from danger. The fear I had carried with me since I had left my Father's home months ago was still gnawing away at my mind. And the tiredness never seemed to go away. Still, I wouldn't have traded it for a safer and more comfortable life.

I wondered what would have happened had we not urged and pleaded with Master Rodney to help us find Jeb. I guess it was good we had been able to plant a seed of doubt in his view of the situation. That we had not been followed out of town was a relief. I only hoped those we left behind would not suffer serious consequences as a result of their kindness to us and Grandmam's brother would welcome us with open arms.

I was sure I wasn't the only one who felt this way. I could feel the emergence of hope from the others with each turn of the cart's wheels. I glanced back down the road, and the sight of nothing but grassy knolls, trees and a distant view of the ocean gave me a momentary sense of freedom and safety. I whispered a "thank-you" for my newly found belief in God, the Puritans and even mankind.

CHAPTER SIXTEEN

A Safe Haven

We arrived at Artie's farm just in time for the evening meal. It had been a long, strenuous day, but one without incident. That in itself was a blessing. On our journey down the coast, Grandmam had stopped us several times to check on her patient. We could tell she was anxious to get Jeb to safety. As we drew ever nearer the farm, she kept telling Tad he could "move tha' cart jest a bit faster."

Grandmam also was getting impatient to see her sibling again after so many years. She asked Tad and Sarah if they remembered having come down to see him. They both nodded in reply. To me, she said," Artie's me only brother. His farm is jest ou'side a seaside village on a bit o' land where he raises hay and goats. He be well pas' his prime f'r workin' 'ard, and the farm gi's him a pleasant way t'spend his days."

Finally, we rounded a bend in the rough road and followed wagon tracks leading to Artie's farm. Grandmam's eyes lit up and welled with tears as she saw the cottage. I think she felt she was coming home. The cottage didn't appear to be large, but looked adequate to house us all. Smoke puffed out of two of the three chimneys and a gentle breeze carried it away into the slightly clouded sky. The thatch roof looked fairly new, as if Artie had recently replaced a portion of the thick straw or had just renovated the whole thing. River rock and mud daub gave the cottage walls a sturdy and secure look. The total effect was warming – a welcome reminiscent of the Miller's cottage where we had spent a night earlier in our trek. So much had happened since then it seemed like an eon ago.

Even before we reached the main door of the cottage, Artie was outside to greet us. He didn't seem afraid a raft of visitors were coming up his wagon path. Tad waved and Artie waved back. Grandmam couldn't contain herself and she rode ahead until she was even with with him. He recognized her and right away was helping her down and hugging her.

"Mercy, it 'as been sech a long time," she said. "I canna' tell ye how seein' y'r face be a welcome sight. Ya' 'member my granchil'ren, Tad and Sarah, don' ye. They ha' grown a wee bit since last we saw ya's lean body and sun burnt face. And this here be a frien' – we call her Lucky, but her given name be Catherine."

"Welcome, welcome," Artie said to the rest of us. "And to wha' do I owe this won'erful visit?"

"It be a long story Artie and we be tellin' the whole tale soon 'nough," Grandmam said. "But here in our cart be a gen'leman frien' who be in need o' nursin'. Do ye ha' a bed t'spare so's I can gi' him love and 'tention? When we found him, he were near dead."

"I do, I do," Artie said. "Wha' 'appened to him? O' my, he do look in need o' ye's herbals an' concoctions. I s'pose ye' still do them. Canna' 'magine anyone gettin' well wi'out ye's tender care."

"Tad, ye and Artie carry Jeb in. I be gettin' me satchel and be right a'hind ye. Artie, where's the missus – be she inside?"

294

Artie turned and said sadly, "Na, she won' be wi' us this visit. God called her 'ome las' winter. It were fever and ague. An' though she did get a bit better, she jest nev'r got her strength back. She finally jest gave up. Tha' I miss her is one o' the biggest trials the Lord 'as given me."

"Be there 'nythin' I can do t'help?" Tad said.

"Sure, come 'long and ye can help get the bed ready. Then we can carry ye's frien' inside," Artie said. "The rest o' ye can come on in or jest wait out here with ye's patient."

Artie turned and went into the cottage. Tad followed him. The rest of us waited, anxiously awaiting a time to sit down in some comfort. Artie returned, leaving the door open. Grandmam pulled back the coverlets from Jeb and felt his forehead.

"He be burnin' wi' fever," she said. "We got t'get him inside and gi' him a big dose o' my potions soon as pos'ble. Do ye have a kettle goin' inside?"

"Yes ma'am I do," Artie said. "An' a couple o' warm fires. Didna' know it, but guess I be expectin' someone t'night. 'Ow 'appy I be tha' it be ye."

"I'll jest go on in and get started makin' some good medicine for Jeb," Grandmam said as she headed for the open doorway.

Tad and Artie carefully lifted Jeb out of the cart. It was a struggle because Artie was not a very big man. Together, they managed to get Jeb inside to the bed Artie had prepared. Once Jeb was lying flat, Grandmam was at his side, coaxing her warm herbal solution down him.

"It looks t'be 'nother long night," Grandmam said as she poured water in the nearby ewer. She found a cloth, wet it down and placed it on Jeb's forehead. And as she had when I needed her help, she told the man to "jest rest, jest rest."

It took a while, but we finally all settled in at Artie's place. Tad and Artie had taken care of the horses and pushed the cart out of the weather and out of sight. Artie seemed to have plenty of room for all of us and we had each been assigned a sleeping spot. Sarah, Grandmam and I were sharing a room, and it seemed Artie and Tad would have to share the other extra room since Artie had given up his bed to Jeb. Sarah and I inquired about what we could do to help with getting some food prepared.

"Don' know why, but I started a big pot o' stew this af'rnoon," Artie said. "Seemed like God were tellin' me t'make ready f'r visitors. And it turned out t'be true. It be a good thin' I helped my wife Emma wi' some o' the cookin' and bread bakin' t'wards the end o' her days. Now I can take care o' myself. So we 'as a loaf o' bread and a pot o' stew f'r our ev'n meal."

"Af'r our last few days, I can say I would be 'appy to share tha' wi' ye," Tad said. "My stomach be a hungerin' f'r some good, hot food. Grandmam 'as certainly spoiled us all wi' her good meals in the pas' and we 'as sorely missed them this pas' week."

When Grandmam came back from administering to Jeb, we sat down to Artie's table. He did indeed make a good stew, or else we were all so hungry we would have eaten anything. After everyone had eaten at least two bowls, it was time to sit back and relax as best we could.

"Well, tell me wha' be goin' on," said Artie. "Why ain' my nephew here wi' ye? Where ha' ye lef' Pap? Back at ye's place haulin' wood?"

"I don' ev'n know where t'begin," Tad said somberly. "Ye best sit back Artie, cause it be a long, sad story."

Tad told the sad and scary story of our last few months, beginning when I first came into the Ringold's lives. It seemed a far-fetched tale that might only happen in a novelette or in such places as London or other big cities in England. It would seem an unthinkable tale about people in the small, tranquil and serene villages of northern England.

"We don' know wha' 'as 'appened to Jeb," Tad concluded. "He 'asna been able to talk since we found him. Tha' we found him at all be a miracle in itself. And as for Pap...."

Tad choked up and couldn't go on with the story. Tears filled all our eyes. Grandmam finished telling the rest of the tale. I am always amazed at the strength of the woman. On more than one occasion I have admired her courage and stamina.

"We 'asna' ev'n ha' time t'grieve 'im prop'rly," Grandmam said. "We been on the run ev'r since. I hope we don' be bringin' our grief and woes t'ye's doorsteps, Artie."

"What do ya' thin we should do?" Tad said. "We be jest so tired and 'fraid o' wha' be waitin' 'round the next corner f'r us. Do ya' thin' we should get on a ship an' get out o' England? I thin' tha' be somethin' Pap thought 'bout a'fore we got t'the coast. But right from the beginnin' o' tha' venture, it seemed we were doomed. Wha' kind o' news do ye hear down this way o' 'ow Puritans be treated?"

"I be sad t'hear ye's 'ventures didna' go so well. So ye thin' my nephew be dead. Oh my, tha' do be a sorry state. I know a bit 'bout the 'ard work ye all do t'help others and Pap will be sorely missed by our faithful community," Artie said. "In my part o' the world though, there jest doesna' seem t'be sech a big concern. I canna' 'member the last time I saw one o' the king's men 'round this area. There 'asna' been any trouble f'r a number o' years. Jest seems like we don' worry so much ov'r this way 'bout wha' be ye's beliefs or politics. We be more concerned 'bout if'n ye be a good person, whether the crops be good and the fish be bitin'. I canna' thin' that ye would ha' any trouble nor be there 'nythin' t'worry 'bout here."

"Well tha' may be true, bu' only if the innkeeper, his wife and stable master keep quiet," Tad said. "I thin we can trust them. Af'r all, they were a big help in gettin' us down the road."

"Could be they jest wanted us out o' their hair. They did seem kind o' eager to get us on our way. An' I jest wonder wha' kind o' 'rangements Jeb made," said Grandmam. "Ev'n now, wi' him lyin' in ye's bed, I canna be sure he werena' part o' the problem. May hap he ga' us away. An' na' 'til I hear it from his lips he werena' helpin' the king will I believe elsewise. I be sorry he is ailin' but I canna' help but thin' it were his own doin'. I jest don' ha' a lot o' faith in him ev'n though Pap and Tad thin' he is their good frien."

"Now Grandmam, I though' we had been all through this and ye were feelin' more kindly t'ward Jeb," Tad said. "His bein' here in the present condition may be o' his own makin' 'cause o' his love f'r ale. Still, I thin' he were tryin' t'do his job and met up wi' some bad comp'ny. I guess we won' know for sure 'til he is well enough t'tell his story."

Grandman waved her hand and made a face. Then she said, "An' speakin' o' the poor man, I best look af'r him and see how he be doin'." She excused herself to prepare her medicinal broth. Drawing a mug of hot water from a pot hanging in the fireplace, she placed a few herbal leaves from her pocket in the water. She stirred the mixture with a ladle and added another set of herbs. Then she headed down the hallway to Jeb.

Artie laughed. "She be the same lady I a'ways know'd. A'ways findin' fault and lookin' f'r the worst in people then treatin' them wi'a bit o' kindness. She be more concerned f'r ye frien' than she be lettin' on."

"I know," said Tad. "But all o' us be grievin' f'r Pap. It ain't jest her loss. And I know tha' is wha' all her talk be 'bout."

"I thin' we 'as ha' 'nough talk for one night," Artie said. "Time t'morrow t'thin' 'bout a plan for ye. Meanwhile, ye be most welcome here f'r as long as ye like. I ha' plenty o' space and I surely can find thin's t'keep us all busy. Tha' will help ease the mind, gi' ye proper time for grievin' an' 'low ye t'pon'er wha' t'do 'bout ev'rythin'. Why don' ye girls go on t'bed and get ye self rested? I can take care o' the cleanin' up. I be well used t'doin' it since my Emma left me. Tad, ye go long too and we can talk more in the mornin.' There be nothin' we can do t'night. I can a'most guarantee ye be safe f'r the time bein.'

I think we were all afraid to acknowledge we may have reached a safe haven. But at this point, we were all so tired that we readily accepted his words. And so with Artie's permission we tottered off to what we hoped would be a good night's sleep. Artie said he would check on Grandmam and soon as he could, he would "shoo" her on to bed, too.

Before long Grandmam came into our room. When we asked about Jeb, she answered that he was resting comfortably.

"Has he said anything yet?" I asked.

"No," said Grandmam as she prepared for bed. "He still be pretty fevered. I ha' gotten a goodly portion o' herbals and potions down him. By mornin' he may be 'wake 'nough to tell us wha' 'appened." The room was large and contained two beds, so Grandmam took one and Sarah and I the other. We bid each other goodnight. I was not expecting sleep to come easily, but I don't remember even thinking much about our day and the travesty that had accompanied it.

Next morning, we awoke to the smell of food cooking. Artie had been busily preparing food since dawn, making bread and a large batch of porridge. A hot breakfast was a luxury we had not had since Millie and Tom's place. After we finished breakfast and completed the morning chores of cleaning up and feeding the animals, we again sat down with Artie to get his feelings about our predicament.

"What I thin' ye should do is nothin'," Artie said. "Jest stay 'round here f'r a time and let's see wha' 'appens. Firs', ye need to wait 'til ye's frien' recuperates. Once he be feelin' better, may be he can shed some light on wha' took place a'fore Pap were kilt. Ye don' know wha' transpired a'tween him and the contact. And it may be tha' ye's journey jest 'appened t'coincide wi' some other event. I thin' tha' 'specially since the sailin' ship were not one o' the king's and some o' the men in the tavern were not English. Let's jest wait a bit. Meantime, ye can help out 'round here. I could use a bit o' help wi' my hayin' and we can thin' then 'bout wha' ye should do later. I do thin' it be 'mpossible for ye t'return 'ome. An' Lucky, I don' thin' ye would be very welcome at y'r father's 'ome either from wha' ye be tellin'. So, let us jest ha' a few days o' rest, do our grievin' f'r Pap and let the world go by f'r a bit."

Grandmam agreed. "I can help our frien' get well. Once tha' 'appens, we can find ou' the truth – ev'n if'n I 'as to rough tha' old Jeb up a bit."

Tad agreed we could all use the rest Artie offered. I was still a bit distrustful of the arrangements, but then I was the one who had killed a soldier. And, the whole family had a lot to lose if ever the king's men found any of us. I did welcome the idea of staying in one spot for a while. In these warm, comfortable surroundings, Artie made us feel at home. It would be a pleasure to return to normal household tasks and duties.

For a few days, we ate, slept, read our Bibles, prayed for those less fortunate than us and worked with Artie around his home. It was good to have a purpose and a routine again, even if it might be short-lived. Artie and Tad worked in the field, cutting the last of the fall hay, carting it to the barnyard and stacking it in a huge mound for the animals. He and Tad spent one day wooding and I offered to help since I was "somewhat experienced" in the task. Us women found ways to be useful in the cottage. Grandmam thought Artie's home could use a serious cleaning and he didn't object when we started washing walls and polishing furniture. The hard work allowed us to keep our minds off the problem of what to do with our lives.

It was on the fourth day of our stay at Artie's, just after lunch Jeb uttered some sensible words and seemed to have tossed off the fever which had racked his body for days. Grandmam had gone in to check on him with her usual herbals. He turned his head towards her as she entered the room.

She smiled and greeted him with a "so ye be returnin' to the livin.'"

"Where be we?" he croaked.

"At me brother Artie's," she answered. "Now don' strain y'rself. Ye 'as been a very sick man and ye need to rest." She urged him to drink more of the healing broth, tucked him in and told him he could talk later. "Jest rest."

Once Grandmam told us he was awake, we were all anxious to quiz him on his actions. But she held up her hand, saying, "Be patient a bit longer. Gi' him a day t'get stronger.

He may not be rememberin' anythin' o' what 'appened even now."

"Are ye' sayin' we may never know wha' was goin' on wi' him and the sold'rs?" Tad asked incredulously.

"Gi' him a bit o' time t'get better. Af'r all, thin' 'ow long it took Lucky to regain her strength and 'member wha' 'appened," Grandmam said.

"And to this day, I still don't remember the actual moment Maudie threw me," I said. "He may have trouble remembering, too."

"Jest gi' him time t'get well be wha' I am sayin'," Grandmam repeated.

I could feel the tension rising within each of us as we waited for a time when Jeb would be up to telling his story. What if we never found out what had happened? Would it make a difference in plans for the future? If we were going to be the target of those who hated the Puritans, how safe would we be here or any where else? As for Artie, I wasn't so sure he could protect us forever. He was getting on in years and it might be nice for him to have the company. But we also could easily add a burden to his life he might not be ready to accept or need.

I finally was able to get Tad alone for an evening. He had gone out to check on the animals and I offered to help. He seemed eager to have my company. We had not had any time alone for what seemed like weeks and I think we both were eager to share a private moment. Even our feelings for each other had been placed on hold until we could figure out what would happen to us or where we could go once Jeb was up and about.

"Tad, I am so worried about the future. How long can we stay here?" I said. "I don't think this is the life we want.

Helping Artie is fine right now, but with ye's background I can't imagine you would be too happy hiding away here in the countryside near a small seaside village."

"Oh Lucky, I don' know wha' we should do," he answered. "I didna' know how much I depended on Pap t'make decisions f'r us. And it may be I don' wan' anymore o' helpin' others – at least right now wi' all the trouble we 'as seen. I am kin'a 'njoyin' helpin' Artie an' w'rkin' his farm. I guess we be caught in limbo. F'r now, we ha' t' jest 'bide by Grandmam's an' Artie's ideas. Grandmam be a pretty smart woman and she knows a lot 'bout Pap's w'rk and 'ow he thought. And she be right, ye know. Thin' how long ye were ailin.' If'n truth be told, ye are still run down from our runnin.' Ain' that so?"

I smiled and nodded. "Do you think we are really safe here?"

"I thin' we be in the safest spot we can be right now," he said. "It all depends on wha' Jeb can tell us."

"I am so worried and feel so alone sometimes," I said, shivering with the fear and apprehension. "I know I can talk to Sarah and Grandmam, but it just seems we haven't had any time for each other. And I do miss Pap."

"Me too," Tad said as he pulled me into his arms. I felt the peace, strength and hope they offered. I could be patient once I knew he hadn't forgotten about me in all the fervor of trying to get Jeb here and getting him nursed back to health. With his arms around me, Tad told me not to worry.

"Ye know God be wi' us, 'though it mayn't seem like it," he said. "Af'r all, he 'as gotten us this far. An' I know it 'as not been wi'out a price. But he do ha' a plan for us.

"I know that is true," I said. "Thank you for the encouragement."

He gave me a quick hug and kiss on the top of my head. "Ye know 'ow much I care 'bout 'ya, and I be doin' my best to keep ye safe. Af'r all, I want ye to be my wife someday."

That brought a smile to both our faces and another warm embrace.

"We best be lookin' after the animals," he said as he reluctantly let me go. "They need our care too."

Finding the animals safe, secure and well fed, we came back to the cottage and found a log to sit on near the door. It was good to sit and chat, bantering back and forth as we had done in the past. I felt the promise of a happy and normal life as we sat together. And although we did not speak directly of love, it was there for us and provided a cloak of safe haven. There was comfort in knowing a future of some kind awaited Tad and me. Shortly, we said goodnight and Tad kissed me before we went inside.

We all began to feel the strain of our past journey ebb as we bided our time at Artie's. We still were caught in a waiting game, but there didn't seem to be the urgency to move on or worry about safety for the time being. We had been there just a week when Grandmam finally allowed Jeb to join us at the dining table. He was a ghost of the man we had once known. His illness made him seem fragile. I wondered that he could ever hurt anyone.

Once we had eaten, Grandmam began to quiz the man.

"Jeb, we found ye in a terr'ble state. Do ya' 'member anythin' o' 'ow ye were treated or wha' 'appened?" she asked. "I know ye be still feelin' the strain o' bein' ill, but we got questions tha' need answers."

It suddenly dawned on him we were missing a body as he gazed around the table.

"Where be Pap?" he asked.

"Ye don' know?" responded Tad.

"What do ye mean? Wha' don' I know?" Jeb seemed puzzled. His wide-eyed expression was filled with fear.

"Pap be gone, thanks to ye," Grandmam shouted at him, tears filling her eyes.

"Ye mean he 'as gone on t'nother job f'r other people and left ye' here t'visit?" Jeb inquired.

"Wha'? Be ye dense man? He is dead and it be y'r fault," Tad shouted angrily.

"Dead? No, tha' canna' be?" Jeb said. "I made the 'rangements and all were set f'r the meetin' and rendevous. Wha' 'appened? Did somethin' go terr'bly wrong? Na, tha' could na' be. I took care' o' everythin' 'cept getting a room reserved for ye."

I thought it was time to step in and take this conversation another direction before there were some angry words and we might never find out what had happened.

"Jeb, can ye tell us what happened from the minute ye got to the coast?" I said. "Did you run into any trouble after we left the Millers?"

Jeb, put his elbows on the table. He raised his hands and placed his head in them. There was a piercing silence and we waited patiently for the man to get his bearings. Finally, he spoke.

* * *

"My journey to the coast was uneventful. I stayed off the main roadways most o' the way, but as I got closer t'the sea, I took one o' the lesser used roads. I didna' see a soul, even on the couple o' nights I stopped at local inns 'long the way. I were a man on a mission, so's I didna' ev'n stop f'r a drink.

I made good time and when I got to Ravenston, I reserved me a room at the inn like Pap and I talked 'bout. It seemed a pleasant 'nough place. It were supper time and I went down t'the tav'rn f'r a bite t'eat. Met me a couple o' nice gen'lemen and they 'vited me t'share a few spirits wi' them."

"I met those two old men. Quite a pair they were," said Tad.

"Indeed they were, an' most helpful in acquaintin' me wi' the village," Jeb said. "I found the contact person tha' Pap ha' set me up wi' but found the man t'be a bit confused 'bout wha' were supposed be 'appenin'. Said it would take a bit o' time f'r the 'rangements I needed, and I trusted him to do so."

"Be he an old sea captain?" Grandmam asked.

"No, he were a young lad, not much old'r than Tad here," Jeb replied. "Why do ye ask? I don' 'member talkin' to any old sea captain a'tall."

"Be ye tellin' us the truth?" Tad asked.

"Ye can trust ol' Jeb here," he answered. "Why do ye ask?"

"Why don' ye jest continue ye's story and we can 'xplain later," Tad said. The anxiety in his voice was coming through plainly.

"Well, as I were sayin, I made the 'rangements wi' this young fellow. I tol' him as I usually do wha' be needed, where he be needed, 'specially for the boat 'rangements and wha' I 'spected t'happen. He nodded his head like he know'd the routine and I didna' question tha' part o' our conversation. Perhaps I shoulda' but he said the 'rangements would be done like I wan'ed. As usual, I gave the man half o' the money and tol' him I would gi' him the rest when the Frosts were safely on the sailin' ship. We 'greed tha' the next mornin' would be fine for the payment."

"I didna thin' anythin' more 'bout it and enjoyed my ev'nin' wi' the two old gen'lemen who seemed t'ha' permanent seats at the tavern. They were a pair an we spent a delightful ev'n talkin' and laughin.' It were the next ev'nin a'fore ye were to arrive at the beach when the innkeeper came t'my room and said there be a gen'leman wan'in' t'see me. I came down then to the tav'rn and met an older man who 'xplained he ha' been hired by a young fellow for a boat trip. I were kind o' confused and wonderin' wha' be goin' on and said so. He tol' me the young man asked him t'find a boat t'connect wi' the sailin' ship. The old'r man seemed t'know all our 'rangements and wan'ed to be paid 'head o' time. I tol' him tha' werena' possible 'cause the 'rangements were a'ready made wi' the young man and tha' he ha' been paid. I said he should talk to the young man for his money transaction. He agreed then tha' he would ha' a boat at the beach and take care o' the rest wi' the man who hired him. I nev'r did find ou' tha' man's name, although I did feel a bit uneasy 'bout the matter. Still it seemed all ha' been set up the way we a'ways did and I so rejoined my new friends in the tavern."

"So ye did meet the old sea captain – a white haired old man with a beard to his waist?" Tad asked.

"I don' know anythin' 'bout an old sea captain," Jeb said. "Firs' there were the young lad and then this older gen'leman. He didna' ha' a beard and he werena' ev'n as ol' as Pap! Neither o' the men I talked wi' seemed to ha' any definite ideas 'bout catchin' up wi' the sailin' ship, but assured me they would check it ou' and ev'r'thin' would be jest fine."

"Wha' 'appened? Didna ev'r'thin' go as planned?" Jeb asked. "The boat were there wasna' it and the man got the Frosts and Pap out t'the ship? They cert'nly got their money cause I ga' the rest t'the young gen'leman next mornin'. He ha' come t'the inn and I thought there were no need t'wait, so I paid him his due amount. Tha' were the day ye were t'be 'rivin'.

"Thin's didna' go as planned," Tad said sadly and launched into what had happened at the beach.

"Oh my God," Jeb said. He grabbed the table to steady himself upon hearing the news. "How awful f'r ye t'watch. I be feelin' so sorry. Me frien' is gone, jest like tha? And we 'as a'ways been so careful wi' our plannin.' I canna' believe it could end like this. But like I said, the young man assured me everythin' was set f'r tha' very ev'nin. I don' know 'nythin' 'bout an old sea captain. Oh my, I thin' we 'as been duped it would 'pear."

Jeb continued: "Af'r I paid the young man, I went back t'my room and was gettin' packed up t'meet ye down at the beach when a couple o' men came t'my door. I didna' recognize them and they didna' seem very friendly. When I asked wha' they wanted, they jest barged in and began goin' through my bags. They seemed more interested in wha' were in them than in me at first, but as I tried t'get out the door one o' the men tripped me and I fell flat on my face. Then he walked over and kicked me a couple o' times and asked me where the rest o' my party were. Tha' were when I got right scared."

"I tol' them I werena' wi' anyone. They laughed with an ugly sneer and one o' the men kicked me again. I asked them wha' they wan'ed and they replied they were hired t'take care o' the bunch o' Puritans tryin' t'leave the country. I asked them if they were King's men and they laughed again. Their reply were they didna' need a King t'take care o' the rabble tha' ran rampant in England. So, I don' know who they were."

Jeb stopped to take a drink and then went on. "Once they tore through my belongin's they stuffed them back into the bags. They picked them up, 'long with me, and forced me down the hall. We en'ered a 'nother room and they didna' waste any time tyin' me t'the bed. I tried to ask again who they were and one o' the men told me na' t'say another word or he would make use o' his saber. They didna' hang 'round long af'r and jest a'fore they left, they stuck a dirty rag in my mouth an' were laughin' and sayin' 'good riddance to Puritan rubbish. Tha' were the last I saw o' them an' from there I don' 'member much. Jest as they were walkin' ou' the door, one o' the men came back and cuffed me really 'ard side o' the head with the butt o' his musket. I thin' I were ou' o' it f'r a while. When I came to, it were dark. I 'member tryin' f'r a while t'yank myself loose but tha' only made my wrists sore an' my head were a blazin wi' pain when I moved. I could feel the blood runnin' down my hands. I kept prayin' t'God tha' ye would find me, but the realty o' tha' 'appenin' came barrelin' in when I tol' myself no one knew where I be. I be thankful ye were persistent, else I would ha' been a corpse."

"Do ye be tellin' the truth there ol' man and not jest makin' a story t'save ye's own 'ide," Grandmam yelled at him.

"Grandmam, ye and I 'as ha' our differences, but I couldna' nor wouldna' put ye, Pap and the fam'ly in sech danger," Jeb said sadly. "I know ye 'as been distrustful o' me and I canna' for the life o' me figure ou' why tha' be. I 'as been a faithful friend to ye's fam'ly and if'n I coulda' changed anythin' I woulda'."

* * *

We all sat around the table in stunned silence. My head was filled with thoughts about Pap and his unfortunate demise. Adding to my confusion was the fact it may not have been soldiers who attacked Jeb. I had already given the idea serious thought.

"Did the men gi' ye any clue as t'who they be?" Tad asked. "I know ye's brain is still a bit fuzzy from the fever and all, but can ye thin' back t'a word or 'nythin' tha' might o' led ye t'wonder wha' be goin' on?"

"I did thin' the second man I talked wi' 'bout the 'rangements seemed kind o' odd and won'ered 'bout the fact he were makin the boat connections. He wouldna' look me straight in the eye when he were talkin'," Jeb said. "But I wasna' sure wha' Pap ha' set up. Sometimes tha' 'as 'appened 'cause Pap don' a'ways know 'bout the connections. Tha' be why I a'ways went on 'head. Pap only gave me a contact name this time and once I got to Ravenston I was t'look him up. Pap said he thought the contact were trusty, though the young fella werena' the usual person we ha' w'rked wi' in the pas'. Said he ha' taken ov'r the affairs o' tha' man, so I trusted him. As f'r the old'r man, he seemed to be takin' the whole thin' lightly. But like I said, they both seemed to know the routine and wha' be 'spected, so I didna' thin' too much 'bout it. In the pas' there 'as been a few times when the contacts set up meetin' the ship and 'nother person gets us the small boat if'n we don' leave from a port. So ev'n as testy as the ol' man were, I nev'r gi' it a though' he mightn be betrayin' us. One o' those men mus' ha' hired the old sea captain ya' be talkin' 'bout. Tha' 'as t'be the answer."

Grandmam noticed Jeb was beginning to tire, so she ended the conversation. "Ye need t'be taken it easy there, Jeb," she said. "We been 'ard on ye an' askin' lots o' questions. May be ye need a chance t'jest set back an' relax. Or it may be ye is ev'n ready f'or an af'rnoon nap. I thin' we can let ye rest and get more answers later."

310

"I thank ye, Grandman," Jeb said. "I do be a bit weary and ye be a kind woman f'r realizin' tha'. If'n ye all will 'xcuse me, I do thin' I will take Grandmam's advice. May hap later we can get t'the bottom o' this."

"Tha' be good," Tad said. "We be at loss for wha' to do and we do need ye's advice."

The rest of the afternoon we all found jobs to keep our mind off of Jeb's story. I still didn't trust him, but he did seem sincere in his answers and it all fit together with what we knew – the ship, the men in the tavern and the two men he had talked to. The old sea captain didn't seem to fit in with what we thought was to be a safe journey for the Frosts. But if Jeb had been double-crossed, there was more reason than ever to worry about our safety here at Artie's. From what Jeb had said, it would seem there were people in this area who were adamantly against the Puritans and their form of worship. Perhaps they had taken matters into their own hands to carry out their own form of judgment and punishment. I wished I had paid more attention to my lessons and learned more about the people who rebelled against the Puritans and the Protestant faith. I wanted to talk to Tad and find out how he felt about all this, but he and Artie had taken a cart out into the fields to finish gathering the hay. And so the afternoon dragged on. Sarah and I helped Grandmam prepare the evening meal. By dark, Tad and Artie had returned.

We were a somber group at the dinner table – each of us just eating and lost in our own thoughts. Grandmam seemed to feel some compassion for him and had given up questioning him about his days just before the explosion. And he had not been able to add anything new the story. He was sort of despondent and seemed to be genuinely grieving the loss of his friend Pap. Jeb would just utter Pap's name, shake his head and moan and groan. He was having a hard time digesting the death.

It was Artie who took the situation into his own hands. I don' know whether he was tired of us all moping around or really felt the need to find a solution to our problems. "I thin' I be takin' a trip over t'Lytham t'pay a couple o' friends a visit t'morrow," he said as we were ending the meal. "I need a few supplies and it be a good time f'r stoppin' in and findin' ou' wha' be the local gossip. It will take me a fair part o' the day t'go ov'r and back. Meantime, ye jest enjoy a day o' rest. Tad I will need ye t'feed the animals and make sure they 'as all they need. I canna' promise I will find out a thin.' But ye never know wha' can be learned when ye be a good lis'ner. And no, Tad, we don' wan' ye t'jeopardize safety t'join me."

Tad laughed and said, "I 'as no thought o' goin' 'long."

"Artie, ye be safe goin ov'r?" Grandmam asked.

"Yes'm, I believe I be safe as usual," he said. "It be a trip I make 'bout ev'ry two or three weeks, so my friends will thin' nothin' 'bout it. So I be safe in goin.' Course ye never know wha' kind o' trouble be 'waitin' for ye 'long the roadway – no matter wha' be the o'casion. But I plan t'be very careful. As I said before, I be a very good lis'ner."

The rest of the evening, we were all quiet. Once we had cleaned up the remains of our supper, Tad checked on the animals and all of us spent a bit of time reading our Bibles. We all feigned tiredness and went to bed early.

The next morning, Artie was long gone before most of us were up. Grandmam had seen him off. She said he declined having anything to eat and seemed anxious to get down to the road leading into the nearby seaside town. We all went about out daily tasks, but an air of apprehension filled the cottage. Jeb was up and about more these days, but still had trouble filling in all the gaps of his treatment at the inn. He seemed to shrink even more into himself once he found out Pap had met his demise.

CHAPTER SEVENTEEN

Surprise at Artie's

*I*t had been a difficult day trying to keep our mind off of why Artie had gone into Lytham. I was sure there had to be more to it than just to visit old friends and pick up a few supplies. Grandmam seemed to think I was worrying for naught. It was just about twilight when we saw two horses coming down the beaten path to Artie's cottage.

"Can ye see who it be?" Grandmam asked. "Don' ye go runnin' out 'til ye see who it be." Looking around, she said, "It be too late t'douse the fire so's they would thin' no one be here."

"It 'pears Artie mus' ha' brought a frien' home," Tad said, trying to see in the dim light.

As for me, my stomach was doing its usual flip-flops and knotting up again. I had the same sinking feeling I had felt on a number of occasions since meeting the Ringolds. "Please God," I whispered. "Don't let it be anything harmful to us. Haven't we given you enough for right now? I know I shouldn't bargain, but please don't let it be trouble."

It was a few minutes later we heard Tad's whoop and holler as he headed out the door.

"Wha' is it?" Grandmam said following him. Then I heard her exclaim, "Oh my Lord – Bless ye, bless ye."

Soon, Sarah and I were behind her. And there just riding into the yard was the best surprise of our life. Artie had company for sure. Somewhere, somehow, he had found Pap.

"Oh mercy, mercy. How be ye my boy?" Grandmam said as she ran to give him a hug. She stopped short, realizing how seriously he was injured.

"Careful there ma'am," Artie said. "Pap is goin' to need ye's potions and lots o' 'tention for many, many days. Jest hold ye's questions 'til I can help him down and get 'im inside. Grandmam, get ye's best potions a boilin' and ready t'bring this man back to health."

Artie carefully helped the ailing man down. Tad offered to help and the two of them managed to walk him inside. Artie urged him to sit on a nearby bench. It was Pap alright, but he was a man who seemed to be lost and not knowing what was going on or what he was doing. His glassy eyes just starred ahead and were huge black spots on an ashen face.

Grandmam mumbled to herself as she prepared one of her famous potions. "Can ye get him onto a bed somewhere?" she asked. "I know we be a bit short, but the man looks like he needs to rest."

"Aye that be true," Artie said. "I canna' tell ye wha' be all his ailments, but I thin' he 'as ha'a blow to the head tha' may ha' knocked out his memory. He doesna' seem to know who he be or where he 'as been?"

"Just like me," I said. "I can tell him about not having a memory. It is one of the worst things that can happen."

It took the cooperation of us all to get him into bed and get some of Grandmam's healing potion down him. He instantly fell asleep and we all tiptoed out of Artie's room. Jeb gladly gave up his accommodations so Pap could have Grandman's healing powers. Tad offered his spot to Artie saying he could easily sleep out in the stable. But Jeb wouldn't hear of it. The two argued back and forth until Artie said they were both being ridiculous.

"There be plenty o' space in the spare room. We a'ready ha' two bunks and we can jest lay cushions on the floor for a third bed," Artie said. "Ye two can figure out who might'n sleep on the floor."

"I'll take the floor cause I'm the youngest," Tad said.

Good," said Artie. "Then tha' be the end o' it."

I think that was the only time we had any real problems or arguments while staying at Artie's. Like Tad said later, "there be too many other thin's to worry 'bout than where I be goin' to lay my head at night."

As we sat down to supper that night, there were prayers of thanks. After the meal, Artie explained what happened on his trip into Lytham.

* * *

"I went t'see a couple o' my fellow Puritan frien's. They live in the back part o' a run-down buildin' sometimes used f'r church services by local Anglican priests. My friends ha' fixed up their portion o' the buildin' and it is quite liv'ble for two ol' bachelors. They seemed very 'appy t'see me and we shared lunch, catchin' up on the latest gossip. They reported there ha' been an awful accident in a nearby sea town north o' here a few weeks ago. They said supposedly a band o' renegades ha' intercepted some Puritans tryin' t'leave the country. My two frien's seemed to ha' a lot o' details – pretty much wha' ye 'as been tellin' me. I asked them how they knew all this."

"My friend Axel said one o' the men from the raid did some w'rk for him las' week and he were braggin' and pretty high on the success o' a mission he did. Axel said the man ha' loose lips and was more concerned wi' his own neck than in bein' loyal t'his renegade frien's. He were boastin', 'bout 'ow proud he were o' the group's deed in thwartin' people from leavin' on a sailin' ship. The man tol' my friend tha' the leader o' the mission and' a few o' the renegades live in an area jest north o' Ravenston. He said the major'ty were men from the n'rth woods and some even from Irelan' and Scotlan'. They all ha' been urged t'help wi' a promise o' gold if'n the raid wen' as 'xpected. My frien's were quite s'prised 'bout the raid an' didna' know such a strong group 'xisted up there. The man didna' know my frien' was a Puritan, and Axel let him jest ramble on. It seems the group doesna' work in connection wi' the king and they really don' do much 'less they know f'r sure they be a group o' true Puritans tryin' t'leave. Seems this wasna' the f'rst time they foiled a 'tempt t'leave the country, 'cording to the man workin' for Axel. From tha' man's story, it would 'pear that it were the second man ye talked to Jeb who turned tail on you."

"I asked my friends how safe 'ny Puritans be in our part o' the country if'n they made themselves known," Artie said. "Axel assured me tha' the man workin' for him said he were plannin' t'move southw'rd where there might'n be more action f'r him and his group. He tol' Axel they ha' done 'nough damage up this way and ha' delivered a strong message tha' would discourage t'others from usin' these ports t'leave the country."

"It were a nice visit wi' my frien's and I didna' mention 'nythin' 'bout wha' be happenin' up t'my place. They asked wha' I ha' been doin' and I said the usual – taken care o' hay an' t'goats. They jest laughed and said if'n I didna ha' my

318

critters life would be pretty bleak. We laughed some more. I was 'bout ready to leave when Axel said he had something to show me.

"I were kind o' puzzled as I followed him t'wards the back o' their livin' quarters. He op'ned a door tha' led into a kind o' sittin' room. There werena' much there for furnishin's and 'gain I were perplexed at wha' were goin' on."

Axel stopped. Turnin' to me he said, 'I 'spose ye be wonderin' wha' I am 'bout. I were hopin' ye could help me identify a fellow I got in the next room. Ye know, Artie, we 'as known each other a very long time and I got to'thin'in' ye might'n know him. I found this fellow 'bout a week ago and he didna' seem t'know where he was. The only thin' I been able to get out o' him is 'the boat, the boat.' When I found him he were down near a deserted beach I sometimes take a walk on. He were jest wanderin' 'round, kind o' mutterin' t'hisself. His clothes were black; him too, like he ha' been in some kind o' fire. He ha' some burn marks on his face and arm. He were skin and bones, still is f'r tha' matte r – I don' thin' he 'as eaten in a while. He jest seemed lost and didna' respond t'any o' my questions. So, bein' a good Samaritan, I gently led him here where we could keep an eye on him.'

'We cleaned him up best we could and offered 'im a warm bed and some hot herbal teas', Axel said. 'I tried cleanin' the burns and covered them with some salve we got from a good lady down the road from us. He doesna' make much sense, but the more I watch him, the more his face seems famil'ar to me. It were only when I saw ye today tha' it came t'me. I thin' he might'n be ye's nephew. I 'member him as a young man when ye were taken him places.'

"When Axel opened the door I crept close t'the bed where the man were lyin'. Ev'n in the dim light o' the room I could

319

see it were Pap. He were 'sleep and Axel said tha' seemed a miracle 'cause the man were greatly agitated and couldna' settle down."

'I ha' no idea 'bout wha' 'appened to Pap,' Axel said. "It jest o'curred t'me he might ha' been a survivor o' the Puritan raid. I don' ev'n know why I ha' tha' thought – it jest crossed my mind. I were kind o' feared for the man's life. Tha' were one reason I brought Pap home and why we didna' call in a physician. I werena' sure wha' we should do. Lucky f'r me ye came to visit 'cause he be in bad shape and was goin' to need some healin' attention. He 'as na' said a word. But he seems to be grateful for the comfort and care offered.'

'It seems tha' God sent me to see ye Axel,' Artie said. 'I jest felt God wan'ed me to come t'town and I couldna' figure why. But ye know tha' when God sends ye a message, ye 'as to obey.'

"When Axel took me t'Pap, I knew why I ha been sent t'town. I woke Pap up gently. His eyes grew wide wi' recognition and he seemed genuinely 'appy t'see me. He tried t'speak, but no words came. I comf'rted him best I could and tol' him I were takin' 'im t'my home. He smiled and nodded his head."

"Nyway, the long an' short o' the story is tha' my frien' and I loaded Pap on one o' his 'xtra 'orses and I guided him back here. I canna' promise Pap is goin' t'be a'right 'gain or ev'n if'n he be able t'tell us wha' 'appened. He be pretty far gone mentally and physically an' it is goin' t'take a lot o' Grandmam's patience gettin' him back t'a healthy man. All we can do is ask f'r God's help t'keep him safe and bring him back to us. I thin' tha' will 'appen in time. Af'r all, God sent me t'get 'im."

"Do you think Pap or any of us are in danger here, knowing what you do about your friends and the man who worked for Axel?" I asked.

"As I tol' ye a'fore, I canna guarantee ye be safe," Artie said. "But I don' thin' ye be in 'ny danger. My frien's are good people and I canna' see them hurtin' 'nyone they know or even 'nyone they don' know. Like the rest o' us Puritans, they 'as seen their share o' troubles."

* * *

Our days became a routine of taking turns nursing Pap – sitting with him to make sure he was resting and not thrashing around like he had been at first. I could tell Sarah, Tad and Grandmam were happy to see their father and son returned to them. And I was next in line. Pap had come to mean a lot to me and I had pledged him my allegiance. We all seemed to relax a little just knowing he was lying down the hall even though he was badly injured. Grandmam said he didna' seem to have anythin' broken, well other than his spirit. She said it is always hard to tell what has been hurt inside and it "jest takes time" for ev'rythin' to heal itself.

Even after the first week, there seemed to be little recognition of anyone. He did smile at Grandmam, but we weren't sure it was because he recognized her as his mother or just because she was giving him potions regularly. She had pulled out the artillery, bringing out some of her strongest herbs and potions to help bring him back to us. It seemed any plans for the rest of us were put on hold one more time as we nursed Pap back to health. Tad and Artie kept busy as usual in the fields and went off to gather more wood. The weather had turned much cooler and Jeb kept the fires constantly lit.

Jeb's spritis had lifted somewhat since Pap was lying abed down the hall. But he still wasn't the same man I had met weeks ago.

As the days grew shorter, Pap seemed to become a bit more lucid. He began to notice his surroundings. When he finally spoke, it was just single words – where, what and happily our names. He was sure Artie and Grandmam were angels. I had to laugh – there was a time when I thought Sarah was an angel. Artie had told us not to worry about staying with him for a while so our only concern was getting Pap well.

"Tha's wha' fam'ly be f'r," he would remind us.

We settled into a comfortable daily routine and watch Pap get better day-by-day. It really was a time of healing for all of us. The trip from the old home and the strain of traveling and dealing with a variety of emotions had left us all a bit broken. We were happy to accept the peaceful environment Artie's home offered. In the back of our minds was the constant thought this was only superficial and we would have to make some serious decisions in the near future. But for now, Artie was the real angel in keeping spirits up and providing a safe haven.

Pap began to regain his strength but he wasn't the same man who had taken us across western England. There were a few moments when he began to resemble his old self – his sense of humor began to emerge and he even winked his eye as he teased each of us a bit. But it was evident the accident had taken its toll on him. We slowly started asking questions and telling him bits and pieces of the story we knew. But he didn't have any answers. We weren't sure whether he couldn't remember or whether he didn't want to remember.

One day when I asked how he was doing and whether he could remember anything about the boat explosion, he only answered: "Lucky, it is ye who 'as kept us all t'gether. Wi'out luck, we wouldna' ha' 'scaped as well as we did. Jest thin' on it – wasna' I lucky Artie found me wi' his friends?"

"I don't know how I am so Lucky," I said. "I was the one who created the problem in the first place."

Pap laughed and said it was God who created the problems. "He jest put ye in place t'help wi' the action."

Time has a way of slipping away and soon the weeks ebbed into each other. Suddenly, it was Christmas week. We all had found a little spare time and were secretly making homemade gifts for each other and planning a family Christmas service. A couple of days before the holiday, Pap finally left his bed. It was late afternoon when he came shuffling slowly down the hall. We had all gathered in the dining area, waiting for our pot of stew to finish cooking. We looked up as Pap slowly entered the room. It was still evident he were not a well man – his face was ashen gray and he shuffled slowly rather than walked. It was all he could do to keep himself upright as he made his way to the nearest chair. Easing carefully down into the seat, he looked around and surveyed his surroundings.

"Whew, tha' little walk made me tired," Pap croaked out slowly. "Artie, ye 'as a pleasant 'nough place here. I hope I 'asna' put ye ou' much in the few days I been restin' here.

He laughed at his joke about having been "restin' f'r a few days" and we all joined in. We spent a couple of hours just enjoying each other's company, keeping the conversation light and telling about the daily things we were doing to keep busy. As anxious as we were to ask Pap what he could remember, we sort of had an unspoken pact to abstain. It was Pap's first meal with us since Artie had brought him home. He didn't eat much but complimented us women on making

323

such good food. It wasn't the old Pap, but it was a Pap on the mend. That in itself was good news.

His stroll down the hall and the meal wore Pap out and it was Christmas Eve morning when he felt well enough join us again. We had a moment of prayer, thanking God for giving us back Pap. Then we sat down to our morning meal. Grandmam asked him if he wanted to talk about his accident.

"I canna' 'member much," Pap said. "Like Lucky, my memory won' cooperate. There seems t'be a big gap 'tween wha' I know an' 'ow I got here. 'Ow long 'as it been?

"Ye 'as been my guest 'bout three weeks now, and y'r family came a couple o' weeks a'fore tha'," Artie said. "Na' to worry, Pap, ye all be most welcome. After all, ye be my only fam'ly now."

"What do ye 'member?" Grandmam asked. "Kin ye 'member goin' t'the beach wi' the Frosts t'meet a big ship?"

Pap looked into space for a moment and then said, "I 'member bein' at our 'ome and goin' woodin' with Tad and my friend Jeb. I 'member Lucky comin' to stay wi' us."

"Do you remember the dead soldier?" I asked.

Pap nodded.

"Ya' know Pap, ye na' be the only one Grandmam 'as nursed back t'health here in the las' month. She be a good woman," Jeb said. "An as f'r the 'rangements – they didna' go so well this time up the coast. If'n it hadna' been f'r these good folk, I would be fillin' a cemetery 'ole. So ye don' 'member havin' t'leave our 'ome and takin' our clients t'meet up wi' a ship near Ravenston."

Pap was silent for a few minutes and we could tell he was trying to revive any memories he could. "Yes, now I thin' on it, I do faintly 'member travelin' wi' those folk," he said slowly, sort of slurring his words. "Sech nice pe'ple. It did seem like we traveled a very long ways. Were there 'ny trouble wi' us gettin' t'the beach? Did our friends get t'the ship a'right? Tha' is right 'bout when my memory fails me."

"Na', Pap," Tad said. "They, 'long wi' ye were in a boat on the way out t'the ship. It exploded. We thought we ha' lost ye and it were all we could do t'carry on 'cause o' our grief. Grandmam got tough an' like ye tol' us t'do, we went t'the inn at Ravenston. Tha' turned out t'be good f'r Jeb."

Tad, Grandmam and Jeb took turns telling Pap the story of what had happened once we got to the coast. Pap just slumped down and held his head low, staring at the floor while the story was being told. When he looked up, there were tears in his eyes.

"It be all my fault," Pap said. "I shoulda' nev'r gotten involved. It 'as been the plight o' my family and it 'as not gotten any better wi' the years."

"Pap, you can't look back on all you've done and regret it," I said. "That's not what I have learned from you. I came to your family, not knowing I would become so involved. But I have and now I am a better person for it. I think each time there is trouble and we come through it, we are stronger. The important thing is sticking together and providing strength, love and forgiveness. Else, what is life all about?"

Tad looked at me and beamed about the advice and help I was offering. "Ye ha' come a long way, Lucky," he said with pride. "Pap, our Lucky isna' the same girl who came t'live wi' us months ago. Ye an' the rest o' us 'as led her t'become a differ'nt person – a better person. Don' ye thin' y'r accident can only help ye become a differ'nt person – a stronger one and more eager to fight f'r wha' ye believe in?"

"I canna' be sure I know wha' I believe 'ny more," Pap said sadly. "If'n God is speakin' t'me these days, he be doin' it in strange ways."

"Wha' ye do need be time t'heal," Grandmam said. "Ye be far from a well man and like I tol' Lucky time an' 'gain – it takes the mind a long time to repair itself – an' the body too. And if'n we don' ha' the time t'do it here, then we will w'rk on gettin' ye well in some other place. The place don' matter. It be the pe'ple ye care 'bout and the strength ye get from them tha' be impor'ant."

"Enough talk f'r one night," Artie said. "Pap, ye 'as ha' a shock t'the body and mind and all we ha' done t'night is reinforce tha' notion. Ye must get down the hall and rest. Tha' be the key t'makin' ye well – tha' much I ha' learned from me sister here. There be t'morrow and t'morrow and many more days af'r tha'. Later we can figure ou' wha' should 'appen."

Grandmam got up and helped Pap shuffle back down the hall. Sarah, Tad and I cleaned up the table while Artie and Jeb checked on the animals.

Christmas morning found us all eager for the day to begin. Once we had shared Bible readings about the birth of Jesus, we exchanged our handmade presents. Artie had carved each of us a cross and Tad had taken straw pieces and twisted them into wreathe tha' were "guaranteed to bring us each good luck." Grandmam, Sarah and I had found some yarn once used by Artie's wife. We made warm socks and scarves for each other.

"I be sorry I ha' no present for ye," Pap said to all of us.

"Oh Pap, don' ye know ye be our present," said Sarah. "We be thankful t'God f'r givin' ye back t'us."

"Amen t'tha' prayer," Tad added.

We spent the day singing songs, eating and reading more Bible stories. It was a day of family. I recalled Christmas time in my past and realized how little it had meant then. On Christmas Eve we would climb into carriages and attend midnight mass – it was often long and when I was little I remember falling asleep. As I got older, it just became a long evening. I have to admit that I did like the music. On Christmas Day, we would have an enormous meal about midday of wild game, lamb, vegetables and lots of tarts and other sweet treats. Afterward we all would traipse around the estate, visiting the people who we employed, taking them baskets of food and sharing our songs and greetings. The house was always decorated beautifully with pine boughs while the smells of holiday food wafted throughout our home and was heavenly.

This Christmas Day, however, had meant more to me than any I could remember. I had immensely enjoyed the gathering of our small family group and felt honored to be included. In looking back, it also makes you think about the future and I pondered on what and when it would happen. Tad and I had managed to get away for a short time and he had given me a straw ring. He officially asked me to become his wife when the time was right. I only prayed there would be a day that could happen. We were still as unsettled as we had been on the day I killed the soldier. No one talked about it any more, but it still clung to us like a shadow on a summer day.

We spent the remainder of the holidays catching up on the news each other had. I thought Tad might announce our plans to wed someday, but he didn't. And so I felt it wasn't my place to share our secret. Day by day, Pap and Jeb would remember bits of information about their near-death experiences and would share them with the rest of us. Boxing Day came and went. Since we didn't have any servants to give the day off or treat with special gifts we pretended we were the servants receiving the gifts. Hadn't we recived the best gift with Pap coming back to us. We didn't even prepare much food and ate lightly so we could celebrate.

It was the second day of the new year, 1642, when Pap and Tad sat down to really discuss what would be our future. It wasn't a discussion restricted to the two of them. Once the question was asked, Pap called for a family meeting. He opened it with a prayer.

"God, we y'r humble serv'nts be gathered here an' ask y'r blessin'. We believe in y'r strength and be askin' f'r help t'make decisions 'bout our future. Ye knows tha' f'r years we ha' gi'en our all t'bring faith t'frien's, neighbors an' those in need. Now, we be in ye's need and we ask tha' ye help us an' guide us t'make wise choices. We know tha' ye ha' a destiny f'r all o' us, but right now we be like lost lambs, searchin' f'r the right path t'take. Gi' us ye's wisdom that we might spiritually experience ye's love and offer our services as best we can. Amen."

"Artie, wha' do ye thin' might'n be the best plan f'r us?" Pap asked. "I don' ha' one an' I be jest too worn ou' t'ha' 'ny ideas right now. Should we stay 'round these parts, per'aps even findin' a nearby farm where we could practice our faith an' live in peace? Or, should we continue t'help wi' the Puritan flight?"

"I canna tell ye wha' t'do, Pap," Artie said. "But ye know, ye ha' gi'en many years to God. May be tha' he be tryin' to say ya' ha' served 'nough time. An' much as I enjoy havin' ye all here, I know it be time f'r ye t'make a decision 'bout y'r own lives and 'ow ye can best live an' serve God."

"Wha' 'bout goin' t'nother country where religious freedom is more op'n?" asked Tad. "Tha' be somethin' ye talked 'bout an' at one time ye thought it might'n be f'r the

328

best. All I know is tha' wha'e'er we do, Lucky will be comin' wi' me. I ha' asked her t'be my wife. An' I know, we may ha' a long wait a'fore we can say our vows, but we be betrothed."

I smiled as everyone offered their congratulations. Pap told me to come his way so he could give me a big hug. And Grandmam was just beaming with pride.

"Welcome, welcome – we be pleased to ha' ye in the family, a'though in my mind ye ha' been here since we firs' found ye," she said.

"Gettin' back to ye's question, Tad, I don' thin' tha' is necessarily a bad idea or a good idea," Pap said. "I know I did mention it as per'aps an alternative if we found the sold'rs pursuin' us. And who's t'say it mightna' become a good idea once we leave the sanctuary tha' Artie's home 'as provided. Per'aps it could be tha' ye young pe'ple might'n wan' to start ov'r in a new place. Tha' canna' be sech a bad idea. But f'r me and Grandmam, it is too late. Personally, I am too tired t'wan' t'start ov'r. If'n Artie would let me, me, I would jest be 'appy stayin' here in his safe haven."

"Tha' could easily 'appen," Artie said. "It 'as been so nice ha'in' my fam'ly close 'gain. Ye an' Grandmam would be most welcome t'join me in livin' ou' the rest o' our lives raisin' goats and makin' hay. There be plenty o' women folk nearby who would welcome ye's 'erbal potions Grandmam."

"As f'r me, I plan t'be movin on," Jeb said. "I thought I might jest take meself down t'London town and find me brother. Las' I heard he were livin' there, w'rkin' in the masonry trade. I might'n be a bit too ol' t'learn, but I cert'nly could find somethin' t'do. An' gettin' lost in the crowd would be somethin' I could easily do. I don' plan t'get involved in helpin' Puritans, Catholics or 'ny o' them other religious pe'ple. Me and God will jest ha' our own pac' tha' don' include others. Matter o' fact, I was goin' t'mention t'ye t'day tha' I be leavin' t'morrow mornin'. I do 'preciate the hospitality ye ha' off'red to a stranger Artie. An' Grandmam, ye be the best lady I know. I know we 'as ha' our differences, an I 'ope ye's feelin's f'r me 'as changed a bit. I will miss arguin' wi' ye, but maybe I be gettin' too ol' to do tha' 'nymore."

"Jeb, we will cert'nly miss ye's face," Grandmam said. "I guess we ha' buried all the old feelin's o' mistrust. Ye 'as been a good frien' and I wish ye the best."

"Tha' goes f'r me too," Pap said. "We 'as seen some good times, ha' we na'? I thin' there will come a time when ev'ryone can choose 'ow they wan' to worship wi'out bein' 'rested and I 'as been 'appy fightin' f'r tha' idea. Bu' ye know, lookin' at the 'istory o' man, there 'as a'ways been dissent a'tween religions. Guess there a'ways will. Perhaps tha' be God's way o' helpin' us become strong an' place our faith in Him. I 'ope ye can find ye's brother and live ou' the rest o' ye's life in peace – though I bet ye be findin' a good tav'rn t'call 'ome a few times a week. Won' tha' be so?"

"Ya' bet – tha'' be a way o' life f'r ol' Jeb," he answered. "Does come a time though when ye 'as, t'slow down an' look at wha' be impor'an'. I thin' I might'n be there. A'right if'n I take a couple o' horses? And Grandmam, if'n ye don' mind, could ye make me a pouch o' ye's good biscuits?"

Grandmam just nodded and winked her eye. Then she lifted her finger and brushed a tear from her cheek.

I decided it was time to get back to options and decisions. I had a lot at stake here and the sooner we decided what we would do, perhaps the sooner I could join Tad as his wife.

"It sounds like everyone has a plan except Tad, me and Sarah," I said. "If we stayed in this area, how safe would we be? I have come to believe in ye's faith and thin' I like bein'

330

able to talk to God when I want and not go through a priest to do so. I like having a destiny – but how do we find out what that is? I guess the real question is what is going to be the safest decision for the three of us?"

"I thin' the three o' ye ha' to thin' 'bout tha' f'r y'rselves," Pap said. "I know tha' if ye leave, I shall greatly miss my chil'ren. But ye ha' the right t'begin ye's own life. For me, the decision o' followin' my faith and fightin' f'r it were a foregone conclusion. I didna' ha' a choice. But I don' wan' tha' f'r ye all. I wan' tha' ye should choose t'find a life tha' is goin' t'be best f'r ye. I foresee a time when there will be less trouble 'bout bein' a Puritan. F'r the pas' few years, we ha' seen less and less trouble. Course there still be a few renegades ou' there – we certainly know tha'. But even those folks be seekin' less and less vindication an' allowin' people t'follow their faith."

Tad had been sitting there listening, but I could see he was trying to rationalize what would be best for all of us.

"Ye know father, I ha' no real trade," Tad said. "I don' know much 'bout any kind o' work 'cept farmin', woodin,' trappin' and keepin' my Puritan friends safe. I don' know wha' kind o' w'rk I could do 'nywhere 'sept on the land. Where can I go? It would be excitin' t'go to 'merica, but I won'er wha' kind o' w'rk I could do there. I would ha' t'w'rk my way there and be indentured f'r years af'r I got there. Same for Lucky and Sarah if they came 'long. So I canna' see goin' t'the 'mericas as a solution, at least right now. An' we canna' return t'our home where I knew 'ow t'make a decent wage."

"Now lad, don' worry 'bout money," Grandmam said. "Ya' know I ha' my savin's and there be more'n I can use. I be only too 'appy to share it."

"Still, I don' thin' the new world is the 'nswer for me – nor Lucky and Sarah," Tad said. "I thin' a farm near a forest would be the best way f'r us t'start a new life. Artie, do ye know of 'ny farmsteads tha' be 'vailable? I ha' felt very comf'rtable and safe here an' I thin' once we settled in we wouldna' ha' trouble wi' soldiers an' such. If'n we not be pushin' our faith on others, I thin' we would be left 'lone."

"I think that might be true," Lucky said. "I could live on a farm. Sarah could join us and the three of us could make it work. Perhaps we could have some dairy cows like Yuker had or just a nice farm like the Millers. I know it takes money to get started and I am sorry I won't be adding any to help. But I can't see any way I can return home and have a warm welcome from my family. Ye are my family and whatever plan is chosen, I want to be with my new family. It would be exciting to go to America, but I think we have all had enough adventure for at least half a lifetime. I know I have, and just settling down to a safe routine seems pleasing to me."

"Wha' do ye thin' Artie?" Be there 'ny farmstead 'round my chil'ren might'n call home?" Pap asked.

"I thin' we can find one," he said. "I like the idea o' havin' fam'ly nearby. Lytham be a good village t'be near, and jest east o' here there be timber an p'rhaps land f'r a farm."

"So is tha' wha' ye wan' t'do, Tad?" asked his father. "I know ye a'ways enjoyed w'rkin' at our ol' 'ome. There were a'ways plenty t'do. I be sorry I didna' get ye into a trade. I guess I thought God would take care o' tha'. And I thin' he 'as. He sure do w'rk in mysterious ways. Who woulda' thought ev'n las' spring tha' our way o' life would be uprooted an' turned topsy-turvy. Yet, God 'as seen us through some 'ard times an' I thin' he won' be done wi' us yet. But f'r now, I thin' he 'as given us fam'ly and I am pleased ye chil'ren see it as a prior'ty."

"Lucky, do ye want t'spend ye's life on a farm, gatherin' hay, taking care o' sheep and goats, milkin' cows and raisin' a family?" Tad asked.

"I do," I said.

Epilogue

Tad and I were married in February 1642. He, I and Sarah found a beautiful cottage large enough for a growing family about a day's long ride from Artie's place. It was hard work at first, but the three of us were ready for the challenge of creating a home. Pap and Grandmam stayed with Artie and for a few years we were able to enjoy holidays and other special occasions with them, either at Artie's or they would come a visitin'. But then life changed again. In 1645 Grandmam caught influenza and died, leaving Pap and Artie to mourn their loss. Pap never really recovered from the boat explosion and remained the shell of a man he once had been. By 1650, both Pap and Artie had died – their bodies had just worn out.

Our farm was doing well and we had made a few friends in the nearby village. It reminded me a lot of the village where I had spent my childhood years. People were friendly and always willing to lend a helping hand. Tad and I were blessed with a family – three boys and a girl. I enjoyed motherhood and became like Father in many ways. I was strict about discipline and education, becoming both mother and teacher to our children. Sarah always worried she was going to become a spinster. But that didn't happen. She soon became acquainted with several area families and was able to become a governess for a local family where she met the love of her life, Tobias. The two were married. She continued her position as governess and they had a small house on the estate farm where Tobias worked. They had a couple of children and longed for their own farm.

The adventuring spirit never really left Tad and me and by 1654 we had caught the fever. A new adventure was on the horizon for all of us – me, Tad, Sarah, Tobias and our children. Tad and I still privately practiced our Puritan faith, but the political and religious winds throughout the years did not give us the comfort and solace we had hoped for by staying in England. We were cautious about even identifying ourselves as Puritans and kept our faith pretty much to ourselves. A civil war encompassed the entire British Islands which eventually ended with the execution of Charles I in 1649. Oliver Cromwell tried to establish a Puritan Commonwealth and we thought there would be more religious freedom for us. But despite his efforts, he was not able to establish a Puritan state. Puritan clergy were expelled from the Church of England and there was much quarreling and bickering amongst the Puritans themselves. There wasn't the violence of the earlier years, but other Protestant communities were just as intolerant as in the old hierarchy. During this time, many Puritans immigrated to America and we heard favorable results about tolerance and freedom to worship our faith. We sold our farm, joined numerous other Puritans and booked passage on a ship to America. I think the seed was planted those long years ago, back in the days of getting the Frosts to their ship. I believe our destiny was sealed even then. We had enjoyed life on our small farm; however, there was no future in England for our children.

The years in America were hard and difficult, but we at least arrived with a bit of money thanks to Grandmam and Uncle Artie. And we had the experience of our farm. Once we got established our two families were able to find land where we could have our own houses and farm together. The years followed years and our children were soon grown, leaving home for their own families.

I often wondered what had become of my parents and siblings. I did make contact with David a number of years after we moved to America. Although there were not a lot of letters, we did correspond for a short time. As the years progressed, he seemed to have forgiven me for not returning home once I wrote to him about my adventure and my family. In one letter he said Father and Mother had taken ill with influenza and were both gone by the 1650s. He had been true to the land and tried to keep the manor going, but so many of the people on the estate also died from influenza and the many wars which plagued the English. Those who were healthy or not involved in fighting slowly, one by one, found employment elsewhere in the area. He never once mentioned a family of his own. In one of his last letters, David wrote to tell me about Marianne's death due to the complications of birthing.

It took a very long time for a response to my last letter to David. When I did receive a reply, it was from David's solicitor letting me know I was too late. There was no one left and I had inherited Grafton Manor. I felt the urge to see the old home place and I persuaded Tad to let me take a trip from America back to England. He wasn't too keen on the idea at first, but when Sarah offered to go with me, he relented. And so, we arrived in England and made arrangements for a coach to take me out to the home of my youth. Sarah had offered to come along, but I told her it was a journey I had to make on my own. Once there, I realized the futility of my trip. It is true. You can never go back and recapture those years of your youth. The only thing I found was a deteriorated home and which only made me sad.

As for the adventure which took me from Grafton Manor so many years ago, there are no regrets. Looking back on my life with Tad and his family, I would do it all again. It was, after all, my destiny.

Bibliography

"Charles II (1660-85 AD);" www.britannia.com/
history/monarchs/mon49.html

The Columbia Encyclopedia, Sixth
Edition. 2001-05: Puritanism

"Elizabeth I (1558-1603 AD (Good Queen Bess),"
www.Britannia.com/history.

"King James I," BIOGRAPHY: King James I;
www.jesus-is-lord.com/kingbio.htm

"Predestination," by Christine Leigh Heyrman, Department
of History, University of Delaware ©National
Humanities Center; www.nhc.rtp.nc.us/tserve/
eighteen/ekeyinfo/puritan.htmPuritanism and

"Protestant Reformation," Young Students
Encyclopedia, pp. 1919-1921, vol. 12.

"Puritan," Young Students Encyclopedia,
pp. 1936-1937, vol. 12.

"Puritanism," The Columbia Encyclopedia, Sixth
Edition. 2001-05; /www.bartleby.com/

About the Author

Jayne Bullock is a retired journalist, published poet and currently doing free-lance articles. She has an Associates Degree in journalism from Marshalltown Community College and a Bachelor of Arts Degree in journalism and English from Iowa State University. *Winds of Destiny* is her first novel, but she has written for several area newspapers and spent 16 years writing feature, arts and entertainment and food stories for the Tribune in Ames, Iowa. She has a published book (2005) of recipes and interviews with area cooks. Since retiring in 2005, she has continued to write food and travel stories for The Tribune and short feature, travel and food stories for The Story County Community Digest, a small marketing magazine. She also has been featured in Poets of now Anthology, Our Iowa Magazine and Capper's Magazine.

Jayne, who enjoys writing and gardening, and her husband Paul, a woodworker, live in Marshalltown, Iowa. Together they enjoy camping, traveling and spending time with their three children and seven grandchildren.

Printed in the United States
93046LV00003B/208-249/A